First published 1979, 1987, 1990
Second edition 1985
Third edition 1995
by the BMJ Publishing Group, BMA House, Tavistock Square,
London WC1H 9JR

British Library Cataloguing in Publication Data

A catalogue record for this book is available from the British Library

ISBN 0 7279 0896 0

Typeset by Apek Typesetters Ltd, Nailsea, Bristol
Printed and bound by Latimer Trend & Co, Plymouth

Contents

III SOMETHING DIFFERENT

Preface

The *How To Do It* series has proved very popular, both in its regular appearance in the *BMJ* and as a series of three volumes. Some chapters have stood the test of time, being as relevant now as they were up to 15 years ago, but most subjects have moved on. We therefore thought that we should ask the original authors to update their chapters. Where this was not possible we commissioned new authors. We have included articles that have been published in the *BMJ* since the last volume was published and added chapters on new topics as they presented themselves. New authors worked hard to preserve an existing style while adding something of themselves.

Considering the old and the new articles together points up some interesting changes in writing style since the late 1970s. No longer is it acceptable to refer to all doctors as "he" and use expressions such as "the ladies' programme" for conferences. It's not only political correctness but also reflects the larger number of women entering the profession—and reading these books. But more difficult to explain is the fact that the new contributions have become more serious, their authors keener to provide a comprehensive account.

The health service has itself changed. Recent reforms have altered procedures, structures, and people's jobs. Emphases have shifted, and some topics such as audit, have grown so much that covering it in a single chapter was impossible. Doctors now increasingly recognise the importance of management, and this is reflected in the revisions and new chapters.

In the previous editions the order of publication in the *BMJ* dictated the order the chapters appeared in the books. The new editions gave us the opportunity to group the chapters together with some sort of logic. The three volumes of the series now have individual themes. This third volume deals with writing, publishing, and publicity, and a miscellaneous category of things that didn't fit under other headings. Unsurprisingly, it contains some of the most sparkling writing of the series. Alex Paton writes, "writers are made, not born"; the chapters that follow in part I will help doctors at all stages of their careers to write well all of the things that they are called on to deliver—reports, papers, books, reviews, Festschrifts, and obituaries. Michael O'Donnell ends the section with his account of how to write for money (but not get rich). The next section contains much valuable advice for budding editors and publicists. Stephen Lock talks of the ups and downs of being the editor of the *BMJ*. How to use the media is described, from holding a press conference to writing to a newspaper as "Incensed of Ipswich."

The section on something different covers a plethora of useful topics, such as how to run a pressure group, give evidence, and attend an inquest. And some character building topics such as how to be a patient, admit you are wrong, and survive a dinner. The final chapter, how to fly, is a good example of how you can never prepare enough for anything.

I would like to thank all of the contributors, old and new, for writing so well and so willingly. I would also like to acknowledge Helen Bodenham, our editorial assistant, who has revealed a detective's talent for tracking down authors, without which these books would be—well—smaller.

Deborah Reece
January 1995

I WRITING

1 Write a paper

Alex Paton

Don't believe people who tell you that writing is easy. Except for the fortunate few, writers are made, not born, and the fashioning is a painful process—a very private struggle between you and a blank sheet of paper. Fortunately for the medical author, there are certain guidelines and plenty of advice, but the challenge remains. Doing the research or collecting case material is child's play compared with the moment of truth when you come to write up (or down) your results. But given that you have something worth saying—and too many papers seem to be written because someone other than the author thought it would be a good idea—get down to it, learn a few basic rules, and write—and write.

The structure

The writer of scientific and medical papers has the advantage of a ready-made scaffold on which to build. This is the IMRAD structure and corresponds with the questions that Sir Austin Bradford Hill said an author should try to answer (box). If you wish you can start with the *Introduction* and work straight through, but you don't have to; sometimes it is easier to begin with *Results*, because this is the core around which the rest of the argument can be written. Most introductions need only a couple of paragraphs, at the most; they do not require a review of "the literature". *Materials* (or *Patients*) and *Methods* should be quite short. You do not need to give details of common techniques, but if your work is based on a new method, you must provide adequate details so that others can repeat

3

Structure of an article (IMRAD)

Abstract
Introduction   Why did you start?
Method   What did you do?
Results   What did you find?
and
Discussion   What does it mean?

---

it. This is not always done with sufficient care, and gives rise to a suspicion, no doubt entirely false, that the author does not want other people to verify his or her work.

Results are results. One of the commonest faults is to introduce snippets of interpretation into this section; the proper place for them is in the discussion. The *Discussion* is always difficult. If you are stuck, begin by giving your results in the light of other people's findings, proceed to discuss their meaning, and end by stating how they alter or advance current ideas. If possible, indicate future lines of research.

There is no need to sum up or conclude at the end of the discussion. Most journals now print an *abstract* at the beginning of the paper, and this is often the only part that people read. Take as much trouble (or more) over composing the abstract as in writing the paper. It must contain the points that you wish to get across as factually as possible, in not more than 250 words. Following the lead of *Annals of Internal Medicine*,[1] more and more journals are adopting *structured abstracts* with headings (box). As with IMRAD, they can

---

Structured abstract

- Objectives
- Design
- Setting
- Subjects
- Interventions
- Outcome measures
- Results
- Conclusions

---

be put to good use as a template by authors, even if they are not needed in the final draft.

The practice

I write it all out in long hand just as it comes, though other people may prefer a word processor. Having summoned up the courage to begin, you cannot at this stage get tied up over niceties of style or meaning and you must keep on writing. It may help to prepare notes of the points you wish to make, and to pepper the pages of the manuscript with headings so as to maintain direction.

Next I type out on the word processor the written draft in double spacing with wide margins all round. If you think that your first attempt was sheer hell and that the worst is over, you are in for a shock, for it is now that the hard work begins. You will find that the manuscript has to be corrected and corrected again, so that it ends up almost unreadable. I spend hours worrying about choice of words and the sequence of ideas, and often have to cut up the script, to cut out sentences and paragraphs and shuffle them around. If you are clever you can do this on the word processor, but I prefer scissors and paste.

Having got as far as possible, you put the manuscript aside to mature. Unless you are working to a deadline (a useful discipline) there is no point in hurrying, however ambitious you are to see your name in print. Editors of medical journals have little sense of urgency and your claim to have discovered a cure for ingrowing toenail is unlikely to impress. I give my paper to someone else to read, someone who will tell me the truth (often unpleasant when it applies to my masterpiece) and maybe give some practical help. I would like to see one or two people in each department or hospital prepared to read and criticise papers, not for the scientific content (that is a matter for colleagues in the same field) but from the viewpoint of the general reader. It might then be possible to dispense with editors.

After a month or so you will begin to feel an irresistible urge to have another look at the paper. You will hardly recognise it and can see at once its many shortcomings. It has to be rewritten once more, but this time the task is easier and there are fewer hang ups. It is now essential to type the revised draft in the style of the journal to which you are submitting the paper; this may be the final or, if you are less confident, the penultimate copy. Note that there have been four, possibly five, drafts; it is not usually possible to get away with fewer.

The package

I hope editors are human enough to be favourably influenced by a nicely presented paper. You don't necessarily need to start writing with a journal in mind, but by the second or third draft you should know where it is to be submitted. You have studied the style of that particular journal, the length of its articles (particularly important in these days of economy), and its notice to contributors. Unfortunately, the variety of different styles and instructions is enough to put off the most dedicated author, and I am an active campaigner for uniformity in matters such as references, but it is bad manners to send off a paper to a journal you haven't bothered to look at.

The final copy of the manuscript must have double spacing, wide margins (for subediting), and be typed on one side of the paper only. Send three clean copies with the minimum of penned alterations —dogeared copies that have obviously been the rounds are unlikely to be accepted. The first (and separate) page should contain the title, together with the names of the authors, their degrees and appointments, and the name and address of the author to whom correspondence is to be sent. It is often useful (sometimes essential) to provide a short title and key words. The abstract follows on the next separate page, and then the text itself. Make sure the pages are numbered. A short covering letter, not a full length apologia, should be signed by all the authors.

The title is very important, both to catch the eye of the reader and for indexing. Many authors seem to think that titles must be long, dull, and "scientific", instead of trying to follow the example of writers like Richard Asher or the anonymous composers of newspaper headlines.

If you are reporting large numbers of patients or experiments, which are split into groups, make sure they tally in text and tables. A reader who finds that figures don't add up rapidly loses interest. Tables should be typed separately from the rest of the text. It is difficult to say anything succinct about illustrations since journals vary in their practice, but if you send photographs label them on the back in pencil with author's name, short title, and "TOP" with an arrow. Photographs have a nasty habit of getting separated from manuscripts in editorial offices or of being printed upside down. Be particularly obsessional about references—it pays to have a librarian or secretary who likes chocolates. Be sparing over acknowledgments, but avoid making enemies for life by leaving out genuine helpers.

The style

I have left to the last what is for the amateur undoubtedly the most difficult part of writing—style. The first (and rarest) quality is brevity: short words, short sentences. Why is it that intelligent people (among whom I include doctors) become imbued with verbosity the moment they put pen to paper? A staccato style must be avoided, though, and the best way to "pace" the writing is to read it aloud. Need I emphasise to a scientific audience the importance of accuracy and the correct word? We all use words not only without knowing their true meaning but also without appreciating their shades of meaning. When you write that "your results revealed . . ." do you really mean that they were "made known by divine or supernatural agency" (*OED*)? It is a valuable exercise to make up sentences in which a key word—for example, the verb—is missing and to see how many alternatives can be used and which are the most appropriate.

Try to avoid vogue words like the plague (and clichés like that). Philip Howard, whose style is worth studying, wrote a series in *The Times* in which he pointed out how the meaning of such words eventually becomes completely distorted by popular usage, words such as parameter, charisma, consensus, obscene, interface. As for "situation", its present vogue is really becoming something of a "headache situation", as I have heard a difficult problem described. There are clichés confined to medicine that make the hackles rise: "disease process", "the patient went rapidly downhill", "the patient presented to hospital".

Watch out too for the circumlocution, the round about talk, the gobbledegook beloved of civil servants and sociologists. Much of the "noise" can be removed altogether or replaced by a single word. In the fullness of time (cliché) we shall be introducing literary audit (vogue word) for medical writers, and one of the more difficult tasks (for specialist registration) will be to précis circulars from the Department of Health. You should develop a special alarm system for in-words, such as "red in colour", "moment in time", and for un-words—"it is not unusual", "it is not unexpected". Finally, try to use short, concrete, Anglo-Saxon rather than Romance words, which tend to be long, abstract, and imprecise. Dr Johnson, as always, provides the apposite example, which we imperfect writers might well display prominently in our studies: "It possesses insufficient vitality to preserve it from putrefaction" can be rendered both simply and devastatingly, "It has not wit enough to keep it sweet".

There are many books and articles giving guidance to the writer and I have prepared a list of my favourites. In them you will find not only good advice but so many warnings of the pitfalls that all but the most daring will be put off. Don't forget that much can be absorbed with pleasure from one's everyday reading. But in the final analysis nothing succeeds like repeatedly doing a job yourself and, to leave you with a few crumbs of comfort, I pass on the words of a respected journalist friend who, when asked how he managed to write with such ease, replied: "The first million words were the worst".

Further reading

Allbutt'T C. *Notes on the composition of scientific papers*. London: BMA, 1984.
Asher R. *A sense of Asher. A new miscellany*. London: BMA, 1984.
Day R A. *How to write and publish a scientific paper*, 3rd ed. Cambridge: Cambridge University Press, 1991.
Fowler H W. *A dictionary of modern English usage*, 2nd rev. ed. Oxford: Clarendon Press.
Goodman N W, Edwards M B. *Medical writing: a prescription for clarity*. Cambridge: Cambridge University Press, 1991.
Gowers E. *The complete plain words*. Harmondsworth: Penguin, 1962.
Hawkins C F. *Speaking and writing in medicine*. Springfield: Charles C Thomas, 1967.
Lock S. *Thorne's better medical writing*, 2nd ed. Tunbridge Wells: Pitman Medical, 1977.
O'Connor M, Woodford F P. *Writing scientific papers in English*. Tunbridge Wells: Pitman Medical, 1978.
Roget P M. *Thesaurus*, rev. ed. Harlow, Essex: Longman, 1989.

2 Be your own subeditor

William F Whimster

Articles pour into the medical journal offices. The editors try to judge them on their scientific and clinical value, but in very few does the value shine out clearly in a "reader-friendly" way. The reading is made into work rather than pleasure by unnecessary words, inaccurate grammar, imprecise expressions, and abbreviations, all of which distract the reader from the author's message. My aim is merely to make the message clear by removing the distractions from the writing, not to indulge in pedantry. At first some people are afraid that this process may also remove their personal style and make their writing dull and flavourless, but they are usually reassured by their own results.

As a freelance subeditor or language supervisor, mainly for papers written by authors whose first language is not English, I have tried to identify the criteria I use to improve clarity. In fact, I find I am looking to see whether the authors have applied the advice given to them by other contributors to this book (see Chapter 1).

As I am a pathologist I start with a low power or macroscopic look at the main sections of the standard original paper: the introduction, methods, results, and discussion. I see if these components are in their correct places and if I can answer the questions "Why did they start?" (introduction), "What did they do?" (methods), "What did they find?" (results), "What does it mean?" (discussion), and, overall, "What is their message?" and "Have they convinced me that their message is true?" Members of journal clubs can obtain valuable practice at this when trying to select papers to present to their colleagues.

Then I turn the microscope on each sentence and look at the grammar in a simple way. Does each sentence have a subject and a verb? Do they agree; that is, are they both either singular or plural? I check all pronouns for the nouns they are representing. I check all adjectives and adjectival phrases and clauses for what noun they are telling me more about and to see if they are necessary or could be omitted; and I take a similar approach to the adverbs and their verbs. If the verb is passive could it be made active? For example, "The patient was treated in the intensive care unit". By whom? "We treated the patient in the intensive care unit" tells the reader more, and more directly. I try to divide long sentences, to spell out abbreviations (unless occurring more than ten times in the paper), delete superfluous words and replace "journal language", which many authors copy from "the literature" and which is unnecessarily formal, wordy, impersonal, and pompous.

The fictitious passage that follows, an introduction ("Why did they start?"), shows how you can improve your own writing. You have to be careful not to be carried away with it and you may need more than one attempt.

Introduction
Approximately 200 g of boro-lithium activated charcoal (BLAC) are said to be needed *in order* to treat each severe case of Amanita phalloides poisoning *at the present time* (Smith and Jones 1984). Ford et al (1985) *were of the same opinion* but they *anticipated* that deactivator coated charcoal would *be of assistance to* a wider *spectrum* of patients *at some future date.*

After treatment *commences* the urine becomes black *in colour comparatively frequently* and *a considerable proportion of* patients *demonstrate skin* rashes *due to the fact that BLAC* still contains impurities. *It may be noted from the literature* that *during the period of the rash* the serum charcoal *level* is *elevated in excess of* 20 mg/100 ml. *It is also probable that* the blood supply to the *lower limbs* is *significantly* decreased *relative to* the *upper limbs* in *female subjects on contraceptive therapy.*

In this situation it seemed to the present authors that, *as already stated,* more *sophisticated* forms of charcoal therapy could be developed, and *they theorised* that experiments in which rats were *sacrificed following* charcoal dialysis would reveal *novel insights* into the interactions between charcoal and the new pomp deactivator, Mediflush.

This communication reports . . .

At first reading I noted that the first sentence is in the passive. In the last sentence people report, communications do not. The second paragraph does not contribute to "Why did they start?" Then I marked the words for improvement in pencil, so the changes could be rubbed out if the author disagreed.

The revised version then reads:

Introduction
Smith and Jones (1984) recommended treating each severe case of Amanita phalloides poisoning with about 200 g of boro-lithium activated charcoal. Ford et al (1985) agreed but thought that deactivator coated charcoal would help a wider range of patients in future.

[*After treatment starts the urine often becomes black and many patients develop rashes because BLAC contains impurities. While the rash lasts the concentration of charcoal in the serum rises above 20 mg/100 ml (reference). The blood supply to the legs probably decreases compared with that to the arms in women taking contraceptives.*]

We also thought that more advanced forms of charcoal therapy could be developed and that experiments in which rats were killed after charcoal dialysis would provide new facts about the interactions between charcoal and the new pomp deactivator, Mediflush.

We report the results of these experiments . . .

I have illustrated these simple techniques because I am sure that all authors, however eminent, have a better chance of acceptance if they "subedit" the paper themselves before submitting it to the editor. It is also useful to have an objective view from a sympathetic colleague who also knows the rules. As the colleague goes through the paper in front of the author, the dialogue can become quite acrimonious, so it is best for the colleague, however senior, to agree to a return match on his or her next paper. In this way differences in experience can be made constructive rather than destructive. Unintentional changes of meaning are avoided by this face-to-face verbal method, which can equally be applied to editorials, review articles, and other types of writing, which differ only in not having a standard structure.

As a pathologist I am naturally fascinated by the most elephantine example of any condition. So it gives me pleasure to conclude with a sentence I once had to subedit, on which readers may spend a few happy minutes practising their subediting technique:

It is suffice to say that although substantial data have been presented demonstrating the antigenicity as well as the presence of tissue and species-specific antigens of prostatic tissue and other associated adnexal glands tissue of reproduction of the various species studied the demonstration of the presence of tumour specific antibodies or for that

11

matter, circulating antibodies to prostatic tissue or secretions by the methods of precipitation and of passive haemagglutination in the sera of patients with benign or malignant diseases of the prostate and/or following cryosurgical prostatectomy has been despite histologic and roentgenologic observations of the remission of distant metastases in cases of metastatic adenocarcinoma of the prostate (stage 3) following the cryosurgical treatment of the primary prostatic tumour for the most part discouraging.

DISTRACTION	TYPE	HOW TO REMOVE IT
Approximately	1	About
in order	2	(omit)
at the present time	2	(omit; not true)
were of the same opinion	3	agreed
anticipated	3	thought
be of assistance to	3	help
spectrum	1	range
at some future date	3	in future
commences	3	starts
in colour	2	(omit)
comparatively frequently	4	often (no comparison)
a considerable proportion of	3	many
demonstrate	4	develop
skin	2	where else?
due to the fact that	3	because
BLAC	5	? spell out
It may be noted from the literature		(reference)
during the period of the rash	3	while the rash lasts
level	6	concentration
elevated	3	rises
in excess of	3	above
It is also probable that	3	probably
lower limbs	3	legs
significantly	1	(omit)
relative to	3	compared with
upper limbs	3	arms
female subjects	3	women
on contraceptive therapy	3	taking contraceptives
In this situation	2	(omit)
it seemed to the present authors	3	we thought
as already stated	2	(omit)
sophisticated	1	advanced
they theorised	7	we thought
sacrificed	1	killed (no ritual)
following	3	after
novel insights	7	new facts

TYPES OF DISTRACTION

1 = imprecise use of a technical word		5
2 = superfluous (usually "journal language")		6
3 = "journal language"		18
4 = wrong word		2
5 = spell out abbreviation		1
6 = needs a technical word		1
7 = unnecessary variation		2
		—
		35

3 Choose a better word

B J Freedman

In nineteenth-century England all doctors learnt Latin at school and some learnt Greek too. In that epoch the use of long words derived from Greek and Latin roots was regarded as the mark of good style. I believe this to have been the natural enjoyment derived from using an acquired skill. It served, incidentally, to render the language more intelligible internationally. Latin and Greek have virtually fallen by the wayside, and in their stead English is fast becoming, or has perhaps already become, the international language of medicine. The trend, therefore, is to return to its Anglo-Saxon roots. This is resulting in shorter, and often clearer, words. At the same time there is a trend to simplify syntax and to express one's thoughts more clearly. There is, however, a steady trickle of polysyllabic latinised neologisms embedded in convoluted clauses, which emanates from a few, mainly American, writers. I suspect that these aspects of style derive from the Italian and German components of the linguistic melting pot.

Lists of words and phrases for which more suitable alternatives are recommended have been compiled by Bill Whimster,[1] Stephen Lock,[2] and Raymond Whitehead[3] and are well worth reading. My purpose here is to mention some of my *bêtes noires*, to say why I think they are better avoided, and to suggest alternatives.

Fashionable jargon

"Overweight" was introduced, I think, to avoid giving offence to the well educated who were obese and to the plebs who were too fat.

14

Through frequent use it has unfortunately established itself in clinical terminology; unfortunately, because it is sometimes diagnosed merely by reference to tables of average or ideal body weight, and without always taking the simple precaution of looking at the unclothed patient. Some people who are overweight by this definition are stocky, muscular, and lean, yet they may be wrongly labelled overweight in the sense of obese. We are currently in a permissive age of vernacular speech. So why not say, "Madam, you are too fat?"

Comparable. Two things are comparable if they can be set together so as to ascertain to what extent they agree or disagree.

If two formulations have comparable bioavailability then we can expect them to have the same clinical effect.

"Similar" is the right word.

Vogue words

"Spiral" and "escalation" are vogue words for "increase", especially in a pejorative sense.

The question of whether the BBC . . . is the best way to preserve public service broadcasting against the pressures of spiralling costs-. . . remains unanswered.

A spiral may be flat, like a volute or the balance spring of a watch, or it may be a helix, like a spiral staircase. It is this latter image, with a vertical axis, that is intended. It may be more than coincidental that the metaphorical use of spiral seems to have begun after the dramatic publicisation of the DNA double helix. When so specified, spirals can also go down.

The dangers of the descending spiral to law enforcement . . . have been repeated for many years.

Escalation is geometrically more appropriate and will probably stay.

Medical negligence claims have escalated rapidly since the beginning of the last decade.

15

When is a synonym not a synonym?

"Treatment" and "therapy" are synonymous terms. "Therapy" is sometimes more suited to a literary style, and it is the rule in combining forms, as in "radiotherapy". The advocates of "fringe" treatments prefer to call their methods alternative therapies, presumably because the magniloquence of "therapy" is thought to invest the discipline with a greater sense of importance than would "treatment". I have no quarrel with this—well, not much—but when the word therapy is used without qualification to mean "alternative therapy", then the word becomes debased.

> VAT . . . is a tax on the freedom of choice for medical attention on those patients who prefer to have therapeutic treatment. (House of Lords)

"Manual" versus "handbook". The reviewer of a book wrote:

> Truly a manual rather than a handbook, it should be recommended to trainees in rheumatology and orthopaedics.

A handbook is a manual (Latin *manus*, hand).

The postmortem examination

"Necropsy", "autopsy", and "biopsy". Necropsy and autopsy are synonyms. Though autopsy is slightly easier in speech, it is etymologically less satisfactory since the derivation implies "seeing for oneself" (corpse understood). By derivation, necropsy specifies that a corpse is under examination. One word is enough, and necropsy is to be preferred. I thought everyone knew that biopsy meant examining a piece of tissue removed from a living subject until I read:

> Full postmortem examination was not carried out but percutaneous biopsy specimens of liver and spleen showed . . .

Pitfalls exist when communicating with Greeks, for whom *necropsia* means external examination of a corpse, while our necropsy is their *necrotomē*. Worse still, their *autopsia* means any sort of specialist inspection, for example, of the scene of a crime or earthquake damage.[4]

When we don't know the cause

"Primary", "essential", "idiopathic", "spontaneous", and "crypto-genic" are epithets used for conditions whose cause is unknown. The first three went into a decline after the second world war, but have regained their popularity in recent years.

"Primary" is used in contradistinction to "secondary". In the 1930s secondary anaemias were those due to bleeding or malnutrition; the primary anaemias were those with no apparent cause, such as pernicious anaemia. For obvious reasons that epithet for anaemia has been dropped, but "primary" is very much with us, and I have seen it currently applied to immunodeficiency disease, glaucoma, Raynaud's phenomenon, erythromelalgia, pruritus ani, and lymphoedema. It should be unnecessary to say that we are not here concerned with primary in the context of tumours.

"Essential" does not mean one must try to get it regardless of cost. A good definition in the medical context is that in the *Oxford English Dictionary* (marked "obsolete"): "dependent on the intrinsic character or condition of anything—not on extraneous circumstances". It has been applied to arterial hypertension and to thrombocytopenic purpura for many years and to these it must now be regarded as fixed, but recent accretions are benign haematuria and thrombocythaemia.

"Idiopathic". The Greek root *idio-* means own, personal, private. In a medical context, therefore, idiopathic was applied to conditions that were not related to anything else. Idiopathic has been applied to epilepsy for many decades, but it has recently burgeoned into Parkinson's disease, ulceration of the small bowel, mediastinal fibrosis, neurogenic anorectal incontinence, scoliosis, "severe anaemia", hyperhidrosis, tinnitus, deafness, persistent hepatitis, and disseminated skeletal hyperostosis.

"Spontaneous", as applied, for example, to pneumothorax, likewise implies an origin *de novo* and without apparent cause.

Every condition has its cause. When we don't know the cause, what better term is there than "cryptogenic" (Gk *kryptos*, hidden + *genesis*, origin)—in the absence of a single Anglo-Saxon derivation? Cryptogenic is the currently used epithet for certain forms of fibrosing alveolitis, cirrhosis, and chronic persistent hepatitis. Whether or not cryptogenic is found acceptable, it is manifestly absurd to have a random choice of five terms for the same thing. If we abandoned the terms primary, essential, idiopathic, and spontaneous, which are incompatible with twentieth-century thinking, in favour of cryptogenic, it would clarify and unify the terminology of the unknown.

Wrong usage

"Healthy" for "wholesome", as in the following quotations.

Fish is healthy food.
Most Germans believe that natural foods are better and more healthy than artificial foods.

Food is not healthy, it may be wholesome and those who eat wholesome food are more likely to be healthy than those who do not. The German *gesund* has both meanings, and the misuse in English may be an importation.

"Methodology" for "method". Methodology is the study of methods, for example, a comparison of different methods of evaluating the same drug. It should not be used when method is the right word.

The methodology of all three papers had much in common.

This would have been better written as "The three papers described similar methods".

"Disinterest" for "lack of interest", and "disinterested" for "uninterested".

The specialist journals are being filled with papers written out of necessity and read with disinterest.

The writer meant "without interest". Disinterested means unbiased by personal interest, impartial.

"Beg" for "ask (or put) the question".

That begs the interesting question—what is the minimum workload for a surgeon (or indeed a physician) if he or she is to maintain competence?
The first question begs another: what is pulmonary surfactant?

To beg the question is to assume what is to be proved as part of the proof. It is an error in logical thinking. It does not mean "ask the question" or "beg leave to put the question".

Wrong spelling

There is little to be said here. I believe that bad spellers are born, and that nothing much can be done to help this minority. For the average speller the remedy is to have a handy-sized dictionary within easy reach. This means, for the occupants of houses, having one upstairs and one downstairs. I recommend *Chambers 20th Century Dictionary*. Learning Latin at school helps, but it is not worth taking it up in later life merely to improve your English.

When writing for publication, you have a subeditor to correct spelling errors (and straighten out the syntax). There are, however, two words that commonly slip through the editorial net. One is "weal", not "wheal". Weal is from Old English and meant originally a ridge, hence now a raised ridge or spot on the skin. The word became confused with "wheal", also Old English, meaning a pustule.

The other is "hypercapnia" and its cousin "hypocapnia", not "hypercapnoea". This error has arisen from a mistaken belief that -pnia has something to do with breathing and should be spelt -pnoea. The relevant root is Gk *kapnos*, smoke. In this context smoke stands for carbon dioxide, whence hypercapnia means too much CO_2 in the blood, or in modern terms, a raised blood CO_2 tension.

Confusion between "who" and "whom" is not a question of spelling, but may conveniently be dealt with here. The tabloid newspapers seem to go out of their way to consolidate the confusion. I quote (not from a tabloid):

> It is now policy to start nasogastric feeding in patients whom we think will be ventilated for a long time.

Omit "we think" and it is obvious that it is "patients WHO will be ventilated".

Ambiguities

"Contemporary" used as an adjective, means belonging to the same time, age, or period. The same time as what? And when? The context usually gives the answer, but not always; and that is where ambiguity may arise.

Most of these defects arose from the limited experimental information

19

available to Carnot at the time and the imperfect state of contemporary knowledge.

. . . premiered in 1877, it links music and speech in a . . . way that won the composer great contemporary acclaim.

"Contemporary" in the above obviously refers to time past.

Contemporary issues in clinical immunology.
Contemporary gastroenteritis in infants.

In these two examples "contemporary" just as obviously refers to the present. It is where the text deals with times both past and present that there is risk of ambiguity, for example:

The characters of Sneer and Mr Dangle are warped prototypes- . . . with more pretensions but less power than their contemporary equivalents.

The foundation of Johns Hopkins Medical School in 1889 . . . led to a scientific revolution . . . illustrated by 51 . . . articles originally published in the journal together with a contemporary comment by an expert.

I suggest that, where there is a possibility of ambiguity, and the context permits, "modern" or "present day" be substituted. "Contemporary" is pushing "modern" into obsolescence. Revive the use of "modern" say I.

"Uncooperative" can mean "unable to" or "unwilling to", and unless the distinction is made clear, serious misunderstanding can occur. This is more likely to arise in case notes than in manuscripts for publication.

To "compromise", in a clinical context, is to put at risk, to jeopardise. Correctly used in:

Many of these functions are compromised . . . in the healthy aged.

"Compromised" has drifted semantically to mean also impaired.

. . . and when this exceeds the normal capillary blood pressure the arterial supply to the muscles is compromised.

Here "impaired", or more specifically, "blocked" would be better. Because present usage of "compromise" may mean either "impair" or "jeopardise" (put at risk of impairment), it is preferable to say which one means.

Lay language

When speaking to patients, use words to which they are accustomed. It is debatable, however, whether the vernacular style is suited to medical writing. I quote:

> . . . vaginal bleeding with an ectopic pregnancy can be mistaken for a period.

Care is needed where the vernacular adopts quasimedical terms. I overheard a colleague inquire about a patient's way of life. He said, "And what is your biggest headache?" In the context of his questioning this was obviously a metaphorical headache, but one that could be taken literally by a simple soul or by a foreigner.

Metaphors

Metaphors are better avoided in scientific writing, even though their occasional use may enliven an otherwise dull discussion. By their unintelligibility they may baffle those readers whose first language is not English, and who are unacquainted with our allusive phrases. For example, it may mean nothing to a foreign reader to be told that a particular sign is the "hallmark" of a certain condition, when we wish to imply that it is pathognomonic. Recourse to a dictionary, only to discover that it means *contrôle* or *Feingehaltsstempel*, will add to the confusion.

Needless syllables

In the opening paragraph I mentioned the entry into medical writing of polysyllabic neologisms and the countercurrent towards short Saxon rooted words, and I implied a strong preference for the latter on the grounds of clarity and better understanding. Unfortunately, once a long word is established it is not readily shortened. Nevertheless, in the past two decades we have seen "valvular" and "valvulotomy" shorted to "valvar" and "valvotomy", and heart sounds that were once reduplicated are now "duplicated". Good for the cardiologists. Practitioners in other specialties please note.

I conclude by offering for thought a few suggestions for change in this direction. I do not, however, expect miracles.

21

Readers will not be surprised to hear that the General Medical Services Committee has reiterated its opposition to the government's plan.

To "iterate" is to repeat or perform a second time; to "reiterate" is to do so a third time or more.

People will continue to micturate in future as they have done in the past, yet I would not be the first to point out that the root of "micturate" and "micturition" is the Latin *micturio*, to desire to urinate. The Latin for urinate is *mingo*, past participle *mictum*. This would give us "mingate" for the action and "miction" for the process. How strange that in speech the sixteenth letter of the alphabet suffices.

1 Whimster W F. Be your own subeditor. *How to do it*. Vol I. 2nd edn. London: *BMJ*, 1987: 220–3.
2 Lock S. *Thorne's better medical writing*. 2nd ed. Tunbridge Wells: Pitman Medical, 1977.
3 Whitehead R. English for doctors. *Lancet* 1956; ii: 390–3.
4 Dafforn-Ierodiakonou E. Necrotomy, necropsy, and autopsy. *BMJ* 1983; 287: 840.

4 Please an editor

Alistair Brewis

Editors are easily pleased—but not often. All they require is a manuscript that describes work that is sound, original, interesting and preferably controversial, and that is presented to their journal before any other. Matters of presentation are a secondary consideration for authors who are able to provide articles that meet these criteria because editors are prepared to take a great deal of trouble improving the arrangement of really excellent work. Most articles submitted to journals are, however, no more than reasonably sound, fairly original, and moderately interesting, and in these circumstances the editor's pleasure will be similarly moderate. The chances of acceptance are then influenced by whether or not the article incurs the editor's displeasure. There are very many ways of doing this.

Preparing for the selected journal

Authors like to have their work published in what are regarded as worthy journals, and there is an unofficial pecking order in most specialties and even among general journals. Even though editors know perfectly well that papers may be submitted to one journal after another before they are eventually published, they like the illusion that they are being offered first refusal, and authors are well advised to present their work in a fresh clean state, free from any marks that indicate that it has already been through other hands. Editors are not cheered by letters addressed to the wrong journal or by papers in a special format clearly intended for another journal; still less are they impressed by copies of correspondence from another journal, which has rejected the paper, recommending that the work be offered to them.

Where there is a choice of journals it is sensible to send the paper first to a journal showing a recent interest in the special area concerned. Editors will be pleased to see a paper developing further a field of interest or a paper contradicting previous published work. Editors are not usually pleased by papers that merely repeat work recently published in the same journal unless the subject is still highly controversial.

Most journals publish "notes for contributors" regularly; the author who wishes to please the editor will follow these to the letter. If the journal requires three copies of the manuscript, send three copies; if an abstract is required at the beginning, the paper should not be sent with a summary at the end instead. The references should be in the format required by the journal. It is worth making sure that the "notes for contributors" are current. The requirements for journals are changed from time to time as editors come and go. Even the address for submissions may change.

The *BMJ* publishes "guidelines for writing papers" regularly. Much of the advice given here is applicable to the preparation of manuscripts intended for any journal. In addition to the guidelines, several detailed checklists are published that guide referees, statisticians, and subeditors in their work. These are highly recommended reading for authors every time they prepare a manuscript.

Presentation of the text

Despite the wide availability of word processors, many manuscripts are poorly typed and badly set out. Simple faults create a bad impression. When it comes to editing the text, the subeditor needs wide margins and true double spacing. This means that the distance between the lines on which the characters lie is twice—not one and a half times—the distance found in single spacing. The type should also be large enough to be read easily. The pages should be numbered, otherwise comments in referees' reports can be uninterpretable, and if the manuscript is dropped on the floor, the task of reconstructing it could prove too much for editorial patience. Editors dislike being sent a manuscript in the form of a zig-zag strip of fanfold paper with the perforated strips still attached to the sides. Most of all they dislike the barely detectable output of a poor quality dot matrix printer operating in draft mode with a two-year-old ribbon.

Many journals now work from authors' disks. Make sure that you supply a correctly formatted disk and comply with any requirement the journal has. These may be given in the Notes for Contributors. Failing this, a quick phone call may save a lot of work later.

Matters of style

Editors like simple, direct English. Simplicity and brevity are admirable but only so far as the meaning remains clear. Papers must be capable of being understood by people who have at least some interest in the subject but are not necessarily super-specialists (the editor often comes into this category). If editors have received conflicting or only slightly enthusiastic referees' reports on a paper, they will read it carefully to make their own assessment. If they find it full of jargon and uninterpretable abbreviations, they will probably give up and reject the paper, judging that the amount of editing work that would be required at a later stage would be worthwhile only if the article was otherwise outstanding.

Parts of the paper

Title

The title is a common blind spot for authors. It should be an honest but inviting indication of the contents. Some titles can be couched in the form of a question: "Do bananas heal venous ulcers?" In general editors now discourage titles that make categorical statements: "Bananas heal venous ulcers".

Abstract

Some journals give precise guidance about length and character of the abstract in the "notes for contributors" and this should be heeded. In general, the abstract should be as informative as possible. The purpose and scope of the work should be indicated very briefly but the findings may be given in detail. The abstract must be capable of being understood on its own without reference to the paper and should not be treated as something equivalent to the trailer of a film in which the contents are suggested but the plot (and in particular the ending) is not divulged.

25

Introduction

The introduction should provide no more than is essential for the average reader of the journal to understand why the study was undertaken. Except perhaps in the case of lengthy review articles, the introduction is not an opportunity to display the depth of the author's scholarship or the breadth of his or her reading. Any references offered should be relevant and useful to other workers in the field.

Methods

Information in the methods section should be sufficient to allow other workers to repeat the study if necessary. When referring to previously reported methods, be sure that the method is exactly as previously reported or indicate departures from the original method and indicate in a few words what the method involves—this helps the non-expert reader. Statistical methods should be described, particularly where these are out of the mainstream.

Results

The results need to be given in detail, but the presentation need not be completely formal and bland. Surprising findings can be described as such and the reason for further measurements or analyses commented on in a logical narrative fashion. Where the results are best presented in a table, they should not be repeated in detail in the text. Where summarising statistics have been used, it is essential to indicate what these are. Mean, median, standard deviation, standard error, range and other parameters all need to be specified. Editors particularly like 95% confidence limits. Missing data should be declared.

Discussion

The essence of the results can be summarised in a few words but the author should avoid repeating the whole of the results section. As well as a comparison of the work with relevant earlier work and a discussion of criticisms of both, there may be room for speculation. When speculating, be modest and brief and make it absolutely clear that you are speculating. It is comforting to finish an article with a rounding off sentence at the end rather than stopping in mid air. Every editor has a sinking feeling, however, when offered the conclusion that "more work is required" and will usually strike through any fond hope "that improved understanding of the underlying mechanisms of the disorder may lead ultimately to the development of a cure (or . . . to its prevention)".

Figures

Figures should be drawn to professional standards. If graphs and similar technical figures in the target journal are redrawn as a matter of course (usually obvious, as all such figures will have an identical style and identical lettering throughout the journal) it may be acceptable to submit extremely clear draft versions. Mark the backs of figures clearly with name, figure number, and an indication of the top. Use a very soft pencil and do *not* use ballpoint or felt-tip pen. Even though the inks may seem to dry immediately they very commonly transfer on to the gelatin surface of prints with which they come into contact even over hours or days later, and the resulting damage can cause unnecessary stress and inconvenience for editors and authors alike. Figures require legends that will make them interpretable to the reader who merely skims the text. All abbreviations in the figure should be explained.

Tables

The first thing editors consider when they see a table is whether it is necessary. The second thing they look at is whether the figures add up. Some editors can hardly resist checking tables even when reading other journals; checking becomes a sport and can deteriorate into an obsession. Simple errors are surprisingly common and result in an immediate drop in editorial confidence in the paper. Each table requires a heading that makes the contents clear to the reader who only skims through the text.

References

References should be perfect. When editors first flick through a newly submitted paper they will very probably look at a selection of the references. If they can detect one or two errors on the spot without referring to other sources they know that indifferent care may have been taken with other parts of the paper and even with the work it reports. Most journals are not now able to check all references themselves and in the end the author must be relied on for accuracy. Mistakes with references are not taken lightly at any stage in the paper's processing. Editors warm to papers whose references are all referred to in the text (in the correct order), are in the style used by the journal, and are perfect to the last comma.

Revision

If an article is provisionally accepted on condition that certain points are dealt with satisfactorily, it helps the editor's work if the author submits an annotated list of points with an indication of how they have been dealt with. The numbering should match the list sent by the editor or referee. If only minor changes are requested and the editor has already edited the manuscript, it is unhelpful to retype or reprint the manuscript, as this will result in the editor having to recheck the whole of the text to see that all of the changes have been incorporated. If you do, however, make changes to the text in this way, it pleases the editor if they are indicated in light pencil or by highlighting on a photocopy. Any changes made by hand should be in pencil, rather than pen, and written or printed exquisitely clearly so that every letter is discernible.

Keep revisions to the proofs to an absolute minimum. Be clear and use proofreading marks if you know them. Errors must, of course, be corrected, but this is not the moment for delicate adjustments to the phraseology or the insertion of a few more results or references. If changes are more than a line in length, type them on a separate full size piece of paper.

Communicating with the editor

Editors are busy people. Most specialist journals are edited by part time editors who have full time clinical or academic commitments. It is easy for authors to forget that the editor of a journal might be handling 100 or 200 papers at various stages of assessment or preparation. Probably the most effective way of getting an editor's back up is to contact him or her directly by telephone and engage in urgent pleading about a paper. It is almost always pointless, as wary editors will avoid making any undertaking until they have had time to consider the matter with the manuscript in their hand and after referring to correspondence and referees' reports. The telephone caller who is not the first or corresponding author, and who does not know who the first author is or the paper's reference number, and is even unsure of the exact title is jeopardising his or her paper's chances.

If authors have something to communicate they should send a

short letter or fax and should quote the *reference number* of the paper as well as giving its title and first author. This allows editors to deal with the matter in the time they allocate to journal affairs and permits them to refer to points in the manuscript and to check on such things as previously agreed conditions for publication.

Authors quite commonly pester editors before submitting an article, asking questions such as whether it is likely to be suitable and whether it can be looked at especially rapidly if it is submitted. The editor's reaction is predictable: "Let us have a look at it and we will assess it in the usual way". Nothing is gained and, if anything, there is a risk that the editor will be irritated by special pleading and consequently be less sympathetic.

If you think that your paper has been unjustly criticised and rejected it may be worth resubmitting it with a compact, quietly reasoned argument meeting the objections. It is sensible to revise it first so as to meet all of the reasonable criticisms. It is very inadvisable to write an abusive letter to the editor. Some authors reserve their best talents for invective of this sort but the end result is usually counterproductive: editors have long memories.

Commissioned articles

So far, pleasing the editor has been discussed as a sensible adjuvant to acceptance of an unsolicited paper. Most journals have plenty of submitted articles to choose from and the editor can reject papers, or refuse to publish unless certain conditions are met, without feeling any need to please the author. When editors commission an author to write an article for a journal (or a chapter for a book), however, the relationship is different. They in effect take a gamble. They hope that the author will perceive precisely what they have in mind and then prepare a high quality manuscript. If the author produces something which is of a disappointing standard or wide of the target, the editor knows that it will require a great deal of tact, time, and probably personal work on the manuscript to recover the position. It will be difficult for the editor to refuse to publish the paper outright. Pleasing the commissioning editor is a matter of (1) writing about the subject requested and not something similar, (2) writing at a level that is appropriate to the intended readership, (3) writing to the required length and, most important of all, (4) getting it in before the deadline.

Editors are human, and like everyone else they are heartened by a

29

letter of thanks. A letter of praise will bring lasting editorial pleasure until it finally fades inside its frame.

Further reading

Lock S. *Thorne's better medical writing*. 2nd ed. London: Pitman Medical, 1977.
O'Connor M, Woodford F P. *Writing scientific papers in English*. London: Pitman Medical, 1978.

5 Write a single-author book

G C Cook

Until relatively recently most scientific texts were single-author works (frequently monographs); those written by Francis Bacon, and in the nineteenth century, Charles Darwin, A R Wallace, and T H Huxley are good examples. Most medical texts in the latter years of the nineteenth and the earlier years of the twentieth century were similarly written by a single individual—for example, Sir Patrick Manson's *Tropical Diseases: A Manual of the Diseases of Warm Climates* (1898), and Sir Ronald Ross's *Memoirs: with a full account of the great malaria problem and its solution* (1923). Such works have some clear advantages: they express the personal views of the author, there is no danger of disparate and contrary views from different contributors, they do not contain a composite accumulation of essays of differing styles with varying degrees of under- and overlapping, and, very importantly, the speed (or otherwise) of producing the manuscript is in the hands of one person. Above all, there is the great advantage of *balance*, something rarely achieved in a multi-author work. A single-author book is therefore a personal achievement based on individual thoughts, ideas, and research in much the same way as an MD or other doctoral thesis. As well as being of contemporary value—that is, in gathering together thoughts, facts, and references from diverse sources—it stands a chance of becoming a historical record, for which posterity will, it is hoped, be grateful. Why has there been this steady and relentless increase in the number of authors of books and papers in recent years? And why are more and more being edited by a team, each member of which contributes very little copy? Clearly, many factors are involved: increasing

31

specialisation in medicine and science is obviously important; the time element has become increasingly critical as the pace and, possibly, the stresses of life have increased; and leisure is now at a premium.

Why undertake it and do I have the time?

There must be an excellent reason for embarking on this enormous task and it must never be undertaken lightly. The reason for writing must be compelling. There has been a vast proliferation of medical and scientific texts in the Western world over the past few decades; most are duplications of other works and they cannot possibly justify the amount of time spent on them.

There are several predisposing or catalytic factors. In some cases a direct invitation from a publisher or series editor provides the stimulus. Another starting point is the desire to bring together, with appropriate modifications, a series of review articles into a single book (not always an attractive option for a publisher); this approach led to my *Parasitic Disease in Clinical Practice* (1990). A third possibility is the expansion of a lecture to a full text; for example, in 1989 I was invited to give a lecture to the history of medicine section of the Royal Society of Medicine, which involved a good deal of historical research, and resulted in *From the Greenwich Hulks to Old St Pancras: a history of tropical disease in London* (1992).

The book may be a straightforward record of original thoughts and new ideas. It might be an up-to-date systematic text, preferably in an area not previously adequately covered. It might be primarily a reference work—an accumulation of facts from the vast and diffuse literature in that particular field. Sometimes the major motive for writing is advertisement of the author's identity; in this case it is of paramount importance that the work is original, preferably unique, and not simply just another book. Thorough justification must thus be forthcoming before the massive task is begun; it is all too easy to underestimate the enormity of the project at the outset. Writing takes up time normally used for patient care and teaching; however, it is research time that is likely most of all to be eroded. Adequate facilities, including a good library that covers the appropriate area, and a clear deadline for completion of the manuscript are essential prerequisites. So time consuming is this venture that a predictable lifestyle, including a stable marriage and tolerant children, is an essential background factor.

Beginning the project

When the decision has been taken, a suitable publisher must be found, that is if the work has not already been requested or commissioned. Only rarely should a book be written before a satisfactory publisher has been identified and the contract signed; finding a publisher retrospectively can be a soul-destroying business. Perusal of the latest *Writers and Authors Yearbook* for a publisher with a relevant list can often be rewarding. With most publishers, the size of the royalty is predetermined; however, if doubts exist, membership of the Society of Authors can be useful for it is happy to advise on such matters.

A satisfactory title that is short, precise, gives an accurate indication of the content, and will enhance the selling power of the finished product is of great importance, but this often takes shape during the genesis of the script. It is essential first to decide at whom the book is aimed: is it for undergraduates *or* postgraduates, or is it primarily a reference work? Who will buy it: individuals or libraries? And in which parts of the world is it likely to be most relevant, and sales likely? Then you need to make a list of chapter headings; it can be altered as writing proceeds, which inevitably happens as new ideas and research come to the fore. You should agree a system for numbering sections, chapters, and subdivisions of chapters with the publisher and strictly adhere to it throughout. You should also write a sample chapter and submit it to the publisher for approval. It is certainly worth visiting the editor before starting the work and keeping closely in touch with him or her as writing proceeds. The length of the text is usually decided before the task has started. Although to most of us "x" thousand words means very little, an approximate number of pages is clearer. And while the manuscript must be as concise as possible, it must also be a complete work in its area of expertise: one that does not cover all that it sets out to do will inevitably receive critical reviews. Figures and tables are usually necessary, and should be accumulated as the work progresses; they, especially clinical photographs and radiographs, should be of the highest possible quality.

Preparation of the manuscript

As with original papers, reviews, and, above all, theses, the most difficult task is to put pen to paper; when this has been achieved the work will, hopefully, "snowball". It is essential that the agreed style—especially the form of references (most now prefer the Vancouver system or a modification of it)—is used from the outset, otherwise a great deal of time can be wasted. Concrete advice on the best way to proceed with writing is impossible: should you start at page one and proceed straight through to the end, or keep a section or several chapters running at the same time? I personally prefer the latter approach, which, to my mind, gives a more even balance. A concise style is essential. Whether it is a reference work or a monograph within a new area containing previously unexplored views, as many original ideas as possible should be included. Attempt to reveal unchartered territory, and suggest ideas for research projects if you can. Comb recent review articles meticulously, especially those from the superior scientific and medical journals; they invariably provide valuable ideas regarding up-to-date literature. How many references to include will vary enormously.

When is the most suitable time to write? Isolation from the "hurly burly" of everyday life is the ideal—either for short periods or, exceptionally, during a sabbatical. As an example, I wrote *Tropical Gastroenterology* (1980) while working in Papua New Guinea; the air-conditioned medical library at the university medical campus in Port Moresby provided an ideal milieu. But few have the good fortune to find that relative luxury. It is usually essential to reserve specific periods—early mornings, evenings, weekends; every spare moment must be utilised! With patient care and teaching, let alone research, life can become very full. Self-discipline and rigidity are essential, otherwise the deadline will rapidly approach and you will still have much to do. And that inevitably strains relationships with the publisher.

For those experienced with the use of a word processor, this method is eminently suitable. For others, not so well equipped, secretarial assistance will be necessary. An easily intelligible free hand and a secretary who can read the manuscript with ease are enormous advantages. It is wise to get completed chapters typed in draft and then to correct them while they are still fresh in your mind. Aim at producing a single draft followed by the final version—otherwise expense can become a problem; for some chapters an additional draft will, however, sometimes be necessary. Use the blue pencil liberally; accuracy is what matters in the final work. The completed top copy must be very carefully corrected, and that applies especially to the references to published work. Using a word processor, page numbering is straightforward; otherwise it is best undertaken with an automatic numbering machine. *Always retain a copy of the entire work, including illustrations, to safeguard against loss or fire*; what a disaster if the only copy is mislaid in the post or goes up in flames!

Finishing touches

The foreword and acknowledgements will, in most cases, be written as the work reaches its conclusion. The publisher will require some notes for the dustjacket; do not be afraid to sell yourself. And, finally, there is the index. This is incredibly important; many books have been ruined by an inadequate index. A good reviewer is on to a bad one like a ton of bricks. It should preferably be composed by the author, for he or she knows and has a feel for the work. If a word processor is not available, a system of index cards is vitally important, and cross-indexing essential. This is a long and tedious chore, which comes when all seems to be over, but it is essential that it is done meticulously. For a reference work the index should be long and detailed. If the publisher allows it, do have important references printed in a bold (heavy) type.

Ultimately, the proofs arrive. It is of great value if the publisher can give an accurate date of their arrival as long as possible beforehand. This is the last time you will see the work before it appears in its final form. Although it is, of course, essential to keep the corrections to a minimum, scientific accuracy is of paramount importance; reviewers and posterity pounce on mistakes, however minor they are. Accuracy of references to published work is particularly important and the only way to achieve excellence is to check them *all* against the original texts; that applies especially if the book is relevant to Third World countries, where it is often necessary for readers to write off to libraries in the West, at considerable expense, for photocopies of original work.

The task completed

Eventually, after a never-ending gestation period between submission of the manuscript and arrival of the book (I still cannot understand why this is so prolonged, when a newspaper can be produced in a few hours!), the project is, for the moment at least, complete. One hopes (and prays) that all of the proof errors have been corrected, and the more obsessional author will meticulously

35

check that that is so. Now, the reviews are eagerly awaited, and on them the book will swim or sink. One hopes that the publisher will also advertise the book widely; this is where the larger firms often provide a significant advantage.

After the publisher has sold copies of the hardbacked version to as many relevant libraries throughout the world as possible, will a paperback edition be produced? The English Language Book Society (ELBS) may do this, but the decision is dependent on their referees. Many factors determine whether this happens, but, of course, circulation and sales are greatly boosted by a cheap edition. Do not expect to "make a mint", for apart from exceptional cases—for example, a widely selling paperback—you simply will not. This must be regarded as essentially a labour of love. And now is not too early to prepare for the next edition, hopefully in some five years' time. All relevant literature should be carefully recorded on a word processor or card index system. The task is never-ending, but, hopefully, worthwhile. There can be no doubt that a well reviewed book brings a great sense of satisfaction to the mind of its hard-working author.

6 Prepare a Festschrift

Greg Wilkinson

The word Festschrift (German *fest*, festival; *schrift*, writings; pl. *-en*, *-s*) is commonly used to designate the volume of essays, papers, and the like prepared by colleagues and friends as a tribute to a scholar or savant on some special occasion—usually on reaching a certain age, stage of career, retirement, or anniversary. "Festschriften", as Gerd Buchdal says, "are for men who have put their stamp on some branch of enquiry during a certain period of time".[1] Although the first recorded use of the word in English was in 1901, there is still no satisfactory English equivalent. The preparation of a Festschrift is most commonly undertaken in the German-speaking countries. Elsewhere, it is much less common, more often a tribute to distinguished figures in the humanities and the basic sciences than in medicine.

Until now there has been no generally accepted method of preparing a Festschrift: varieties differ considerably in form and content. The typical format is most often that of a special issue or supplement of a learned journal, or of an obscure publication, rarely read (except by the recipient) and destined for a neglected library shelf. Many, if not most, examples of the genre, whether emanating from the arts or sciences, emerge as no more than an ephemeral medley of stale material, reminiscences, and anecdotes, flavoured with flattering commentaries on the person concerned.

As a consequence, the task of preparing a Festschrift is often perceived as a dutiful chore, a secular act of devotion designed to give pleasure to the recipient but mainly heartache to the editors. Too much effort surrounds the preparation and too little thought is given to the purpose.

Accordingly, when my colleagues and I decided to embark on a Festschrift for Professor Michael Shepherd, we decided to try to construct a new model, one that would be original and constitute an enduring work of academic scholarship in its own right, becoming an essential point of reference for the subject, and indicating new points of departure. The theme of such a Festschrift should ideally derive from the work of its dedicatee and in this case the theory and practice of the epidemiological approach to mental disorder was the obvious choice.[2] Until his retirement in October 1988 Professor Shepherd had held the chair of epidemiological psychiatry at the Institute of Psychiatry, the first of its kind in the world, and his own contributions have played a major part in indicating the scope of the field as it has emerged over a generation.

Genesis

The proposed volume was conceived as bringing together theory, experiment, and practical applications, and was subdivided into six sections. The first, a brief introduction by the editors, outlined the purpose and scope of the work; the second was concerned with the scientific principles that underpin epidemiological investigations; the third was divided into three subsections, each of which concerned a particular area of inquiry within the general field; the fourth was concerned with the evaluation of psychiatric intervention, and was divided into subsections that focused, respectively, on the organisation of services and the assessment of specific treatments; the fifth provided international perspectives; and the sixth and final section gave a personal overview of Professor Shepherd's achievement.

To represent the range and nature of his influence, our aim was to bring together a group of colleagues who had had professional association with him at a number of levels. We then contacted a likely publisher, sending a detailed outline, including details of chapters and the names of prospective contributors. Financial and administrative aspects of publication were also dealt with at this stage.

Next, we invited an international group of around 40 distinguished clinicians and academics to contribute, giving them specific instructions, an example of which runs as follows:

38

We are inviting you to write a chapter for the section on the scientific principles that underpin epidemiology, and would like you to discuss the relevance and importance of statistical understanding for the prosecution of research in epidemiological psychiatry. We expect that each chapter will be about 5000 words long, and we hope to deliver the manuscript to the publisher in nine months' time.

The invitation had to be qualified as follows:

Although you will receive a free copy of the book, the publishers regret that in view of the large number of contributors, it will not be possible to offer a fee. We also regret this, but hope that you will none the less agree to contribute. If, as we hope, you do agree to participate, we will write to you again soon to clarify the nature of your contribution and the details of the publishing schedule.

We sent contributors precise guidelines, including a copy of the most relevant parts of the publisher's house style booklet and a full list of contents and contributors. We took care to give individual guidance on possible areas of overlap. We emphasised that we did not want irrelevant or anecdotal mention of Professor Shepherd in the text, though his work could be referred to in a conventional manner when necessary.

On course

There were few early complications. One of our contributors had to drop out but we quickly found a replacement. Later, there were more thorny problems: one contributor's instructions had evidently not been explicit enough; one wrote twice as many words as requested, so the typescript was returned; another insisted on having numerous references printed in an unconventional style; a European contributor, though fluent in English, submitted his work in native tongue. Duplication and redundancy were minimal. Several figures and tables needed to be redrawn for publication, and a few contributors had changed address and title.

In the course of time we increased the number of chapters and contributors as our ideas crystallised. We drafted introductions to the various sections of the volume—a relatively easy task, as instructions to authors were so specific. Close to the stated deadline we wrote an encouraging letter of inquiry to far flung contributors and tackled those closer to home more robustly.

As anticipated, the material was submitted to the publisher six months over schedule. The planned 140 000 words had snowballed to reach 250 000. The subeditor's textual queries appeared with, as usual, many peculiar and unexpected errors to correct or clarify. There were abundant problems with references. Total commitment and lengthy national and international telephone calls with contributors were required, thus ensuring that all difficulties were dealt with within the allotted week. Shortly afterwards proofs arrived: because of time constraints we decided not to send them to authors. The main finding—a quarter of one chapter had been duplicated. We also found it particularly important to check contributors' names, titles, and addresses, the lists of contents and contributors, chapter headings, and index. Lastly, we provided the publisher with an (approved) photograph of our subject for a discrete position on the dust-jacket.

The book, some 550 pages in length, was officially launched at the beginning of 1989 and has been well reviewed.[3,4,5]

The following illustrative extracts bear on structure and quality:

> It serves as a "compleat" introduction to epidemiological psychiatry in the broadest definition.[4]
> The editors followed in the master's footsteps by making a teaching device of their efforts, so that others would not fail to learn what a festschrift volume could be.[5]
> But it is really quite a remarkable book, showing well the advantages of multiple authorship without the usual disadvantages. There is tremendous diversity of subject and tone throughout these essays, the breadth is greater than any single author could encompass, and yet there is a pleasing unity. This must indicate that the editing is inspired.[4]
> The most striking aspect of the book as a whole is its high level of intellectual sophistication, its reflexive awareness of its own methodological presuppositions. This is what is commonly (and naturally) missing from journal publications and what makes this book a near ideal introduction to the subject.[4]
> Happy reading. You'll enjoy the book.[5]

After publication one contributor was temporarily aggrieved because a portion of her submission was edited without consent; another was wounded because his recently elevated status had not been acknowledged; a surname had been misspelt in the list of contents. Several colleagues complained that they had not been invited to contribute.

Finally, to celebrate the publication we organised a dinner for contributors and publisher, at which Michael Shepherd was presented with a leather-bound copy of the Festschrift. A photograph was taken to mark the occasion and was sent as a souvenir to everyone concerned.

Unexpectedly, the form of our Festschrift has already attracted some attention as a possible model for tributes of this type. We have come to the opinion that its construction might provide a more appropriate and more permanent accolade on such occasions. In view of the associations of the word Festschrift, however, perhaps another form is needed; we have wondered about tributary volume.

1 Buchdahl G. Nagel's message. *Nature* 1971; **231**: 399.
2 Williams P, Wilkinson G, Rawnsley K. *The scope of epidemiological psychiatry. Essays in honour of Michael Shepherd.* London: Routledge, 1989.
3 Johnstone E C. The scope of epidemiological psychiatry. *Lancet* 1989;i:588.
4 Charlton B. Wider still and wider . . . *BMJ* 1989; **298**: 1193–4.
5 Robins L N. Social psychiatry in the European mode. *Contemporary Psychology* 1991; **36**: 121–123.

7 Review a book

Harold Ellis

Even though I have done so myself on several occasions, I am always amazed that anyone ever succeeds in actually writing a book. To collect all the ideas and the facts first, then to put them down on paper in clear English, choose the illustrations and references, check them, and then to guide the whole lot through the intricacies of galley and page proofs, indexing, and tables of contents strike me as almost impossible tasks. And as for writing a novel or a play—they seem to me to be feats beyond human endeavour. Thus, when an editor asks me to review a book, my first thought is, "What a remarkable person this author must be to have got all this into print; he or she must be an extraordinarily knowledgeable and industrious fellow, and I doff my hat to him or her."

I feel I ought to make this confession (of which I am not the least bit ashamed) at the outset of this chapter because it accounts for the fact that I have the reputation of being a "kind reviewer". I suppose most people who have written books fall into the category, very much in the same way that a mother with six children is more likely to be sympathetic towards a girl in labour than a spinster or, worse still, a bachelor might be.

A duty to readers

I did my first medical book review 45 years ago and I suppose now I average about two dozen reviews a year. These are mostly of textbooks and monographs on general surgery, but also include volumes dealing with other specialities, including surgical anatomy, history of medicine and a few books of general medical interest or on paramedical subjects. Most of these I read right through fairly conscientiously, often as bedside reading, or late at night or at weekends. I admit that I only dip into the interesting parts of massive textbooks, read the new sections of further editions of those standard books that I already know fairly well, and I do *not* undertake to read medical dictionaries through from cover to cover. I read with a notebook alongside me so that I can jot down any comments as I go along, and I pay particular interest to the author's preface and to the "blurb" on the dust-cover.

In preparing a review I believe I have certain duties to perform on behalf of my readers. Firstly, I like to give some sort of background to the book's subject: is this of particular topical interest—for example, transplantation, medical education, or the social aspects of mastectomy; does it fill a gap hitherto left open (I have just thought that there is no book entitled *Anatomy for Hospital Administrators*, and I will just make a note of that); or does it report on some important symposium (and, if so, how soon afterwards has the publisher got it on the market)? If possible, I then like to give some information about the author or authors, especially if I know them, and of their experience of the subject that they write about. Then I need to detail what the book contains, and to state whether or not it is readable, the print legible, illustrations relevant and suitably pictorial, and the bibliography reasonable and up to date.

After this, being a book lover, I consider whether it has that indefinable quality of being a book that it is a pleasure to own. Under this category are included such factors as the quality of the paper, binding, typography, and, of course, the smell. Finally, and very important indeed, I must state which members of the medical fraternity (if any) I would advise to purchase the commodity. On this I like to make up my mind. Reviewers are particularly allergic to dust-covers that state "This important volume will prove invaluable to teaching hospital neurosurgeons, professors of urology, district hospital physicians, house surgeons, clinical and preclinical students, physiotherapists, and members of NUPE" unless, I suppose, it refers to the Holy Bible. In fact, with the degree of specialisation extant today, more and more books have appeal for smaller and smaller groups of specialist readers.

Constructive criticism only

I hardly ever mention the price of the book—unless to comment in those rare cases where it is surprisingly cheap. Being an unworldly academic, I do not think it is for me to argue with the publishers about the price they charge. Presumably they wish to make their book as cheap as possible, compatible only with making some sort of profit, because they know that they can easily price themselves out of the market. After all, I would rather have a first class book, which I can own for ever, than a first class meal, at the same price, whose pleasures are only transient and which is far less good for me. No, in my opinion, the price of the book is the concern of the purchasers and not the reviewer. It is they, and not I, who need to decide whether or not they can afford it.

I also never enumerate a list of typographical errors in my reviews. I certainly state in no uncertain terms that a book is riddled with mistakes (usually associated with the related phenomenon of illustrations, especially x-ray films, being upside down), and by and large such a book should be carefully avoided. If the authors have not checked the typography, they are equally likely to have been careless with their references and with the accuracy of their material. I do indeed make a note of any errors I come across (and I am sorry to say that careless proofreading and slack production are becoming yet another "English disease"), and post the list to the authors. They are always grateful for such help and it is amazing how the same minor but annoying slip can go unnoticed in edition after edition of standard textbooks.

In my more depressed moments—usually when reviewing a book late at night—I naturally wonder whether the whole thing is really worth while; wouldn't it be better for journals to use their precious space for something else? When I cheer up again, however, I reassure myself that reviews of books, like those of films and plays, do have some important functions. Firstly, they act as a genuine guide to the purchaser, and I think many doctors decide whether or not to buy a book after reading one or two reviews about it. Speaking for myself, I buy medical books either because they are standard ones that I simply must possess for my work, or because they are written by friends of mine, or because I read about them in reviews and decide that they are for me. I am sure that many others follow these same guidelines. Secondly, reviews do act as a conscience and a quality control for our medical textbooks. A shoddy, badly written book will certainly receive its just punishment at the hands of even the kindest reviewers; a promising first edition will blossom out into a worthwhile revised version if the authors take cognisance of constructive review criticisms, and a world-beater will get to the public all the quicker when review readers realise this is something that must not be missed. Finally, and of this there is no doubt, book reviewing makes me read about a dozen more books each year than I otherwise would, and for this I am duly grateful.

8 Write an obituary

A G W Whitfield
Revised by Liz Crossan

What is the purpose of an obituary? Certainly not to notify death, for bad news travels fast and patients, colleagues, and friends will usually hear of a doctor's decease within hours rather than days. Its main objective, like the address at the funeral, is to give solace to the bereaved family. To read their loved one's achievements and good qualities extolled in carefully chosen words of eulogy undoubtedly gives comfort and a feeling of pride which to some extent mitigates grief. A kind and good obituary evokes gratitude from those who mourn, while one that underestimates its subject is swiftly met with resentment and anger, and nothing can "wash out a word of it".

An important secondary objective is of maintaining *esprit de corps*. If when a St Monica's doctor dies, colleagues all attend the memorial service, one giving an oration thereat, while another writes a generous tribute for *The Times* or *BMJ*, it all helps to maintain the prestige of St Monica's, and this applies in the same way to the medical community of a town, the medical service of the navy, army, or air force, or any other medical body.

A third function of the obituary is to provide posterity with a fragment of accurate medical history of the period. The purpose of an obituary is certainly not to try to convince the world of the greatness of the person who has died, whose existence was unknown to all but a few when he or she was alive.

The length of an obituary will be decided largely by the journal for which it is being written and to which it must be exclusively submitted. Unless your subject was someone of very great national importance, half a dozen double column inches is the maximum that

The Times will be able to print and if a cabinet minister or film star happens to choose the same day on which to die even this may be curtailed. On the other hand, an obituary written for inclusion in *Biographical Memoirs of Fellows of the Royal Society* may stretch to any length the writer has the strength to produce. Medical journals, particularly the *BMJ* and the *Lancet*, are under great pressure for space and the editor of the *BMJ* now asks for contributions to be restricted to at most 250 words. Naturally this allows little scope for non-essentials.

Speak of me as I am

What therefore should an obituary include and exclude? While none of us of course knows, it seems unlikely that in the next world we shall have to apply and compete for consultant vacancies. In fact, in that undiscovered country it may be that we shall be allotted humble and distasteful work as a counterbalance to the privileged position, the high salary, and the index-linked pension that we have enjoyed here. Obituaries should not therefore just list qualifications and experience that could be used for job applications on the other side of the river. In fact, the obituary's content should be confined to what is interesting and important, and it should endeavour to paint a portrait and capture the spirit of the person. No one is without blemish and no life is free from fault; to stress the good qualities is essential but the canvas must also show the special attributes and skills, the humour or lack of it, the leisure interests, and the many different attitudes and beliefs that together made up the person whose life we are striving to honour in generous perspective. Strict factual accuracy is essential. No children reach for their pen more quickly than those whose parent is erroneously recorded as having been president rather than the assistant secretary. The *BMJ* asks for the cause of death to be mentioned, but other publications may prefer not to do this.

Gathering detail for an obituary may prove difficult. *Who's Who*, the *Medical Directory*, the *Medical Register* and college lists may provide a good deal of information, but it is usually necessary to approach members of the family about some items and it is a revelation to find how often they are unable to help in filling the gap.

You should include a photograph if you can obtain one; the family, hospital, or medical school or a friend will usually be able to find one that they are willing to lend, but, if not, the portrait libraries hold an enormous number and can often help.

The family of the deceased should be mentioned, particularly if any of them have entered the medical profession, but however distinguished they may have become it is important to do little more than mention them—it is not their obituary that you are writing.

The opening paragraph (or, for the *BMJ*, the final one) should state, "John Henry Smith, the well-known physician from Much Binding in the Marsh, died in hospital on 1 April", and then the date and place of birth, parentage, and short particulars of scholastic, university, and postgraduate education should follow. Two or three lines are all that are required for this unless there are some features that would be of especial interest to readers. The *BMJ* does not include this paragraph in its 250 word limit, but the remainder of the obituary should not repeat any of the details given here.

Many hospitals and medical schools, realising the importance of good obituaries, insist on anyone appointed to their staff completing a proforma of biographical details and updating it every five years. In addition, many designate a senior member of staff to be responsible for writing, or persuading a suitable colleague to write, an appropriate tribute when the time arrives. Although such coordinators are sometimes said to add another terror to death, if some arrangement of this nature is not made, hurtful omissions are inevitable. If it is left to the subeditor of a journal to invite an obituary, the request may reach someone who did not hold his or her deceased colleague in high regard, with embarrassing results. Certainly you should decline a request to contribute an obituary of someone for whom you had feelings of contempt or dislike, and an editor or subeditor might perhaps most suitably approach the appropriate professor when seeking an obituarist. The best obituaries, however, tend to come from those who have been colleagues and personal friends of the subject, and his or her family will often express this preference or make their own approach.

Advance notices

Many editors keep obituaries ready for publication for figures of great eminence or advanced age or who are known to be mortally ill so that they may be promptly published. This is not only good journalism but is a very acceptable compliment to the deceased. In fact, an obituary loses a proportion of its value with every day that passes between death and publication. An additional advantage is that it allows the editor time to consider who would be the most fitting person from whom to request the tribute. The undesirability of delay is reflected by the rule of the editor of the *BMJ* not to publish an obituary received more than three months after a person's death.

"Write your own" is just beginning and it has the advantage that obituaries so compiled are likely to be factually correct and that they will be ready for publication as soon as death occurs. The obvious difficulty is the modest and self-effacing undervaluing their worth, and the egoistic and self-satisfied painting too flattering a portrait of themselves.

There are many volumes of biography made up of obituaries of varying quality. The standard of those in the *Dictionary of National Biography*, *Munk's Roll*, *Plarr's Lives*, *The Times*, the *BMJ* and the *Lancet* is high, but writing an obituary is, like any literary skill, an art that requires time and practice to acquire, and some never succeed. An obituary is as much a measure of the writer and his or her relationship with the subject as it is of the subject, and many are so apt and moving as to become part of our nation's heritage. Dr Samuel Johnson's obituary poem to Robert Levett, whom he had known for over 40 years, was a wonderful example of how to write an obituary, and his tribute to his lifelong friend, David Garrick, whose death "eclipsed the gaiety of nations and impoverished the public stock of harmless pleasure", will live forever.

9 Referee a paper

D A Pyke

There are three arguments in favour of refereeing. First, no editor can know his or her subject well enough to be an expert in all its aspects. This must certainly be true for a general medical journal, such as the *BMJ*, but I think it is true even for specialist journals. My particular interest is in diabetes. That sounds a narrow subject but there are at least six English language journals, each containing about 100 pages an issue, devoted entirely to this one subject. A quick look at the list of contents shows how varied are the papers: clinical, biochemical, pathological, statistical, and immunological. I do not know anyone who would claim to be an authority on all these aspects of diabetes. My view seems to be shared by the editors of *Diabetes* and *Diabetologia*; both these journals use referees.

Second, it takes a long time to establish a journal's reputation, but it may soon be lost if a few bad or hastily written papers or papers without proper acknowledgment of other work are published. It is the ease of making bad mistakes and their disastrous consequences that support the need for expert refereeing. (Referees make mistakes too—there is only one sure way of not publishing bad papers, which is not to publish any.)

And third, most manuscripts can be improved by advice from referees. This may have nothing to do with grammar or style but may concern a reference that has been missed, a conclusion that is over bold, or a technique that needs description. The referee may see, in a way that an editor cannot, how a paper can be improved by amplifying or explaining part of the work, or that the paper would be better if deferred until more material has been collected or more experiments done.

The two arguments against refereeing are, first, that it causes delays. Recently the process of publication has been speeded up in most of the more general medical and scientific journals (*BMJ*, *Lancet*, *Nature*); refereeing takes time, so omit it. But referees can be prompt. In practice the time taken to referee a paper is only a fraction of the whole submission-to-publication time.

The second argument against it is that refereeing does not lead to the best selection of papers. A general editor can do just as well. My bias is against this, and I think poor selection of papers shows, at least to the expert reader.

I have set out some of the pros and cons of refereeing, but why must we come to any definite conclusion? Why not have variety? I am, in general, in favour of refereeing for medical journals but I am glad that there are some editors who never referee and some who break their own rules. The editor of *Nature* in 1953 cannot have needed a referee to advise him to accept that paper by Watson and Crick.*

If I were chairman of the journal commitee of the BMA I would say to the editor: "I hope you will go on using referees but I also hope that you will use your own judgment, not merely on bad papers, which I am sure you can easily reject without advice, but also on good papers, whoever the authors may be. It may be easy to decide to accept a paper by David Weatherall or Cyril Clarke, but you may also get a paper that you like by someone you have never heard of, and then I hope you will take it."

Editors' decisions

Editors must know what they want from their referees: straight advice on whether to accept or reject, or, in addition, criticism of the paper and, if so, in detail or only in outline?

Editors must choose their referees and referees must have certain qualities: they must be reliable and punctual (unpunctuality is an incurable curse). Editors soon learn whose judgments cannot be trusted. My guess is that most referees tend to err on the side of recommending rejection and the editor may have put on a slight bias

---

* But even that great paper could have been improved! The first seven words of the famous last paragraph—"*It has not escaped our attention that* the specific pairing we have postulated immediately suggests . . ".—are superfluous.

to compensate for this. On the other hand, a referee who recommends acceptance of a paper that is then demolished in correspondence should probably be dropped. Individuals may have been good referees once but cease to be so because they do not keep up with their subject or take on too many other commitments. They should be dropped.

Should editors use one referee or more? If they use a second referee, either simultaneously or after the first has reported and they disagree, what then? Use a third, or disregard them both? It is probably better, as a rule, to use only one referee but there are many exceptions. Indeed, referees may themselves suggest that the editor takes another opinion because they are unsure of their own judgment or are not familiar with the whole scope of the work being considered.

Should editors transmit the referee's comments verbatim to the author? Rude comments such as "waste of time" or "useless work" will offend the authors, and there is no need to pass them on. All authors, whatever their protestations of indifference, are as sensitive as mothers at baby shows and just as protective. If editors want to reject a paper, they can do so politely and, unless there is a special reason—for example, that the paper would be better in another journal—without giving a specific reason. Some may disagree with this advice on the ground that it lacks courage or is secretive, but I see no point in rubbing salt into the wounds of rejection—and another editor may accept the paper.

Should referees be named or anonymous? In theory referees should be named: the authors know whom they are dealing with and everything is open and acknowledged and referees are restrained from indulging their whims and prejudices. I believe this is a facile argument and that referees will usually give better opinions if their identity is protected. They are spared the embarrassment, for example, of being seen to recommend rejection of a paper by a senior colleague or personal friend. Of course, the editor has to choose referees carefully when they are privileged by confidentiality and reject those with obvious bias, but that is part of good editing.

How to choose referees? In most subjects there are many experts in the country and from them good referees can soon be selected, but in some highly specialised fields an editor may have to reach across the world to find the right person.

If editors reject a paper they should be ready, if the author challenges them, to think again and perhaps consult another referee.

Referees must accept that they are not the only adviser an editor may use and that they are giving an opinion, not making a decision.

The referee

Some simple rules:

(1) Don't lose the manuscript. A former chief of mine had a bad few hours before his secretary found a manuscript he had accidentally thrown away on the town rubbish tip. If you lose the author's only manuscript I advise immediate emigration.

(2) Be prompt. If you cannot read and comment on the manuscript (which does not usually take long) within two, or at most three, weeks, return it at once. It doesn't take any longer to read the paper today than in a fortnight, and it won't go away if you put it in the bottom of the "in" tray.

(3) See what exact questions the editor is asking you. For example, the editor of the *BMJ* asks specific questions about a paper: Is it original? Is it reliable? Is it clinically important? Is it suitable for the *BMJ* or would it be better in another journal?

(4) If in doubt add a bias in favour of recommending publication. A borderline paper published is not a sin, but a reasonable paper rejected is a shame. The temptation is for the referee to be superior and advise rejection. It should be resisted. The purpose of medical journals is to convey information, not to block it.

(5) Don't nitpick. There is a strong tendency of referees to find little faults. A referee may prefer one way of expressing results but if the author prefers another there may be no harm in that. The referee is not the author. In short, don't be bitchy. Your opinion may be confidential but write it in such a way that if it were published you might be embarrassed but not ashamed.

(6) Don't be overawed by the authors: famous people can do bad work and write bad papers. And papers from famous departments may be badly prepared and may not (or so one must suppose) even have been read by some of their illustrious authors.

(7) Don't ask silly questions of the authors. Don't ask them if they have collected results that it is obvious they have not. If the absence of those results invalidates the paper, advise rejection; if not, keep quiet. Likewise, don't suggest new work. You are judging this paper, not the next.

(8) Don't get bogged down in details. At the first reading take

the paper at speed to get its general feel and then turn to points of technique or detail.

(9) If you have comments that you specially do not want the authors to see, make that clear to the editor.

(10) Try to resist the temptation to advise acceptance of a paper merely because it makes frequent (and favourable) reference to your own work.

(11) Don't get in touch directly with the author, least of all by telephone. If referees are meant to be anonymous, they should stay so.

Conclusions

I come back to a few points: referees usually improve a journal; they should be anonymous, but they should write as if they were not; the editor should not usually give detailed reasons for rejecting a paper.

Finally, there are no absolute rules in this matter; variety is of the essence of progress, which is what medical publishing is for.

10 Edit a staff round

Robert Winter

Examination of the *BMJ* over its 151 years shows the staff round to be an established forum for clinical teaching, criticism, and advancing ideas. The weekly medical staff round at the then Postgraduate Medical School of London has been recorded in the *BMJ* at various times, the first clinicopathological conference appearing in 1959 and describing a 30-year-old man with lupus nephritis and endocarditis.[1] Publication of clinicopathological conferences in the *BMJ* continued more or less regularly until 1960, occasional contributions continuing up to 1978.

Colleagues in North America have had the impressive weekly records of the case records of the Massachusetts General Hospital for 80 years since their foundation by Richard Cabot.[2] The case records were first published in book form, but in 1915 Cabot's secretary began recording the discussion, including this along with the clinical and necropsy reports in the material circulated to a restricted list of physicians. Later still, these records were published in the *Boston Medical and Surgical Journal* (now the *New England Journal of Medicine*), marking the start of a series that later won world renown and which has continued without interruption to this day—a notable record. The records now form an important part of that journal; the section has a full-time staff, and accounts of the records in the form of 35 mm colour slides and other audiovisual material are provided for educational purposes. Discussion of a single case in its wider context has a particular appeal, perhaps because for most the craft of medicine is learnt from treating individual patients and from sharing the experiences of others.

Most hospitals now hold a weekly staff round. This provides a formal occasion for clinical problems and their management to be discussed. Although the standard can vary, these presentations often provide an excellent overview of a clinical subject. This brief account describes how I have edited the medical staff round at Hammersmith for the *BMJ* and gives guidelines to those planning to submit cases for publication.

Selection of cases

Cases published during the past two years have covered most main specialties. Those that have worked well include reports of rare complications of common conditions, such as thrombocytopenia in sarcoidosis,[3] and of disorders whose incidence seems to be increasing or whose diagnosis may be easily overlooked—for example, systemic candidiasis.[4] Advances in the management of common conditions, such as using antibiotics to treat hypergastrinaemia for bacterial colonisation in peptic ulcer disease,[5] or the application of topical techniques that non-specialists have read of but not seen used, such as the molecular analysis of human genes,[6] also make good reports. It helps if there are good radiological and pathological features. I have tried to select cases that are appropriate for a general clinical readership, as more esoteric cases are better suited to specialist or basic science journals. When uncertain about whether a case is suitable for publication I have sent a synopsis to the journal and left the final decision to editorial staff; this has prevented would-be contributors spending time and effort on a case that may not be publishable.

Writing the report

The headings of introduction, clinical history, comment, and discussion have been used throughout the series. The introduction, clinical history, and comment are written by the team presenting the case, who take responsibility for its accuracy. The introduction should state clearly the reason why the case is being reported. What are the interesting points? Why should the reader read on? The clinical history should summarise the salient clinical points, giving relevant information about presentation, physical signs, and abnormal and relevant normal results of investigations. Space does not allow the case to be written up as a whodunnit in the style of the *New*

England Journal of Medicine and it was not the intention to try to emulate this series. The usual guidelines about good medical writing apply: short words, short sentences, and no abbreviations. The account preferably should be written on a word processor, as this helps subsequent editing even though the journal does not accept the final account on disk. The floppy disk can, if needed, be borrowed by other participants, who may wish to add references or to change text. Spell checking (and virus detecting) software is useful to scan the various contributions.

Discussion

Steering the discussion of a case is a skill, and the Hammersmith tradition, apparent from the earliest accounts, of putting staff on the spot by asking for specific comments leads to interesting and pithy discussion. Responses that do not deal adequately with the subject are picked up on as a matter of course. Seniority provides no immunity here—often the reverse. I have tried to convey some of the cut and thrust atmosphere of the discussion in these reports. Direct rather than indirect speech is used and contributors are identified by their initials, the discussion group being named fully in the footnote.

A tape recording is essential for editing the discussion. Many hospitals have an audiovisual department, and at Hammersmith their assistance has been invaluable. We found that a perfectly good recording could be obtained by using simple, inexpensive equipment, with the presenter using a neck microphone (needed for amplification in our lecture theatre) and by having a single free-standing microphone positioned to record audience discussion. If several cases are to be recorded tapes should be labelled clearly with date, title of case, and presenter.

Considerable editing of the discussion is needed as spoken and written English differ. It is a well known journalistic maxim that we use about twice as many words to describe something orally as we would use in writing. I transcribed the discussions directly rather than use secretarial help because it seemed easier to make the transition from spoken to written from the tape rather than from a verbatim transcript.

Figures and illustrative material

With all radiographs and clinical slides it is important to remember that features clearly visible on the original can be lost in the process of reduction and reproduction. An accompanying line diagram can clarify points of interest, and with histological slides annotation on the photograph can help the reader to orientate a figure. Clinical slides and other material submitted for publication should be free from any numbers or names by which the patient could be identified, and the patient's consent should have been obtained for clinical photographs. Most of the illustrations in the staff rounds have been taken directly from 35 mm slides or black and white prints, and I have generally taken a copy of these before sending them in case of loss in the post or mishap at the printers.

Approval of participants

It is important to get the approval of all participants, especially so that they feel that their contribution has not been misrepresented. Sending each person a copy of the report for comments before submission is a good way of checking accuracy and also allows participants to add to their contribution or to include references to support their statements. Circulating the final draft to all concerned is particularly important because, aside from maintaining goodwill for the exercise, the discussion benefits from clarification and additional comments.

Those who have made a particular contribution to patient management should be acknowledged. This especially applies to colleagues in radiology, histopathology, echocardiography, and surgery. When appropriate we have also acknowledged the referring physician, to whom a final copy of the report has been sent for comment before publication.

Proofs and editor's responsibility

There is greater potential for error when an article contains several contributions from different individuals. It has therefore been our practice for two people to check the proofs. The system reputedly used by the staff of the *New Yorker* magazine of putting a pencilled dot above each word as it is checked is probably the best advice to those who have little previous experience.

Because each article has many contributors it is also important that one person assumes overall responsibility. The editor is in a position to see an article through from case presentation to the final report in print, and the interval is seldom less than six months. The

---

Steps for producing a staff round

1 Choose case
  - Suitable for general readership?
  - Need to send summary for editorial approval?

2 Commission article
  - Agree deadline for first draft

3 Illustrations
  - Will they reduce?
  - Line diagram or annotation needed?
  - Patient anonymity maintained?
  - Check copyright

4 Discussion
  - Abstract from tape recording
  - Circulate draft to participants

5 Merge discussion with the case history and comment

6 Check accuracy with participants and contributors

7 Acknowledgments

8 Check proofs

---

editor's task is to liaise with all contributors and with editorial staff and to have overall responsibility for the manuscript. The box gives a checklist for those intending to prepare a case presentation for publication.

In summary, staff rounds are an important forum for sharing clinical experiences within a hospital. Clear and well illustrated reports of these discussions will help extend their educational benefit.

Acknowledgments

I acknowledge the advice of colleagues in the department of medicine in preparing this article.

1 Kincaid-Smith P S. A case of many lesions. *BMJ* 1959;i:224–9.
2 Cabot R C. *Differential diagnosis.* Vol 1. Philadelphia: W B Saunders, 1911.
3 Larner A J. Life threatening thrombocytopenia in sarcoidosis. *BMJ* 1990;**300**:317–9.
4 Bates J. Systemic candidiasis: an unusual complication of eating mutton. *BMJ* 1989;**299**:557–8.
5 Levi S. Campylobacter pylori, duodenal ulcer disease, and gastrin. *BMJ* 1989;**299**:1093–4.
6 Cox T. An independent diagnosis. *BMJ* 1990;**300**:1512–4.

11 Enhance your practice annual report

Stefan Cembrowicz

Since April 1991 doctors have been obliged to provide their family health services authority with an annual report containing some basic data about their practices. This data must include details of:

- ancillary staff,
- alterations to the premises,
- patient referrals (both outpatient and inpatient) by specialty,
- other commitments of the doctors,
- details of the complaints mechanism, repeat prescribing system and whether a practice formulary is in use.

These reports make dull reading and are of questionable value. How can they be enhanced?

Our practice started producing an annual report in the mid-1980s. It began in a simple way, stimulated by an interest in recording the variety and volume of our work. It has now grown to fulfil a remarkable number of uses within and beyond the practice.

We operate a rotating medical editorship, with a different partner taking charge every year. Every doctor and each group of team members, including the cleaners, is "invited" to contribute and given a deadline of 1 January.

Our report starts with a foreword or introduction from a local personality or celebrity, such as a councillor or the mayor or member of parliament. This can be followed by an editorial review.

What to include in your annual report

- Foreword or introduction
- Editorial review
- Description of practice—premises, equipment, staff, etc.
- System of care provided
- Audit
- Finance
- Reports from each group on the staff
- Brickbats and bouquets
- Illustrations, charts, photographs, poems
- Obligatory data for family health services authority

Structure of the practice and its team

Write a short background of the practice including a description of the premises and catchment area. Briefly describe the sort of records that are kept and whether you have a computer or word processor with specialised programmes. If necessary mention the communications available within the practice—whether bleeps, car phones, or hand held phones and the type of switchboard used. Mention the range of publications in the practice library and list special practice equipment—for example, a video, resuscitation equipment, oxygen, nebulisers, electrocardiograph, and the facilities available for minor operations and family planning.

When you list the team members make it clear who are the principals, assistants, and trainees, and to what extent locums and deputising services are used. The rest of the staff can then be included.

System of care

Under the heading "system of care" give the surgery hours for both the main surgery and branch surgeries. If specialist clinics are held, such as diabetic or well women clinics, these can be listed separately. This is a useful place to deal with your system for repeat prescriptions and any dispensing arrangements.

Audit

Audit has an important place in any self-respecting practice report. How this is laid down is a matter of individual preference.

61

Comparisons can be made between practice statistics and local, regional, and national figures for items such as attendance rates per patient and per year and patient turnover—that is, new patients and loss of patients because of death or moving away. Demographic details of the practice population should also include information on temporary residents. Much of this information can be relegated to the appendices.

It is worth having a section devoted to unusual aspects of the practice which could be a peculiarity of your catchment area and to mention some particularly interesting patients who have been seen during the year. For instance, in our practice, during the year of the Olympics we saw three cases of gynaecomastia among weightlifters who took illicit steroids.

Finance

It is important to provide information on the cost of the practice. We include such items as the number of auxiliary staff per general practitioner and the costs per capita of general practitioner services. It is illuminating to itemise prescribing costs from the Prescription Pricing Authority review and include the amounts of certain drugs prescribed such as benzodiazepines. Local and national comparisons are available, and we considered a "financial supplement" comparing our income from items of service payments with national averages. These figures can be gleaned from magazines such as *Medeconomics* and *Financial Pulse*.

Individual reports

In our health centre we have several dozen staff (including part-timers), and we think that it is important for each staff group to have a say in the report. The brief is to define workload this year, aims for next year, and special problems.

We encourage collecting simple statistics and performance reviews. Many statistics are already collected by various team members but never gathered together.

Research, training, and teaching projects should be included, as well as papers that have been written. This might be followed by listing any outside sessions and other commitments such as occupational medicine or work for the Department of Health. Consider drawing a pie chart of the working day and saying how it could be improved. This is an ideal space for individual opinions to be aired, whether about special problems that have been experienced or ideas for the future.

A short piece on how study leave is used makes interesting reading, and perhaps you can finish by naming the best medical book read during the year.

Layout and publishing

Keep the reader's attention by breaking up the pages with graphs, illustrations, pie charts, histograms, photographs—and even poems. Insert anecdotes, include some items on newsworthy local issues, and make use of a "brickbat and bouquet" section to publicise those who have caused problems or helped to solve them. Items from the waiting room suggestion box or comments from the patients' participation group add spice.

No one wants to read densely packed typewritten pages. Avoid solid blocks of type on the page; divide the pages into columns and use subheadings for each topic introduced. Some expert advice from an experienced journalist friend, relative, or patient can help you to avoid dull presentation. Copies of the *BMJ*, the *Lancet*, and even *Private Eye* are good examples of expert layouts.

Contributions can be typed on A4 paper and illustrations stuck down in the relevant places. Photocopy the whole lot and bind with plastic spines and a cardboard cover. One year a generous patient let us use his photocopier in exchange for a donation to charity.

Typing and editing on a word processor can produce a "letter quality" printout, which can be printed or photocopied commercially. This cost us £120 for 120 copies last year. The health authority or family practitioner committee may be able to help by allowing the use of its photocopying and collating equipment. One year the Royal College of General Practitioners charged £200 for producing 200 photocopies. Commercial printing would have cost a little more.

Colour snaps are relatively cheap to use for a team photograph, particularly if you use your high street photo processing centre. One of these photos glued to the front cover makes it more likely that the report will be kept—at least by those in the picture.

Practices that have access to more up-to-date hardware can

produce the layout with desktop publishing and use laser printing direct from a floppy disk.

Insert an assessment slip into the report for readers to return with their comments.

Circulation list

The circulation list might include: all staff; friends and neighbouring practices; interested colleagues at home and abroad; members of training groups and research groups; the Royal College of General Practitioners; the regional adviser in general practice; the postgraduate tutor; local university departments of general practice; the district general manager; nursing officers and administrators; the community health council; the family practitioner committee; your member of parliament.

Patients can be overlooked as a valuable resource to a practice, so decide at an early stage whether you will give them access to a report, for instance, in the waiting room, on request, or through a patient participation group.

What it can achieve

Within the practice

Producing our annual report has been a painless introduction to simple performance review. This in turn has led to more detailed audit, which has stimulated improved practice management—hesitant partners can be encouraged to contribute with the prospect of improved financial returns.

We find it a safe way of letting off steam, as it airs issues that may not come to light during team or practice meetings. Visitors, students, trainees, and job applicants use it as a source of information, and we have found it useful as a reference store for projects and audits that may bear fruit in the years to come.

As a method of expressing common goals and tasks the report is invaluable and is a reminder that team members with widely differing backgrounds can share similar aims. As time goes by it is fascinating to read old copies and realise how much change there has been over the years, and it provides us all with a tangible record of the richness and diversity of general practice. This approach also makes providing obligatory data less of a chore.

Outside the practice

As general practitioners working in a health centre we are aware that owing to shortages of cash the health authority is unable to maintain premises and supply staff in accordance with our original agreements. Mentioning these matters in a report that is widely circulated does seem to help.

I also find it is a way of keeping in touch and of exchanging ideas and enthusiasms with friends and neighbours whose practices may be greatly dissimilar from ours. It can also stimulate helpful suggestions from the most unexpected quarters. Doing a simple report is just another way of looking at the quality of care in practice and adding our support to the Royal College of General Practitioners' initiatives.

Standing back and looking at your work will help you to avoid being overwhelmed and burnt out by it, and will remind you of your rewards from it.

Don't be daunted by all this. A two-page report may be more interesting than a 40-page report. Remember:

- start small,
- define your aims,
- have a good look at someone else's report,
- involve everybody,
- enjoy doing it.

12 Write—and use—the annual report of the director of public health

John Middleton, George Pollock, Kathy Binysh, Valerie Chishty

Before the health service and local government were reorganised in 1974 medical officers of health had a statutory duty to produce annual public health reports.[1] Subsequent, and continuing, organisational changes have necessitated a re-examination of the aims and objectives of producing, *and using*, such reports.

The Acheson report on public health in England defined public health as "the art and science of the prevention of disease, the prolongation of life and the promotion of health through the organised efforts of society".[2] The linked implementation circular HC(88)64 required health authorities to appoint a director of public health (DPH) and for this director to produce an annual report on the state of the public health in the district or region.[3] Further guidance, issued under cover of HSG(93)56, emphasised the need for all authorities and agencies to work within a coordinated and comprehensive public health strategy to achieve the best possible health for the population.[4] HSG(93)56 stresses the key role of the annual report as the cornerstone of the NHS planning cycle, providing the health needs assessment from which should flow the purchasing plans and corporate contracts of district health authorities. This chapter concentrates on district public health reports because of the changed situation resulting from the later stages of the reforms of the NHS.[5]

Districts have now had four years' experience in producing annual public health reports. This account is not intended to be an analysis of these documents; neither can it be a comprehensive guide to how these reports must be produced. Each director of public health must

Health service commissioning: advice to the health authority

- To assess health and health care needs
- To assess health service deficiencies, clinical effectiveness and actions
- To inform decisions on priorities and choices in health and health care provision
- To inform and formulate local health policy and strategy.

Advice to other agencies and developing healthy alliances

- To advise the local authority, family health services, voluntary sector, industry and trades organisations, the police, and combined justice system, church groups, and other bodies on their contribution to improving health
- To draw attention to social problems that affect health, and can be resolved only by action by other local agencies, or by national action
- To "market public health" to show the work done by the department of public health, indicating its relevance to decisions being taken by the health authority and other agencies, and advertising its expertise as a resource for the local community.

An information resource

- To be a source of data for local providers and the local community
- To be a cumulative source of in-depth studies on a wider range of subject areas, for example by including an index of previous reports' subjects
- To report local health studies undertaken during the year and recommend action based on these studies
- To report local epidemiological artifacts and advise on further research needed
- To report and restate public health successes, such as fluoridation of water supplies or clean air acts
- To be an archive for reference in the future.

Fig. 1 Aims of the annual health report

bring his or her own personal mark to the report for it to maintain its value and its appeal. This article is based on our personal endeavours in Coventry,[6,7] which predated the Acheson Report, carrying through to individual district reports in the case of two of us (VC and JM) alongside certain responsibilities for national surveillance and development of the public health function held by the remaining two (GP and KB).

Aims of the public health report

The public health report is aimed primarily at health authorities, as a tool for commissioning health and health care services (see fig 1). It appears that the purposes to be served by the annual report have increased greatly in number since 1990. Many of the "new public health" reports produced during the 1980s by health authorities, local authorities, and pressure groups were statements of local health strategy.[8–12] What was missing was political respectability, allied to centrality in the managerial system. Now, the NHS reforms and central policy directives such as *The Health of the Nation*[13] have given health policy greater prominence over health service delivery, and placed directors of public health at the centre of local health policy development; their annual reports have therefore become essential tools for health policy, planning, and commissioning. They have also been allowed to become advertisements for the development of local healthy alliances, giving mainstream respectability to a "Health for all" principle, "multisectoral working".

The assessment of epidemiological health needs, always practised to an extent by community physicians and public health practitioners in the past, has also been elevated to a health commissioning tool, sitting comfortably in the context of the new NHS as a device for rational planning and, by implication, for rationing of health and health care resources.[14] There is much expectation on the part of NHS managers that public health reports will give them the answers they need about how much of a service they should buy. The reports are also expected to contribute significantly to local debates about priorities and choices.

The change in outlook in annual public health reports has been one of status, focus, and emphasis: many of the first wave of annual reports after the Acheson report were wide-ranging, but limited in the depth of the information they contained and offering general, multiagency, health-for-all philosophies for local health policy.[6,8,15,16,17] More recent reports have become more focused with health needs analyses based on local priorities and much greater emphasis on health-care problems, and they have been reported in greater depth.[18,19,20]

Two aspects of the report have not changed. It is essentially a reflection of health issues at *local* level and the perception *is* personal to the public health physician who holds the overview position locally. The document presents the independent, professional view of the director of public health, but it is likely to be an ineffective and hollow document if its recommendations cannot command the support, and therefore the resources, of local managers, clinicians, politicians, and the communities they represent.

Content of the report

This chapter will not cover in detail the potential contents of annual public health reports. The appendix gives a list of possible sources of local and national data that can be looked into for the wide-ranging style of health profile, or selectively for in-depth needs analyses. The health needs assessment toolbox prepared by Muir Gray and colleagues on behalf of the Faculty of Public Health Medicine and the Department of Health is a useful pack to assist directors of public health, particularly through their first annual report.[21]

A number of national resources have been developed in the last few years in support of local needs assessment work. The Public Health Common Data Set is an important database for directors of public health, giving local data set in the context of regional and national figures for a range of demographic, mortality, and limited morbidity indicators.[22] It has been available by district health authority and by family health services authority boundary, and is issued to directors of public health each year. In addition, a Department of Health working party is currently looking at environmental indicators and morbidity indicators that could be included in the database.

Other national resources available to directors of public health are:

• *Effective Health Care Bulletins*, issued from the Nuffield Centre for Health Services Research in Leeds; these have covered subjects such as screening for osteoporosis and brief interventions for alcohol misuse[23]
• the series of health needs assessment documents issued from the Department of Health; these cover topics such as hip replacement, diabetic care services, cataract operations and mental health needs[24]
• the Clinical Outcomes group at the NHS Management Executive[25]
• the Cochrane Centre for the assessment of effectiveness in health services[26]
• the national perinatal outcomes database, a very specific example of a resource offering up-to-date information of the clinical effectiveness of antenatal and perinatal care.[27]

These resources are some of the more recent developments; the Office of Population Censuses and Surveys, the Communicable Disease Surveillance Centre of the Public Health Laboratory Service, and the regional cancer registers remain among the larger longstanding sources of public health information available to directors of public health.

Style of the report

At an early stage the style of the report will need to be decided; this will be determined by the intended audience. By definition, the audience includes health authority members and health service commissioning officers. If the report is to be effective, it will also need to be addressed to health service providers. It is likely that the audience will include local authority services, particularly social services, environmental health, housing and education, but also leisure services and the much-neglected town planners.[28] The report needs to be written for the "educated lay audience" of health authority non-executive members. It may also include, or be accompanied by, "technical annexes" for use by officers of the authority for planning purposes.

Directors of public health should then consider the need for a covering report for other agencies, and summary reports for different audiences. Some summary reports have been produced as glossy A5-format flyers, inserts and advertisement features in the local press, and A4 triple-fold leaflets; these can carry simple messages to larger numbers of people and attract new interest in the subject matter.

Tiplady and colleagues in East Cumbria produced an annual report on six sides of A4 glossy card which was accessible to a large number of people.[29] Gentle used a series of cartoon illustrations to liven up the presentation of his report on health in Exeter.[17] The West Midlands Regional Health Authority reports have used high quality full colour printing to enhance the attractiveness of their reports.[18] One Sandwell report, *The Album*, involved over 400 local residents in its production—from voluntary organisations, a school, women's groups and ethnic minority groups and "vox pop" interviewees in the street.[30] If the health authority produces a newsletter, or its own newspaper, put out to all residents on a local free-paper distribution, this should also be used to send out annual report information. Annual reports have also been produced on video.

The public health report in the NHS planning cycle

HSG(93)56 suggests that annual public health reports should be published by the end of May each year, unless agreed otherwise locally, to ensure that they take up a key position in the NHS planning cycle. The reports can then influence health authority discussions about priorities in June and July. These are then expressed in the purchaser intentions letters in September. Priorities are consolidated into the outline commissioning plans and draft community care plans that go out to public and provider consultation in late October and November. The draft and final corporate contracts contain the stated objectives of health authorities for the next financial year. These should be published, once financial allocations to districts are known, between February (draft) and April (final). Public health reports can include a chapter on progress in health improvement during the previous year; this coincides with the health authority's "out-turn report", the report of action taken in the previous year, usually due also in May/June. HSG(93)56 expects the report to be an annual report, which some directors of public health find a burden.

Taking May/June as the publication date for the report, directors of public health can use a critical path analysis to determine how far ahead the process of preparing the report should begin. The stages include identifying subject areas; requesting information from outside agencies; gathering and analysing information from in-house databases; drafting report chapters; convening an editorial board to review first drafts, and particularly the recommendations deduced from the data; agreeing the final draft; preparing an executive summary and translated materials; producing desktop published material and camera-ready copy for the printer; time at the printers; time in advance of the health authority distribution; and time for other distributions.

Much of the material that can be published in the report will have been initiated as part of the routine work of the department and not specifically for the annual report. However, it would be desirable that the annual report follows through a consistent strategic theme and is not simply a randomly compiled collection of reports that just happen to be ready in time for the deadline. It is beneficial to undertake a round of provider consultation on the first draft chapters where these are heavily health-care orientated.[18,19]

The editorial board may comprise only public health department staff; it may include other commissioning staff; it may include non-health staff if a particular theme is being pursued, for example environmental sustainability, community care, or community safety. Where other departments and organisations are being invited to contribute material, the status of their involvement should be clearly understood: the director of public health is responsible for the report and therefore holds final editorial say over content.

Turn around times for commercial printing have reduced dramatically with the development of computerised print systems. Public health departments can speed up the process further and reduce costs by desktop publishing the report in-house, and delivering camera-ready copy to the printers. (One trick here is that when you are behind your publication deadline, you produce enough photocopies in-house for the health authority meeting and then publish the glossy report when it gets back from the printer!) Desktop publishing does require a skilled operator, but these skills are becoming more commonplace in health authorities.

These time considerations will vary from district to district, and the director of public health will have to judge and plan the time needed for the various stages of the report production.

Using the report

The health authority should receive the report in full public session. It should also make available sufficient resources for the report to be published and distributed to its intended audience. The launch should be a media event. A press release should be prepared while the report is still at the printers. A distribution list should be drawn up at the same time (fig 2); putting the list on a database for labels will reduce the workload in future, but the lists will need to be updated. The authority should readily observe the value of the document as the statement of the public health interest that must inform all its activities and which needs to become an essential working document in relation to its commissioning and purchasing processes.

Pre-existing good relationships with local media will do much to assure supportive publicity when the report is presented. Directors of public health must be prepared to take on a higher than usual public profile with regard to press releases and conferences, interviews, and phone-in programmes. Training in media skills will enhance their effectiveness in delivering the key messages from the annual report. They must anticipate contentious areas in the report and be prepared to field the trickier media questions.

Personal presentation of the report to local authority service committees and the community health council and professional representative bodies will produce a greater impact and encourage

Department of Health
- Chief medical officer: 6 copies required[4]
- Health ministers

Regional health authority
- Director of public health
- General manager
- Chairperson

Health authorities and hospitals
- Senior officers, heads of department
- One copy for each department, ward, health centre, and clinic
- Medical executive committee members
- District medical committee members
- Nursing professional advisory committee members
- Staff trade union representatives
- Reception areas (fixed copies)
- Hospital patient libraries
- Medical and nursing education centre libraries

Family health services
- One copy for each general practice
- Members of local medical committee
- Members of local dentists, pharmacists, and opticians committee

Community health council
- Council members
- Members of joint consultative committee

Government
- Members of parliament
- Representatives of all political parties
- All councillors
- All local authority chief officers
- Additional copies to other key local authority officers, particularly those who have provided information, such as departments of planning, economic and information; road safety; environmental health; social services; education and leisure services.
- Racial equality council members

Local services and organisations
- All school headteachers
- One copy for each secondary school library
- One copy for each chairperson of school board of governors
- District or neighbourhood housing offices
- One copy for each public library
- Police, fire, and ambulance chiefs
- Coroners
- Voluntary services coordinator, and all agencies on mailing list if available
- Church organisations
- Members of chamber of commerce
- Members of other industrial or business organisations
- Training and enterprise councils
- Development corporations
- Members of trades council

British Library

Fig. 2 Possible distribution for the annual health report

the development of health alliances in the district, including fund-holders.

Similarly, presentation to general practice fundholders, local provider units, clinical directorates, and neighbouring providers to the district's residents will reinforce the sense of being involved in a common enterprise.

Evaluation and audit of the report

Some directors of public health have enclosed evaluations sheets with their reports; few have experienced good returns of these, even when offering prize draws. Formal evaluation by peer review should take place in medical audit forums involving groups of districts. The Mersey Regional Health Authority and Nuffield Institute for Health Service Studies' *Audit in Public Health Medicine Guidelines* are extremely useful in this.[31] Some directors of public health invite independent professional review by journal editors and academics. Evaluation can also be against the objectives set for the report at the outset. For example, an objective for *The Health of Coventry*[6] and for *Life and Death in Sandwell*[15] was to have health seen as an issue of civic pride in which the local authorities should be pursuing active policies; in both cases the reports were regarded as successful in their objective.[7,32] Annual reports can also be evaluated against the achievement of their specific recommendations. Other process measures can be used to assess impact, for example, column inches of press coverage, minutes of local radio air time, numbers of organisations and individuals consulted about the report, and commitment of non-NHS resources to health projects achieved through annual report recommendations.

Conclusions

The health report still retains its function as the "community diagnosis"; as with the clinical diagnosis, it is not an end in itself, but provides the information on which to base the "community treatment".[33] It is not sufficient to produce glossy reports on the problems faced by our communities; it is necessary to use the information in these reports to campaign on behalf of the public health and to involve people in their own local initiatives to improve health.

We believe the annual public health report must still retain its campaigning qualities. However, it now holds the opportunity to secure improved health for the population through its central position in NHS policy and planning. Public health physicians as advisers to primary health care services and local authorities can also use these relationships to extend their influence constructively into other sectors of the community.

The production and use of the annual report by directors of public health is a valuable source of power to "drive" the development of a comprehensive local health strategy, to inform purchasing priorities, assess health and health care needs, and to develop healthy alliances in order to *improve health.*

Appendix: Subject areas and possible sources of information for an annual health report

Demography

Population

At census; estimates; predictions; crude birth rate; crude mortality; fertility; single-parent families; migration; ethnic minorities [Office of Population Censuses and Surveys (OPCS) census, local authority planning and information departments, regional health authority statistics department]

Major determinants of health

Housing

Housing "spaces", private, council, other; overcrowding, lacking basic amenities [census]; housing condition surveys; council waiting lists; homelessness; medical priority for rehousing [local authority, homelessness agencies]

Poverty

Benefit claimants [Benefits Agency]; housing benefit claimants (indicator of very low income) [local authority]; percentage unskilled workers [census, local poverty action groups, and Low Pay Unit surveys]

Employment

Census of employment by standard industrial groupings [Department of Employment, local authority economic units or planning and information departments]; employment by socioeconomic groups [census]; industrial accidents [Health and Safety Executive, hospital programme data sets]

Unemployment

Local authority economic units [Department of Social Security]; water supply, quality and sanitation [Water company reports, local authority technical services or city engineers]

Education

Provision of nursery education; school population; percentage school leavers entering higher education [local authority education department]

Violence and personal security

Crime statistics [county councils or metropolitan police authorities]

Hazards

Fires

County councils or metropolitan fire and civil defence authorities

Pollution

Air monitoring and hazardous materials surveys [local authority environmental health departments]; water quality and pollution incidents [local authority environmental health departments]

Environmental control

Pests, public health nuisances [local authority environmental health departments]

Maternal and child health

Obstetric care; birthweight; congenital abnormalities; perinatal and infant deaths; legal abortions [district health authority and information departments and OPCS]; notifiable infectious disease [OPCS, local authority, district health authority]; immunisations; child abuse [local authority social services departments]; home and road accident statistics [additional data from local authority environmental health departments and police authorities]; dental health [district health authority local surveys of missing, decayed, and filled teeth in school populations]

Physical and mental handicap

Physical disablement, blindness, and deafness registers [local authority social services departments; local surveys and proxy measures from national studies]

Adult health

Indicators from primary care [Royal College of General Practitioners' spotter practices, local practice databases and annual reports; contraceptive use [health authorities, district information services]; prescriptions for major groupings of pharmaceuticals [Prescriptions Pricing Authority]; notifiable infectious disease; accidents; AIDS; sexually transmitted diseases; local information from lifestyle surveys, coronary heart disease risk factors; smoking related diseases and coronary heart diseases [information similar to that presented for districts in the Health Education Authority reports; for example, *The Big Kill, Broken Hearts, Smoking Epidemic*]; home, road, and work accidents statistics; drugs [local drug agencies, local authority social services departments, Home Office statistics, accident department and hospital episode system, Prescription Pricing Authority, and health authorities]; alcohol [local agencies and social services; district information system; regional information system; extrapolate national estimates for local proxy measures]

Major uses of hospital specialities

Major causes of hospital admission; major uses of hospital facilities; hospital performance; mental health [standardised hospitalisation rates can be calculated by ward from district health authority, regional health authority; Department of Health and John Yates' performance indicator packages; hospital minimum data sets district implementation system; Hospital Inpatient Enquiry, Mental Health Inquiry, District Information System; Regional Information System]

Major causes of death

Mortality statistics, numbers [OPCS SD25/VS1 series], rates over time, standardised mortality ratios by ward for major conditions, three or five year aggregated data for all ages and for selected ages (for example, 15–64), with confidence intervals [Public health common data sets]

Clinical effectiveness and outcomes

Public health common data set; *Effective Health Care Bulletins*; Department of Health needs assessment series; clinical outcomes group; chief medical officers' reports; communicable disease report (Communicable Disease Surveillance Centre); National Confidential Enquiry Stillbirths and Deaths in Infancy; Confidential Enquiry into Maternal Deaths, regional perinatal audits; national perinatal outcomes database; National Enquiry into Perioperative Deaths; register of health needs assessments (Institute of Public Health West Midlands); Office of Population Censuses and Surveys data

Special reports and local research

1 Middleton J, Binysh K, Chishty V, Pollock G. How to do it: write the annual report of the director of public health. *BMJ* 1991;**302**:521–524.
2 Department of Health and Social Security. *Public Health in England*. London: HMSO, 1988. (Cmnd 289.) (Acheson report.)
3 Department of Health. *Health of the population: responsibilities of health authorities*. London: Department of Health, 1988. (HC(88)64.)
4 Department of Health. *Public Health: responsibilities of the NHS and the roles of others*. London: Department of Health, 1993. (HSG(93)56.)
5 Department of Health. *Managing the new NHS: a background document*. London: Department of Health, 1993.
6 Binysh K, Chishty V, Middleton J, Pollock G. *The Health of Coventry*. Coventry: Coventry Health Authority, 1985.
7 Binysh K, Chishty V, Middleton J, Pollock G. The health of Coventry—use of a health profile to stimulate community health promotion. *Health Education J* 1989;**48**:94–96.
8 Central Birmingham Department of Community Medicine. *A picture of health*. Birmingham: Central Birmingham Health Authority, 1987.
9 Ashton J. *Health in Mersey: a review*. Liverpool: University of Liverpool, 1984.
10 Nottingham City Council Unit. *Health for all in Nottingham*. Nottingham: Nottingham City Council, 1988.
11 Thunhurst C. *Poverty and health in the City of Sheffield*. Sheffield: Sheffield City Council Environmental Health Department, 1984.
12 West of Scotland Politics of Health Group. *Glasgow: health of a city*. Glasgow: West of Scotland Politics of Health Group, 1984.
13 Department of Health. *The health of the nation: a strategy for health in England*. London: HMSO, 1992. (Cmnd 1986.)
14 NHS Management Executive. *Assessing health care needs: a DHA project discussion paper*. London: NHSME, 1991.
15 Sandwell Public Health Department. *Life and death in Sandwell*. West Bromwich: Sandwell Health Authority, 1989.
16 Walsall Public Health Medicine Department. *The health of Walsall*. Walsall: Walsall Health Authority, 1989.
17 Gentle P. *Better Health 1990*. Exeter: Exeter Health Authority, 1990.
18 West Midlands RHA Directorate of Public Health. *Gaining better health*. Birmingham: West Midlands Regional Health Authority, 1991.
19 Sandwell Public Health Department. *Sandwell under the knife*. West Bromwich: Sandwell Health Authority, 1993.
20 Wolverhampton Department of Public Health. *Report on the public health of Wolverhampton 1993*. Wolverhampton: Wolverhampton Health Authority, 1993.
21 Muir Gray J. *The public health toolbox*. 3rd ed. London: Faculty of Public Health Medicine, 1991.
22 Public Health Common Data Set. Prof. R. Balarajan *et al*. Institute of Public Health, Chancellor Court, The Surrey Research Park, University of Surrey, Guildford GU2 5YL.

23 Effective Health Care Bulletins. Nuffield Centre for Health Services Research, School of Public Health, University of Leeds, 30 Hyde Terrace, Leeds LS2 9LN.
24 DHA Project: Epidemiologically based needs assessments. NHS Management Executive, Quarry House, Quarry Hill, Leeds LS3 7UE.
25 Clinical Outcome Group, NHS Management Executive, Quarry House, Quarry Hill, Leeds LS2 7UE.
26 The Cochrane Centre. NHS Research and Development Programme, Oxford OX2 7LG.
27 The Oxford Database of Perinatal Trials. Oxford: Oxford University Press, 1991.
28 Pulford M, Middleton J. Street talk. *Health Services J* 1993 Sept. 27.
29 Tiplady P. *Health of East Cumbria*. Carlisle: East Cumbria Health Authority, 1990.
30 Sandwell Public Health Department. *Sandwell health: the album*. West Bromwich: Sandwell Health Authority, 1991.
31 Mersey Regional Health Authority, Nuffield Institute of Health Service Studies. *Audit in public health medicine guidelines*. Leeds: Nuffield Institute and Mersey RHA, 1992.
32 Middleton J. Life and death in Sandwell: where public health and economic health meet. *J Local Government Policy Making* 1990;16(4):3–9.
33 Ashton J. Health in Mersey: an exercise in community diagnosis. *Health Education J* 1985;44:178–80.

13 Write a classic paper

Anthony David

A classic paper is that elusive blend of art and science, a piece of scholarship that changes the way people think but also delights each new readership that rediscovers it. Words like "elegant" and "lucid" are the adjectives most often used to describe one. This is not to be confused with a citation classic, which need not be worthy of such accolades. These are often technical articles describing a laboratory technique (such as gas-liquid chromatography) or a rating scale (such as the general health questionnaire), or they may contain statements designed to be tendentious and annoying, stirring up colleagues to write refutations (more or less anything by Eysenck). No, classic papers are different. For one thing they tend to happen by accident. But here are a few guidelines to follow so maybe one of us will get lucky.

Getting in the mood

First of all you have to make a major finding or conduct a substantial study. This article assumes you have done that already. If you haven't, don't stop reading: you may get some ideas. After all, they have to start somewhere.

Next are some practical hints. Get yourself a word processor. No one ever wrote a classic paper in one sitting, believe me. Some word processors can check your prose and cut out words like "inasmuch" and "moreover", which you never find in a really important work of science.

You should allow yourself to get into a writing mood. Finish the background reading, the review of the literature, and the work to date. You know it inside out. Relax. Take deep breaths. Just let it flow. Many people find music a help, but choose carefully. Something light and formal, not intrusive or demanding. Mozart obviously. A lot of people like Simon and Garfunkel. Avoid the romantics and counterpoint. Fugues make demands on the left hemisphere and could effectively muzzle your writing ability. Steer clear of anything Italian, especially opera. Jazz (such as Louis Armstrong or early Ella Fitzgerald) is all right so long as it is not too rhythmic and evocative; you'll end up tapping in time on the keyboard and this could slow you down or you may even start smoking again. Sonny Rollins is absolutely contraindicated for obvious reasons. And if you must drink coffee, stick to decaffeinated. Wear comfortable clothes; a sweater and jeans are fine.

The title

I cannot emphasise too much how important the title is. Colleagues of mine persevered with "Microprocessor assisted clinical assessment and management of minor psychiatric disorders" and suffered rejection from journal after journal. Someone suggested "The computer will see you now" and the *BMJ* lapped it up. Titles beginning with "On" are good, such as *On the circulation of the blood* (Harvey), *On the origin of species* (Darwin), and *On aggression* (Lorenz); they suggest the monumental, something enduring. Other titles echo through the literature. In my own subject *Sex and the single girl* became *Sex and the single hemisphere* (Witelson) and (note the twist) *Psychotherapy and the single synapse* (Kandel). Another was *What the frog's eye tells the frog's brain* (Lettvin), which became *What the mind's eye tells the mind's brain* (Pylyshyn), and many others. "Towards" is a bit like "On" in that it conveys portent without bragging. For example, *Towards a theory of schizophrenia* (Bateson), which heralded the double bind, and later, *Towards an aetiological classification of schizophrenia* (Murray), a less famous but quite influential work. Question marks in titles are corny, and colons are the refuge of a coward. The authors thought of a snappy title and then spoilt it by sticking in a colon followed by "pathological findings" or "a new theoretical framework" or even "physiological studies in the newt".

81

Style matters

Whatever you do, do not mention statistics (terms like logistic regression, factor analysis) unless you are writing about them specifically. Otherwise it is just going to alienate your audience. The same goes for code names or numbers for new drugs and the precise locus of the new gene you have just identified. Put these in parentheses or use a footnote. Some people like quotations. Be careful it doesn't come over as pretentious: French and Latin are out; anything by Shakespeare, Bertrand Russell, and Peter Medewar is safe.

What follows should not be a problem: the study itself or your new theory. Just let it come out, don't force it. Find a style that you feel comfortable with. Be a bit old-fashioned—that can give the paper a sense of solidity and trustworthiness. "Notwithstanding" is perfectly acceptable in the 1990s if used sparingly, so is "with respect to". "Heretofore" is going too far and "the aforementioned" makes you sound like a lawyer. Try not to let the reader see that what you have to say is going to knock their socks off, let it creep up on them. Modesty and understatement is the best policy. Remember Watson and Crick and the double helix? "It has not escaped our notice that . . ." this is the most mind blowing discovery of the century. Use phrases like "it could be argued that . . ." and "one possible explanation is . . ."; you don't have to shout.

The discussion is the most important part of the paper. People skip the methods and most of the results sections. Remember to criticise yourself first before anyone else gets the chance. After all, in a couple of decades or centuries you may turn out to have been slightly wrong. Things like "some observer bias cannot be entirely excluded . . ." and "it remains possible that some of the responses occurred by chance . . ." go down well with the sceptics, but save yourself for "however" or "nevertheless . . . steps taken in the experiment render this highly unlikely" and "this would not explain the central finding", etc. Generally, keep it short and to the point. It is not a novel you are writing. If you get stuck, take a break. Leave the draft by your bedside. Sometimes a phrase just comes to you and it's a shame to lose it.

Conclusion

Well, that is all the help you can get; from now on it is up to you. If it doesn't work out, try not to get disheartened; you will have made a contribution. Those hours or days spent listening to soothing music, daydreaming of Newton, Einstein, Darwin, and Freud have not gone to waste—you will have learnt what it means to write a classic paper.

14 Write for money

Michael O'Donnell

I'm a bad person to give advice about writing for money. I usually write what I want to write then try to find someone willing to publish it. It's not a course I'd recommend to anyone concerned with making money. I could call my bank manager as witness. The nearest I get to a direct bid for the lucre is when I accept a commission for an article, or a script, on a subject I haven't chosen for myself and try to deliver what I hope is expected. But even then the most valuable reward is not the payment—though it can produce a comfortable feeling in the pocket—but the discipline that the exercise imposes.

Write and keep writing

Like everyone else, I find writing hard work and I'm sure that if my working habits came under the scrutiny of marketing experts they'd say I spend too much time writing things that offer a low financial return per mmol of sweated blood. They'd advise me to desist from writing novels and return to writing the TV plays I wrote when I was harder up, or advertisements for Snibbo or for Thoroughgood's Thoroughgrip Trouserettes. Just as they would demand that I should never again contribute to those ill-paying publications for which I sometimes write because it's fun. The problem with marketing folk, of course, is that while they are good at measuring returns, they have no measure for rewards.

That said, let us consider this business of earning money. Doctor writers, if they can make any show of competence, should find it easier than other writers to get their work published. Thanks to the money spent on pharmaceutical promotion, medical publications have proliferated almost as exuberantly as NHS marketing persons. One or two are first rate but the content of some reveals the strain their editors are under to find something to keep the ads apart. These are useful places for medical writers to learn their craft. Nearly every cliché uttered about writing is true. (Struggle as we must to keep clichés out of our prose, we can't keep them out of our lives.) So I don't apologise for repeating the truism that the only way to learn how to write is to write, and to keep on writing. This dreary business of churning out words can be lightened by occasional publication, and doctors are lucky to have a group of editors who are more likely to read their work, comment on it, and even publish it, than the hardfaced persons who sit in editors' chairs elsewhere.

Doctors also have an advantage when submitting their work to non-medical magazines and newspapers. People, not surprisingly, are interested in their health. More surprisingly, they are also interested in the antics of doctors, so practising doctors who write about their work simply, directly, and with enthusiasm, have a good chance of selling "A doctor writes . . ." style of article. The late Dr Alfred Byrne, one of the first doctors to become a full-time newspaperman, used to call it "working the bronchitis belt".

Easy reading, hard writing

The key words in that last paragraph are "enthusiasm", "simply", and "directly". If, when you write an article, you can generate no enthusiasm for its subject—a state into which it's easy to lapse if you concentrate only on the lucre—the article will quickly bore any reader foolish enough to dip into it, no matter how much technical skill you deploy on its construction. Similarly, unless you can express what you want to say in simple, direct prose, much of what you write will remain unread.

It's not easy to be simple and direct. One writing doctor, William Somerset Maugham, claimed: "To write simply is as difficult as to be good". If anything, he understated the problem. Yet achieving an appearance of simplicity is the central skill of the writer's craft. Luckily, help is at hand, set out in useful textbooks. My favourite is *Elements of Style*[1] by Strunk and White; a slim volume that contains everything we need to know but will never master in our lifetimes. For more specialised help, I recommend another slim volume: Tim Albert's splendid *Medical Journalism: the writer's guide.*[2] Despite its title, this book offers practical advice to all writers and not just to aspiring journalists. Both books describe the simple techniques that underpin our craft. The techniques are easy to understand; the problems—and the hard work—come when we try to apply them. Most successful writers will tell you that if you want to forge simple, direct prose you need to rewrite, rewrite, and rewrite. And then rewrite. An article such as this, for instance, needs to be rewritten at least 20 times. But once again help is at hand in the shape of that electronic marvel, the word processor.

Help at hand

Any writers who still use typewriters or who, as I once did, use pen and paper, are burdening themselves with unnecessary manual work, which is not only tedious but wholly unproductive. The only drawback to using a word processor is that we no longer know how many times we rewrite, and that is a drawback only to the boastful. Gone are those piles of paper, smothered with crossings-out and arrows, waiting for a competent typist to produce the final "clean copy", which, of course, never was the final copy and had to be retyped again and again as the words sank beneath the inky tide of corrections. Thanks to the word processor, writing and rewriting are welded into a seamless process and even a stumbling typist like me can produce printed words, which, if naught else, are at least legible. God help us but it's true that some publishers and editors still make their first judgment of the quality of a manuscript on the neatness of its presentation. So if you get your magic machine to type your words double spaced on A4 paper, you're off to a flying start.

That's when you'll need another class of textbook. The best guide to where the money lies is the *Writers' and Artists' Yearbook*,[3] which lists all the people likely to buy your wares, tells you what they're after, and hints at what they're likely to pay. When it comes to protecting yourself within this jungle, the medical profession is, once again, twice blessed. Two patients' support groups exist to help innocent doctors who stray into the threatening world of editors and publishers: the Medical Writers' Group within the Society of Authors and the General Practitioner Writers' Association.

When contracts grow complicated, as they can with books and television programmes, it's well worth acquiring an agent. A brazen agent will get you more money from publishers than you'd dare ask for yourself—usually more than the 10 per cent, which is the only commission a reputable agent will demand. The *Writers' and Artists' Yearbook* includes a list of agents and advice on how to approach them.

Yet no matter how brazen your agent, only you can earn the money. So it's back to simplicity, directness, and a word processor, which, when deployed with enthusiasm, may warm the heart of your bank manager and allow you to eat occasional slices of cake instead of bread. If, however, you are tempted to try to make writing your main occupation rather than a part-time one, you may have to make drastic changes to your way of life. You will need to cultivate a way of living that feeds your imagination, and you may need to indulge in some cold-blooded introspection to try to discover more about the creature who produces the words, the voice that speaks to the reader when you write. For, unless you write with some honesty of purpose, and try honestly to express the complexities within you and that you see around you, your writing will smack of triteness.

To write from any motive other than honesty is to write propaganda. That may not deter you if your only aim is to make money. Propaganda is certainly a profitable form of writing. It demands the same skills and techniques as any other writing and suits many people as a well-paid part-time occupation. Some professionals produce it to buy time to write what they really want to write and it does them little harm as long as they retain insight into what they're doing and why. Sometimes, however, beguiled by good pay and work that's not too demanding, they do lose insight. And that's a pity, for propaganda is thin gruel to sustain the enthusiasm of a full-time writer. You can measure its charm by reading advertising brochures or watching party political broadcasts.

Profit of penitence

I've left the most practical advice until last because it is also the most painful. I've yet to meet anybody who finds the business of setting down words a pleasurable way of passing the time. All of us who write yearn for diversions that will take us away from the desk or from the keyboard or, even better, some urgent matter that will prevent us from even starting. Most writers I know compel themselves to write a certain number of words, or to spend a specified time at their desk, every day. Some of the best prose they produce may come during a session that got off to a reluctant start; some sessions that grow out of bubbling enthusiasm may produce only rubbish.

The secret of successful writing is, as Mother Mary Catherine hinted on my very first day at school, a matter of self discipline. And the appropriate working garb is sackcloth and ashes. Still it seems to do no great harm to most of us to play the penitent for a few hours every day—and it does bring temporal rewards. The greater the suffering while the stuff's being hammered out, the greater the joy when we reach the last full stop. Forgive that late intrusion by Samuel Smiles (another doctor writer, as it happens) but I can sense that the joyful last full stop is on its way. The cheque, I trust, will soon be in the post.

1 Strunk W, White E B. *Elements of style*. 3rd ed. New York: Macmillan, 1979.
2 Albert T. *Medical journalism: the writer's guide*. Oxford: Radcliffe Medical Press, 1992.
3 *The writers' and artists' yearbook*. London: A & C Black.

II PUBLISHING AND PUBLICITY

15 Become a medical journalist or editor

Fiona Godlee, Stella Lowry, Richard Smith

Making an informed decision

Plenty of schoolchildren climb on the conveyor belt that turns them into doctors with only a hazy idea of what being a doctor entails, and it is when the belt delivers them into disagreeable and unforeseen circumstances that their minds turn to journalism. So we hope that those seeking a career in medical journalism will not repeat their mistakes and will instead try to find out more about what it is like to be a medical journalist or editor. They will find this difficult because medical journalists are a small and heterogeneous group. One or two make much of their money writing colourful articles for colourful lay publications; the odd one here and there is a medical correspondent for a national newspaper; some write potboilers; and some write literature; but most plug away editing and writing for medical publications that are read mostly by other (and proper) doctors.

A distinction must be drawn between being a journalist and being an editor. The doctors who work for the *BMJ*, the *Lancet*, and other scholarly publications spend most of their time editing—that is, selecting papers for publication and preparing those that are selected. People who want to be creative and who "really want to write novels" will not be happy sifting through piles of complicated papers, arguing with dissatisfied authors, and fretting over whether a colon should really be a semi-colon.

Pure medical journalism, without the editing side, may seem more attractive, and the media's appetite for medical stories means that there's always work for the good freelance writer, especially if he or she is medically trained. Most Dear Doctor columnists and radio doctors are practising general practitioners, and magazines tend to prefer people in the swing of medical practice. Their own staff can add the necessary gloss.

Medical journalists and health editors on newspapers are usually full-time journalists who either joined the paper after taking a degree or started out as general reporters—often on provincial newspapers. Some colleges and universities offer courses in journalism—for example, the London College of Printing.

A few warnings for those interested in a career in medical journalism. The field of academic medical journals and medical editing is small and openings are rare. The same is true for the medical newspapers such as *Pulse* and *Hospital Doctor*, which tend to use doctors on a consultant or freelance basis. The recession has hit medical publishing less than publishing in general, but there is always the risk of a journal folding and leaving you without a job, something the NHS is less likely to do.

Those who contemplate metamorphosing from doctor to journalist should also remember that doctors (believe it or not) are highly regarded by most people in Britain, whereas journalists (and editors are rightly tarred with the same brush) rank no better than politicians and union leaders, and are thought of as mendacious, unfeeling, greedy, and drunken. In reality, of course, there are just as many wicked doctors as journalists, but this sudden drop in status may put some aspiring journalists off, while it may positively attract others.

Getting into journalism

If despite these warnings you are still interested, you'll need to find a way in. Look for advertisements in the medical press. Get some articles published—anywhere. But above all, get clinical experience.

Wide medical experience is said by almost all the editors to be important, and so it is, but many successful medical editors and journalists are thin on both postgraduate qualifications and medical experience. It is impossible to say what use a training in journalism would be because we know of no medical journalists who have had a training before applying for a job. Such a training shouldn't count against you (although in such a fickle world it might), and most editors say they would prefer more *medical* experience.

Something that will undoubtedly impress editors is having had something (and preferably lots) published. Even an article (but not a portrait) in the *Sun* will count a little, but two articles in *Nature*, a five-page essay in the *New England Journal of Medicine*, and a first review in the *Times Literary Supplement* will impress much more. (A book of poetry we suggest you keep to yourself.) Getting into print is not difficult, and even swallowing rejections will do you nothing but good. So if you do fancy a career in medical journalism, reading and writing a lot and sending articles off to publications will be useful. Editing the medical school magazine may also help, although most editors don't seem to be much impressed by this achievement.

It may help to get in touch with the journal or paper you'd like to work for and let them know that you're around. Hustling is part of the stock in trade of journalists, and you may get a free lunch if not a job.

The *BMJ* has two schemes for giving people a taste of journalism and editing: the Clegg scholarship, which is a three-month student elective, and a one year editorial registrar post for doctors with postgraduate qualifications. Both of these can lead to more permanent involvement with the journal. *JAMA* and *CMAJ* have schemes and other journals may follow.

Another way round the problem of there being only a few openings might be to look ahead. In France, for example, most of the medical correspondents for national newspapers are qualified doctors, but we doubt if many British graduates will have a good enough grasp of French to earn their living in that language. More sensibly and traditionally, they will look to other English-speaking countries, which means in this context the United States, Canada, and Australia (all the other countries are too small to employ doctors full time as editors or journalists).

Conclusion

The last thing we would want to do is to encourage people to give up medicine. Medical journalism is not a way out of medicine, but a way into something very different. Nor is it a career for the fainthearted, but it may be an endless source of amusement to the thick-skinned divergent thinker. If you can combine it with practising medicine, so much the better.

16 Improve a student medical journal

Colin M Barron

I was always interested in magazines. At the age of 7 I produced my first, a 14-page collection of jokes, drawings, and stories entitled *The Weekly World*, and later I hand-produced a number of comic magazines for my own amusement. It was quite natural, therefore, that I should become interested in student publications, and during my undergraduate days I became involved with several magazines, especially *Surgo* (Glasgow University's medical journal). Initially, I was just a cartoonist, then a writer, later the advertisement manager, and finally I did a two-year stint as editor. During these two years we were able to improve the production standards of *Surgo* considerably by applying a number of principles derived from years of success and failure. I hope they may be of value to others.

Key principles

Let's start at the very beginning. You're the editor of a student magazine that looks like half-a-dozen sheets of lavatory paper stapled together; the layout is abysmal, the articles are boring, and no one will advertise in it. Worse still, no one reads it. Just how do you start improving it? The first key principle is enthusiasm, optimism, and a genuine desire for improvement. If you do not enjoy being editor and do not want to make every issue better than the last, then you are in the wrong job.

The next important principle is to have a working knowledge of printing, because an editor who knows nothing about printing is like a surgeon who knows nothing about anatomy. Most public libraries stock a few books on the subject.

Production team

Having worked up some enthusiasm for your job, you should then assemble your production team. Ideally, this should consist of several experts, each skilled in one particular subject. At the very least you will need an advertisement manager and a finance manager. If you intend to have much artwork in your magazine, you would be advised to have a couple of resident artists and a photographer. If you do not have any design sense yourself, one of the artists should serve as layout and art editor.

It is also useful to include in your production team some interested persons who can serve as general dogsbodies—writing book reviews and snippets, for example, making coffee, and, most important, coming up with ideas.

Once you have assembled your production team, encourage them all to contribute to the magazine in some way. It is wrong, I've found, to be *too* democratic; in the end the editor must have the final say, because an unchecked committee will spend hours arguing about what colour of staples to use.

Layout and design

A common failing of student magazines is layout and design. Student editors are often content to present articles as page after page of unbroken type. In fact, the most interesting article in the world becomes unreadable when presented in this way, so if you want people to read your magazine, learn about layout.

Unfortunately, few books have been written about this and much of the craft seems to have been passed down by word of mouth, but you can learn by studying professional magazines. The next time you're browsing through *TV Times*, stop and look. Observe the way that text, illustrations, headings, and white space have been blended to produce a page that is attractive, eye-catching, and easy to read. It is worth building up a collection of professional magazines with good layout for occasional references. If you are really stuck for a way to lay out a particular article, then go ahead and copy the layout from a professional magazine, inch for inch. Articles are copyright, but layouts aren't.

One of the basic principles of layout is that text should be broken up into small, easy-to-read blocks. There are several ways of doing this. The simplest is using headings in bold type surrounded by the correct proportion of white space. As it is rather unlikely that the author's original subheadings will occur in the most aesthetically pleasing part of the page, you may have to move them. More commonly, you will have to write subheadings that didn't exist in the original manuscript. Whatever you do, however, don't waste the design value of a subheading by leaving it sitting at the top of a column.

Breaking

Another effective technique for breaking up text common in modern publications is the use of crossheads. These are single words in bold type lifted from the following text and sited above paragraphs. The word "breaking" a few lines above is an example of a crosshead.

Layout and design have been revolutionised by the introduction of desktop publishing computer systems. The best known system is the Apple Mac, which enables journalists to lay out their own articles. There are many other simpler and cheaper systems on the market that give excellent results, some of which are compatible with home computers. Most universities now have some form of desktop publishing system available on the campus.

Drawings and illustrations

Almost every article looks better with some sort of illustration, and you should remember that it is usually the picture that makes people stop at a particular page. If you use drawings, they should be done in pen and indian ink, not ballpoint or felt-tip pen, which look unprofessional. A Rotring-type indian ink drawing instrument is a good investment at about £6, while halftone areas can be effected with self-adhesive dots such as Letratone.

Drawings look better if produced larger than required and then scaled down to size, and you can save on costs by having this done at a photocopying agency. Many of the latest copying machines produce enlargements or reductions of artwork whose quality is similar to bromide prints but at a fraction of the cost. Any photographs should be 35 mm black-and-white prints.

Avoid the temptation to cut out graphics from professional magazines for use in your own: as well as being a breach of copyright, it is a rather obvious ploy. One student journal I saw had to call its news page "Talking Shop" so that it could use a graphic from a professional journal.

A two-column format is believed to be easiest to read, but if you use a lot of illustrations, then three or more columns allows a more flexible layout.

Cover design

I have singled out the cover for special mention because it is an area of graphic design that is often botched up in student publications. This is a pity because it is the most important page in the journal. Think how many times you have picked a magazine from the newstands because of an eye-catching cover.

The rules of cover design are quite simple and in the figure I have indicated the correct way to lay out a cover, and some of the common errors. Your title should be set in a simple, easy-to-read, bold typeface and should occupy the greatest vertical height possible. Avoid handdrawn lettering: it never looks as good as lettering originated by transfer lettering or computer. Do not be tempted to use some of the more elaborate typefaces—medieval and futuristic styles look ridiculous on the cover of a medical journal—and remember that the simplest typeface is usually best.

Advertisement manager

The advertisement manager is the unsung hero of the production team: without his efforts the whole show would not be possible. Regrettably, it is not a popular job and this is because people imagine that it involves many hours of letter writing, often with little result. But the job can be rewarding and fruitful, and drudgery can be kept to a minimum if the right techniques are used. Letter writing can be dispensed with for selling advertising space, and the telephone used instead. The telephone is the most effective way of selling advertising space: in my experience it has a success rate of over 50% as compared to 10% for letters.

When you are on the phone, try to put yourself in the shoes of the person on the other end of the line. What information would convince him or her that it would be a good idea to take an ad? The readership, for example. If a few copies of your magazine lie about

Do's and Don'ts of Cover Design

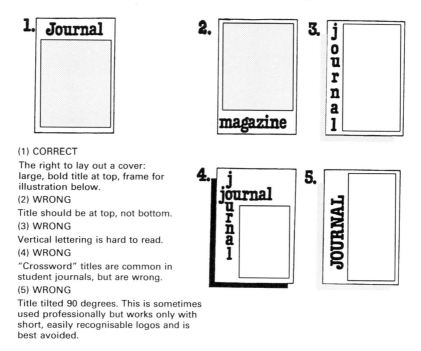

(1) CORRECT
The right to lay out a cover: large, bold title at top, frame for illustration below.
(2) WRONG
Title should be at top, not bottom.
(3) WRONG
Vertical lettering is hard to read.
(4) WRONG
"Crossword" titles are common in student journals, but are wrong.
(5) WRONG
Title tilted 90 degrees. This is sometimes used professionally but works only with short, easily recognisable logos and is best avoided.

hospital reading rooms, then you would be justified in saying that your magazine is "widely read by doctors".

You should always try to present your magazine as favourably as possible, even if you have to exaggerate somewhat. If your magazine is still of poor quality, you should try to avoid showing a copy; you can do this if you sell space by phone. Advertisers are more interested in taking space if their product is in some way connected to features in the magazine. If you have a motoring section, for example, dealers will probably be delighted to take ads if you ask them to supply road-test cars. If there is an annual ball coming up soon, try to get a clothes hire service to advertise, and if you've got a book review section, you should have little difficulty in attracting medical publishers.

Getting articles

The main complaint of student editors is that no one will write articles. There are several ways of getting round this problem. First of all, get as many regular features as possible. If someone writes a particularly good piece for one issue, then make it into a regular feature. Regular features, once established, almost seem to write themselves and the editor need only send timely reminders as the copy date approaches. These regular features should be put on the same page on each issue to make them easier to find. If you're trying to get people to write for your magazine, it is better to give them a subject or title. A person who is asked to write about anything usually ends up writing about nothing.

Another problem is contributors who do not produce their articles in time. If this happens, often it is a good idea to produce the article by interviewing the potential author and recording the conversation on tape. This can then be written up either as a formal interview or as an article with a few quotations. Most articles will need to be rewritten to some extent to make them more palatable because the average contributor will be inexperienced. Even if you shirk rewriting the entire article, it is often worth rewriting the opening paragraph; as with other activities the opening line is important and a better one can often be found a few lines further on. The title is important, too, and, in my opinion, it should be eye-catching rather than just informative.

Finally, the golden rule is perseverance. Even if you have early failures, it is important to keep trying. What I have described so far is the 1% inspiration. It is up to the student editor to provide the 99% perspiration.

17 Edit a specialist journal

John Swales

It was really quite straightforward, I was assured, by the man who had preceded me as editor 30 years before. Papers were submitted and you read them. If they were good, you accepted them; if they were not, you did not: and that was clearly that. Unfortunately for prospective editors of a specialist journal, times have changed and they will find themselves at the centre of a rather more complex operation. And so, when the ego-boosting invitation arrives, dear novitiate, it is as well to be prepared. You will, of course, have had some experience with scientific journals: you will certainly have been an author yourself; you will have acted as a referee; and you will probably have served on the editorial board. As a result you will probably have some ideas. If you have not you should probably decline the offer: you do not have the motivation to carry the task through. On the other hand, you may well suffer from some rather unrealistic ambitions. Perhaps you dream of a completely revamped journal stunning in appearance, each issue expectantly awaited by a rapidly increasing number of subscribers, the unchallenged leader in its field. It is as well to have some such praiseworthy but largely unattainable aims. My only advice would be to proceed with due caution and stealth. If not, most of your editorship will be spent trying to mitigate the errors of your first few months. Your failings will be displayed to a wide and attentive group of your peers. It may well be more worthwhile to take a fresh look at the content rather than appearance of your journal. There are some innovations that are certainly worth considering. Invited reviews, for instance, are more likely to be read, cited, and perhaps even enjoyed than original papers, and such reviews fulfil one of the major functions of your journal—which is to inform and stimulate.

The editor and the editorial staff

The first thing to appreciate is that you are an amateur. Editing will be a part-time task for you while you continue your clinical and academic work. You will, however, be supported by a fully professional staff at the journal editorial office. The senior staff will have had many years' experience in producing journals and of dealing with the wilder eccentricities of editors and referees. If the editorial staff has no such experience, then let someone else take on the editorship: the journal is heading for the rocks. Like most partnerships, that between an editorial office and an editor can become difficult if relationships are bad: that in turn is likely if roles are not defined. The staff at the editorial office (editorial managers, assistants, subeditors, etc) are responsible for the production of a journal from the manuscripts that you have selected and edited. Your job as an editor is to ensure that those manuscripts are of acceptable standard, both in form and content. You will therefore be responsible for seeing that the authors say what they have to say clearly and honestly. This may involve a good deal of work on the manuscript. The editorial office will then ensure that the printed version of the work will conform precisely to the style of the journal. This will involve a painstaking process of checking and "marking up" for the printer. These are professional procedures: if you as an amateur attempt them, you may well cause more rather than less work for the editorial office (who may well be too patient and longsuffering to tell you). Your task should end therefore with a manuscript that reads as you wish it to read. Before the first paper leaves your hands you should know what is being done by means of an amicable discussion with the people involved. You should also determine the point at which a manuscript has been so altered by your efforts that the author should be asked to check and retype it before subediting is attempted. Setting up agreed procedures for dealing with these mundane matters is much more important than proceeding with your grand plan to change the covers of the journal to scarlet overprinted with the titles of the major articles in black. It is probably best to leave such things until a reasonable working relationship has been established between all concerned.

You will also inevitably be drawn into financial matters however much you protest that your role is purely editorial. To the outside world you are more closely identified with the journal than are the publishers. Here your lack of expertise may become even more painfully brought home to you, particularly if you have to participate in delicate negotiations between a learned society and a commercial publisher. I can offer only one guiding principle: by and large, the average specialist journal makes a healthy if not spectacular profit for its publisher. It is possible to test this, when a learned society owns the copyright, by putting the journal out to competitive tender. You will be surprised by the interest stimulated, an interest that is clearly not entirely altruistic. You may at this point decide that your own altruism is also limited and demand appropriate remuneration for your labours. You will certainly bear this in mind when asking for secretarial help.

Using referees

These aspects of editorial work may not have crossed your mind before. As an author, however, you will have your own ideas about how manuscripts should be submitted and judged. This is a face you will present to your peers and you will yourself be judged just as much by this as by the appearance of the journal you edit. Whatever your feelings about the use of referees, as an editor of a specialist journal you really have no choice if you intend your production to have scientific credibility. Usually you will inherit an editorial process for seeking the opinion of referees. If not, you have a fundamental decision to make. Do you intend as editor to send papers to referees and reach your final decision unaided (except of course during unavoidable absence) or are you going to delegate some of your powers to assistant editors or members of the editorial board with expertise in different areas of your specialty?

The decision you reach will depend to some degree on the number of papers you receive; more importantly, however, it will depend upon the breadth of interests represented by your journal. If the journal covers a wide area, you may well not have the expertise to know who the reliable referees are; indeed, you may well not understand the points at issue. It is not for you to resort to the more comfortable approach of the general medical journals: "If the editors cannot understand it, our readers will not understand it either and we should therefore reject it". Your journal is not communicating reputable work as widely as possible. Very few people actually read what you publish. You and the subeditor will probably be the only people to read the journal from cover to cover. You have a duty to transmit to a select few and to act as an archive for valuable information that will provide a foundation for future work. You may therefore have to select a group of expert assistants from your editorial board who will seek the opinion of referees and advise you on what should be done with the manuscript. In this case your decision will probably be in most cases automatic or you may further delegate correspondence with the authors and the final decision to your assistants, retaining for yourself only papers that lie in your own area. You will need to be fairly perspicacious in your choice of assistants: willingness is not always correlated with efficiency.

Choosing and delegating

If you have tears to shed, they will be shed over your dealings with the referees. To select a referee you have to form a shrewd idea of what the authors are trying to say by examining their manuscript briefly. You will then be able to decide on which of the subspecialties the paper impinges. Some journals leave this to the editorial office. I believe this is quite wrong for two reasons. Firstly, you are asking referees to give a considerable amount of time to the task of assessing the manuscript. They are more likely to oblige a colleague whom they know than an editorial secretary. Secondly, the editorial office does not have the special knowledge to appreciate all the nuances in what may be a fine exercise of judgment. This is particularly true of work submitted to medical scientific journals where several discreet areas of expertise may be relevant. Let me put an imaginary example. An impressive paper may arrive reporting a startling increase in toenail uranium in patients with ischaemic heart disease. The authors conclude that uranium is a major risk factor. You send the paper to a leading international authority on the biology of uranium, who reports that the methods are impeccable and the conclusions therefore of major importance. There are journals that would regard such a report as definitive: usually they belong to the small number of journals that attempt to cover all aspects of science from radioastronomy to molecular biology. When they venture into the medical world they tend to attach disproportionate importance to laboratory method. You, however, dear editor, will be painting on a much broader canvas. Who are the people with ischaemic heart disease? Is it possible that their toenail uranium owes more to the fact that they are older and fatter, that they smoke and have quite different dietary habits from the authors' fellow scientists who served as controls in their study? You certainly need a uranium expert as referee: you will also need someone well versed in clinical research and epidemiology to advise you about confounding factors. You will thereby avoid propagating howlers that may help your position in the citation league as later studies refute the conclusions of the uranium paper but will certainly not have helped the progress of clinical science. Your referees will therefore need to come from quite separate disciplines. This accounts for one of the two problems with referees that will dog your editorial career—discrepancies and delays. Your uranium and your epidemiological referees may well reach radically different conclusions about the adequacy of the manuscript. This does not mean that the refereeing process has failed. It simply means that you are (unconsciously perhaps) asking two quite different questions of different people. You may indeed indicate this in your covering letter to referees and reassure your epidemiologist that he or she does not have to worry about the validity of uranium measurement. This cannot be done by a subeditor or secretary inexperienced in the subject.

Briefing and report forms

When reports are returned certain considerations have to be carefully weighed in reaching a judgment based on referees' views. Most journals use report forms to help in this task. The top sheet is for the eyes of the editor only and helps to concentrate the mind of the referees on the aspects of the paper that they are being asked to evaluate. Is the work scientifically acceptable? How valuable a contribution is it? How well is the work presented? Are there ethical problems? A limited number of options can be presented, from the hopeless to the outstanding. The top sheet also serves a secondary function in having cathartic value for referees by inviting them to summarise their views and communicate any opinion that they do not wish the author to see. This section can be remarkably revealing. One of the first lessons that you will learn is that science at this level is not dispassionate.

On the second sheet the referee writes a report for the benefit of the authors. This also requires careful editorial study. Apart from the libellous, beware of statements that usurp your function, such as "This paper would be acceptable if . . .". Authors have a habit of selecting the most optimistic assumptions upon which to act and you may find yourself having to justify an apparently anomalous decision that does not reflect the referees' views.

Whatever your personal views about the matter, you are under an obligation to preserve at all costs the anonymity of referees. You are demanding enough of them without subjecting them to a potentially vituperative correspondence with wounded authors. The report sheet helps this by revealing only what the referee wishes to reveal. Without it you may find that one of your assistants has unwittingly transcribed rather more than you wished from a personal letter sent by a referee. If referees identify themselves on the second sheet unwittingly and you overlook this fact at least some of the blame belongs to them.

Maintaining goodwill

The behaviour of your referees will span the complete spectrum of human potential from the obsessional to the anarchic, from the meticulous to the delinquent. Some will refuse to use your report forms, some will continue the remarks to you as an editor in the report for the authors. Some will tell you that the work is acceptable or not and leave it at that or simply that they disbelieve everything a particular author writes. In most of these cases you will make a mental note (or programme your computer) to dispense with the services of that particular individual. The worst form of referees' behaviour, however, is manifested by delay. Your editorial office will, of course, monitor the progress of the manuscript and will send regular reminders to the referee according to a plan that you have designed. At the end of six weeks the referees will probably be requested to return the manuscript with or without a report. Soon you will suffer the recurrent nightmare of the referee who after a delay of two or even three months returns the manuscript with a curt note of apology and no report. It is difficult at first to believe that there are many reputable authorities who behave in this way but your term as an editor will prove a revealing experience. No man is a hero to his valet and some scientific referees are by no means cast in the heroic mould as far as their editors are concerned. You are then left with a manuscript with one (occasionally no) report and an author who is scanning the post each day in vain. Some authors maintain their sense of humour under these circumstances, like the one who inquired whether we worked on the principle that a good paper like good wine improved with age. Other authors are less amused by delay. To deal with this situation you will have at your right hand a group of rapidly acting reliable referees who will provide a report (when the situation is gently explained to them) within a few days. The reputation of your journal and yourself depends upon the goodwill and efforts of such scientific saints.

On rare occasions you may feel it is necessary to preserve the goodwill of your referees by not sending a paper out to referee at all. This is a serious decision and not to be undertaken lightly, but most journals receive the occasional crackpot paper or work that is quite inappropriate. When your clinical journal receives a paper on steroid levels in an obscure marine mollusc you will not wish to send the work to a long-suffering precious steroid referee, who reports that the work is technically good only to find that you have rejected it on grounds that should have been evident to you in the first place.

Handling authors

Now that you have your reports you are confronted with the delicate task of communicating with the authors. Your words will be studied in minute detail. Indeed, the authors will probably spend longer on dissecting out the subtle implications of what you write than you have spent on composing it. Your aim is to present the conclusion that you have reached and provide guidance for the authors. To achieve this you must be quite clear what your decision is. If you feel that the work is not suitable for your journal, it should be declined with appropriate expressions of regret. It is best to avoid detailed reasons describing where you feel the authors have gone wrong. At the most perhaps you should refer to the referees' reports, which should normally be sent with your letter. There may be a great many criticisms of the work and if you list only a few you risk tempting the authors to resubmit a manuscript that meets these points. You then have to explain that there was more to your original decision than you stated or gracefully give way. Some authors hold the view that most editors will give way if pressed frequently enough with a revised manuscript. It is up to you to disprove this hypothesis.

If the paper is probably acceptable you have to decide how you want the authors to revise it to meet the criticisms presented by the referees and yourself. If the necessary changes are trivial it is a reasonable courtesy to point this out and indicate that the work is, in principle at least, acceptable. Many editors do not accept this view and, presumably in terror of the possibility that they might enter a binding commitment to publish, invariably begin their conclusions with the statement "I regret that your paper is not therefore acceptable to us". They then proceed "If, however, you . . .". This risks anticlimax when the major suggestion is to replace a couple of commas with colons and divide page 9 into three paragraphs. Often, of course, more major changes may be necessary. Here your letter becomes quite critical. The referees will have listed points that may, if you are fortunate, overlap but which may be quite discrepant. On occasions statements may be made that you feel should be ignored. You have to guide the authors through this maze, describing what they must do to provide an acceptable paper. In some cases you may have to leave the final decision open and dependent on whether the authors can provide further data, which they may or may not have. "I am afraid we could not accept your paper therefore unless you can present values for toenail uranium in a properly matched population as detailed by referee 2". Occasionally you may suggest a more modest paper in the light of the referees' comments. "We would therefore be happy to reconsider a paper describing and validating your method of measuring toenail uranium".

It is reasonable to provide your referees with some return for their work by sending them a copy of the other referee's report (unidentified of course) and a copy of your letter. This will also help to ensure that justice is seen to be done.

If you have left the door only slightly ajar a revised manuscript will almost inevitably appear on your desk. The authors will also provide you with a reply to the referees with a list of changes that they have carried out. Your task is to assess their case and, if you think it justifiable, send the paper again to the referees for a second opinion. Where the points at issue are minor this is unnecessary. To enter the refereeing cycle a second (or third) time round is to invite profoundly irritating delays. Your role is that of a judge, not a tennis umpire, who watches helplessly as author and referee send the ball to and fro across the court.

And then, when you have finally decided that you have an acceptable manuscript, you will read it from beginning to end, carrying out your editorial task before handing it on to your editorial office. Your grand design for the journal may well by now have been forgotten in the face of the need for sustained detailed work and your personal popularity may suffer in some quarters but ultimately you should have some tangible justification for your endeavours. You will have learnt something of your specialty and a good deal more about your fellow human beings.

18 Survive as an editor

Stephen Lock

So you're congratulating yourself on being appointed editor? Fair enough, but think again for a minute. You will:

- use all your spare time
- think of nothing else
- lose friends and certainly make none.

Few people, you will find, will read your journal, and within only a few months 90% of what it has published will be wrapping up the fish and chips. And yet, . . . Publication is how science advances; editing is as powerfully addictive as opium; and, to speak personally, there are few more enjoyable methods of transit from walking the wards to leaving for the grave. So the decision is yours. Here I will assume that you have decided in favour, and will be editing part time, almost certainly a specialist journal, and discuss how to survive in terms of structure, process, and outcome.

Structure

Most probably your journal is owned by a society, occasionally by a publisher. Publishing is big business, and it makes money, so don't be fobbed off by protestations that there isn't enough to do what you want. Five hundred paid subscriptions is a viable commercial proposition and any extra means profits, some of which should be yours to pay you a realistic honorarium as well as your expenses and some secretarial help (which may include computerisation of the editorial office). Universities have now begun to realise that for years they have subsidised journals edited by their academic staff on their premises. Major journals, particularly in the United States, have come to arrangements with universities whereby they pay the latter the true overhead costs and part or all of the editors' salaries, so that they can work part or full time. And, increasingly, editors are asking for a voice in "commercial" decisions—for example, on the design, pricing, and promotion of their journals. All these requirements are no moonshine: for many years the BMA publications group has recognised them, paying its specialist journal editors full expenses and a fee related to the number of original manuscripts received every year, besides involving them in commercial decisions.

Right from the start you must establish relative rights and responsibilities. Who makes which decisions on important matters for the journal—the editor, the society, or the publisher? Who accepts and places advertisements? Do all society notices and addresses by its great and good get published automatically? Who decides about house style (scientific and linguistic)? Who hires and fires the editor? Is there a fixed, renewable term of office laid down? And what about a legal contract of employment? Many of these problems may never surface during an editor's tenure, but you ignore them at your peril.

Process

Robbie Fox, perhaps the greatest medical editor of all time, defined the functions of a journal. It should "amuse, interpret, stimulate, criticise, integrate, reform, and even perhaps amuse". Then he was speaking of the general journal, but today the criteria are no less true for many specialist journals, which now have leading and review articles, book reviews, and correspondence columns. Often all of these are more widely read than the original articles, yet it is the quality of the latter that determines the journal's standing. Once established, quality tends to be self-perpetuating, so it is vital to ensure it. Despite the admitted imperfections of editorial peer review, there is no better way of achieving quality. Establishing and running such a system remain major priorities for editors, with two aspects being particularly important: ensuring a wide range of referees and getting to know their strengths, weaknesses, and biases.

The best way of achieving both these objectives is to appoint a good deputy or associate editor (the nomenclature varies; for some, but not all, journals "deputy editor" implies a crown prince, whereas "associates" clearly have a less close relationship to the editorial succession). Even very specialised journals have arcane subfields and a deputy or associate who can advise on the right person to assess a particular paper or to write a review article is invaluable. For this reason many "general" specialist journals (say, in paediatrics) have half a dozen associate editors in the various subdisciplines, some of whom may have additional specific tasks, such as responsibility for arranging book reviews, editorials, or review articles, or for statistical advice.

Together with other members, the deputy and associate editors make up the editorial board, which should be a working one. Hence you must resist your publisher's blandishments to put aged Nobel Prize winners on it as mere window dressing (it is not all that unusual to find printed in a journal the names of board members long since dead). Conversely, given the choice between two members of equal quality, an editor should remember the possible need for a geographical spread of the board and prefer youth to age. Age under 40 is a known crucial feature for a good referee and I suspect it applies equally to editorial board members. You should also resist a publisher's suggestions about having many international members of the board, unless the publisher is prepared to pay their air fares and expenses for the annual meeting. For the latter is a necessity, and, though such meetings may be inordinately tedious, if they are structured correctly, they can be both useful and fun. Often, however, only too self-evidently, nobody apart from the editor either reads or cares about the journal, and a board meeting may be merely a monologue taking the form of an apologia *pro vita sua*.

The way to ensure an interesting meeting is to make some of the board members contribute, by asking them to review a specific part of the journal. One, say, can introduce a discussion of his or her statistical audit of a 1 in 10 sample of the past year's articles; another an analysis of the type and content of the book reviews. Other suggestions are to have a presentation by an invited speaker on, for example, peer review, confidence intervals, or the paperless journal, concluding with a buffet meal. Again, this will cost money, and, again, it is no use your publisher pleading poverty; instead, you must point out what a continual wealth of free skills he or she is getting from the board, which is the only way of ensuring quality, and hence profitability.

I could fill this chapter with details of how to manage the

individual sections of the journal, and how to decide on the level of subediting to be done (by yourself or a skilled technical editor), not forgetting the important side aspects: appeals against editorial decisions, for instance, or editors' and reviewers' conflicts of interests. But fortunately these are dealt with fully in several books, listed at the end of this article.

Outcome

There are three special personal risks for editors that threaten the journal's reputation: loneliness, stagnation, and hubris (in ascending importance). The first can be combated by talking to colleagues on the board and maintaining a dialogue with both authors and referees. But editing is inherently lonely and in any case you are likely to alienate some friends by rejecting their papers (which you must steal yourself to do if your criterion is excellence).

Stagnation can be avoided by innovation, auditing, and research. You should join one, and preferably both, of the major scientific editors' organisations: the European Association of Science Editors (EASE) and the Council of Biology Editors (CBE). New ideas abound in their bulletins (better with the former than the latter) or at their annual meetings (crisper with the latter than the former), and you can always find somebody with experience of what you are proposing to introduce. You should be auditing the quality and usage of the various sections for the meetings of the editorial board, using the customary haphazard and imperfect, but non-superseded, methods of personal impression, discussion, citation, and subsequent correspondence. At least together these will give some impression of what others like and dislike or find useful or superfluous. Finally, serious research into journal structure, process, and outcome (journalology) is only just starting and you have a wide choice for your own studies: what happens to the articles the journal has rejected; is blind better than non-blind refereeing; is one referee better than two, and how much inadvertent duplicate publication is there?

Lastly, there is the difficult problem of hubris. It may be merely my impression associated with aging, but increasingly editors seem to be throwing their weight around, dominating meetings by always asking the first question or scoring points off rivals. To be sure, nobody wants editors to be shy and withdrawn, but equally their place in the scientific community is limited. As the Bloomsbury

111

diarist Frances Partridge said of C P Snow, "Once people have become public figures all they want to do on social occasions is to show off, and secure to themselves admiration, which is hardly necessary in view of their own tremendous opinion of themselves".

Hubris tends to be acquired rather than to be innate and outsiders can probably avoid personal contact with much redactorial yobbery. But one of its features that will affect them directly is the increasing tendency of editors not to reply to or thank people for communications, whether these be contributions, referees' opinions, or comments on a previous letter from the editor. Who wants to continue contributing to a journal, or refereeing for it, when the editor's only response is silence? Who wants to submit an article to one whose editor will decline to instigate an appeal or persistently fail to reply to reasoned correspondence? And who wants to subscribe to a journal whose editor is so obviously conceited and arrogant in public?

If you have appointed the right editorial team, one of them should be able to tell you that your head has swollen. And another way of reducing hubris, rather than having to descend the whole way to nemesis, is continually to remind yourself just how unimportant you and your journal are in the eye of history. In the meantime at least take advantage of the fact that it has never been easier to thank somebody using a standardised letter from a word processor and personalising it with a few handwritten words. If you write too many thank-you letters, the worst that can happen will be a reputation for old-fashioned dottiness. If you write none at all you will rightly be stigmatised as an unfeeling boor. I am sure you are not that, but just in case you have tendencies, why not put up a sign in your office quoting Oliver Cromwell's famous words to the Scottish Church Assembly: "I beseech you, in the bowels of Christ, think it possible you may be mistaken".

Further reading

Bishop C T. *How to edit a scientific journal*. Baltimore: Williams and Wilkins, 1985.
Huth E. *The CBE style manual*. Cambridge: Cambridge University Press, 1994 (in press).
Lock S. *A difficult balance*. London: BMJ Books, 1991
O'Connor M. *Editing scientific books and journals*. Cambridge: Cambridge University Press, 1988.

Addresses

CBE: Suite 1400, 11 South LaSalle Street, Chicago, Illinois 60603, USA; telephone: 312 201 0101; fax: 312 201 0214.
EASE: Secretary-Treasurer Ms Maeve O'Connor, 49 Rossendale Way, London NW1 0XB; telephone: 0171 388 9688; fax: 0171 383 3092; E-mail: ease *moc* @ cix. Compulink Co. UK.; Compuserve: 100410, 1326.

19 Set up a newsletter

Tim Albert

Few newsletters are worth the devastation of rain forest to which they are contributing. They are conceived in haste, often by general practitioners, consultants, or managers who realise that their new expensive software has a desktop publishing facility. They are executed reluctantly, often by a junior member of staff who has neither the training nor the enthusiasm to be an editor. And they are scoffed at by would-be readers as blatant propaganda, or left unread in embarrassing piles, until about the third edition, when the enterprise quietly collapses.

Yet effective newsletters are an important asset. They can distribute information cheaply and effectively. They can improve morale. And they can act as a focus for change, encouraging participation by those at the bottom as well as the top, by patients as well as providers.

So what makes the difference? How can editors overcome their many problems (see box)? How can they ensure that a newsletter is worth the paper it is printed on?

Editing

The worst thing to do is to rush into print. A newsletter is launched only once, and time spent on planning will repay itself once the glow of being a press tycoon has died down.

The most important decision is: who will be the editor? By this I do not mean who wants to be listed as such (leaving others to do the real work), but who will have, and be allowed to exercise, the

---

Top 10 problems faced by newsletter editors

I don't know what readers really think	60%
Everyone is too apathetic to write for me	55%
I find it difficult to write headlines	55%
My contributors can't write	50%
I need more money	50%
I can't afford good photographs	50%
I never know what's going in until the last minute	45%
The pages in my magazine look grey and dull	45%
I find it difficult to start writing	45%
I have trouble cutting articles down to size	35%

From a survey of 20 editors on effective newsletter courses

---

responsibility for commissioning and approving articles, ensuring regular publication, and taking the blame if things go wrong?

The editor is the hub around whom the publication turns or grinds to a halt. He or she must motivate and monitor a range of people: writers, editors, photographers, illustrators, typesetters, publishers, and distributors. At the same time he or she will have to balance three often conflicting needs: reliability, resources, and readability.

Reliability

Any publication set up to serve the needs of an organisation must avoid subverting that organisation, whether knowingly or (more commonly) unknowingly. As editor, you can minimise that risk. Firstly, make sure that your lines of reporting to a group of colleagues (editorial board) or your immediate superior (who then becomes editor in chief) are clear. This should simplify the political task of the editor by avoiding the trap of having too many masters or mistresses to please.

Secondly, agree with the editor in chief on the purpose of the newsletter: draft, discuss, and write down a clear mission statement. Many strains are caused by the editor producing one publication while the editorial board or the editor in chief (and his or her superiors) want another. Clear aims are important: there is a huge difference between a newsletter for staff and one for patients, and between one intended to provide information and another to

114

stimulate debate. Agreeing in advance will not only reduce friction but also determine style and content.

Thirdly, decide what refereeing systems you need. Sending copy to interested parties is time consuming, encourages endless debates over the exact usage of a semicolon, and leads to safe, often sycophantic, material. But it does reduce avoidable errors and ensures that unexpected time bombs can be defused before publication. The choice is yours, but if you decide on a refereeing system, make sure that your schedules (see below) reflect that.

Resources

Editors must ensure that they have enough resources from the start. The obvious costs will be typesetting, printing, paper, distribution, contributions, and illustrations. Less obvious are overheads and staff time, yet these are vital. In particular, make sure that those working on the newsletter are not expected to take on new tasks without being allowed to shed old ones (unless they are underemployed). If this is unrealistic, consider outside help. Do not be put off by the fact that this will show the real cost: work out the unit cost (per person per edition). Then decide whether it is worth it or whether you can make do with something cheaper, such as two pages of black and white instead of 12 pages of full colour. Do not forget to take into account the savings that you can make by winding up existing, less efficient, ways of communicating.

Readability

Readers are the third element of the editor's infernal triangle. They are often neglected. Many publications fulfil the needs or egos of managers, or explore the minutiae of technical matters, but are left unread or despised by their intended readers. They have failed.

How can editors attract and keep readers? Mainly by keeping them their main priority at all times but also by careful planning, sensible selection of articles, shrewd appointments, effective team leadership, and a wise use of training courses. Cherish your contributors: if you feel they are apathetic, ask, "What's in it for them?" Give rewards, such as prominent bylines, parties, meetings (but make sure that these keep to an advisory role). A neglected technique is the simple "thank you", which costs nothing.

You will soon realise that the goal of pleasing your readers conflicts with the goals of playing safe and saving money. For instance, an article exposing the sexual peccadillos of the senior anaesthetists will be avidly read, but your editorship is unlikely to survive long. A drive to cut costs will save funds but could force down the quality so much that readers stop reading. Such conflicts, however, are the essence of editing, and good editors will enjoy the challenge.

Production

Once you have set up an effective structure, work out how you are going to produce your newsletter.

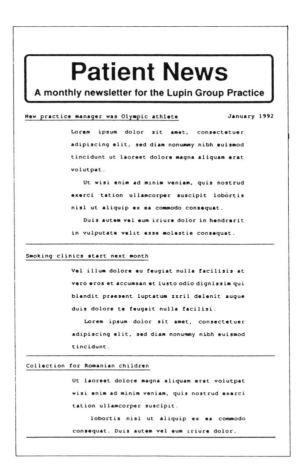

Fig 1 Typed copy can be perfectly effective

Typesetting and layout

Typesetting and layout are the processes whereby subedited manuscripts or disks are turned into finished pages, ready for reproduction. The simplest method is to type the copy neatly (fig 1). Word-processing packages allow you to edit manuscripts on screen, arranged in order from the top of the page to the bottom. Desktop publishing systems, such as Quark Xpress, Ventura, and Pagemaker at the top of the scale, go one stage further and allow you to import articles from a word-processing package, edit them, and then paste up text and graphics in any order on simulated pages on screen. This gives you much more flexibility. A final method is hard copy, in which manuscripts are sent to a professional typesetters, who will provide galley proofs to read and then paste up according to your rough design. This is old technology: it is relatively easy but time consuming, and you will have less control.

Reproduction

Photocopiers are practical, though they reproduce photographs badly and can become expensive for long print runs. Laser printers provide better quality, but the unit cost is higher still. Many newsletter editors use outside printers, who will make their plates from your laser-printed copy; if you have a Postscript printer, you can obtain a positive or negative from a bureau at about £8 a page, which gives a much sharper image.

Which method you choose will depend largely on your budget (a full colour eight-page newsletter with a run of 3000 will cost about £1500–£2000 for printing alone), the equipment you have in house, and, most important, what your staff can operate.

Schedule: April 1995 edition

Friday 10 February	Planning meeting
Monday 13 February	Commission articles
Monday 27 February	Copy submitted
Friday 3 March	Last day for authors' corrections
Monday 6 March	Layout pages
Thursday 9 March	Pass final page proofs
Monday 13 March	Final copy to printers
Monday 27 March	Delivery to editorial staff

Once you have decided on the means of production, construct your own production cycle (see sample schedule). Produce schedules for the rest of the year, and you will know when to block off time. This should ensure that you publish your newsletter regularly.

Design

The next stage is deciding how your finished publication will look—in other words, the design. Your final product should be simple and have its own identity or personality.

Structure

Remind yourself what you wish to achieve. Reread your mission statement, then work out the type of contents you will need to achieve your aim: news, features, letters, columns, editorials, small ads, etc. Decide on the number of pages you can afford and construct a master flatplan (fig 2). If you are using a professional designer, this will be a major part of your brief.

Your newsletter must have the same structure issue after issue. We all like our favourite publications to be familiar. Those that have experimented by moving parts around have received a clear message from their readers: "We don't mind where you put things, but please stop moving them around".

A clear structure helps the editor as well as the reader. Many inexperienced editors use a scattergun approach, in which they ring up anyone who could possibly contribute, waste valuable time chasing them all up, and end up having far too much material. It is far more efficient to work out what you want for each page and then write or commission accordingly. This won't solve the problem of writers missing their deadlines, but it will ensure that copy chasing is directed to the right places.

Style

Once you have the structure, decide on the style. Start with the masthead, or the publication's title. This should have four elements: (*a*) the publication's name, (*b*) an explanatory line (for example, "A monthly newsletter for patients of the Lupin Group practice"), (*c*) the date and issue number, and (*d*) the logo. One word about logos: you may not like yours (few people do) but you must use them for the sake of what marketing people call your corporate image. It is

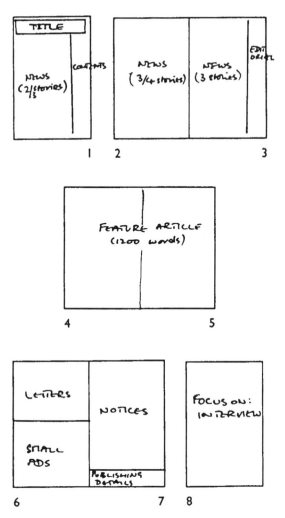

Fig 2 Flatplan of master edition of newsletter

worth going to a professional for this part of the publication: a local art school might welcome it as a project.

You should also consider your headers and footers: the lines or other graphical material at the top or bottom of each page. You can use these to replicate your title, reinforcing your newsletter's identity, or to denote certain parts of the newsletter, such as Letters, News, or Noticeboard.

119

Fig 3 Not only does this page have too many fonts; it also lacks a logical progression in headline size, uses white space between paragraphs rather than framing the page, and, because of the reverse block at the foot of the page, has as its focal point a minor story

Decide on the size of the paper. Most people choose A4, which is familiar and convenient; choose another size only if you have a good reason. Coloured paper can help to build an identity, but make sure that it is pale enough to display the type clearly. Don't change the colour for each issue: you might understand that white comes with the February snow and green with the new grass in May, but the reader will not.

Work out how many columns you will use. There are two rules of thumb. Firstly, for ease of reading, use no more than about 65 characters in each line. Secondly, the more columns there are the more complicated the layouts; most wise but inexperienced newsletter editors choose two or three columns. White space is important:

there should be adequate margins on all four sides so that the words are pleasantly framed.

Next comes typography. Resist polyfontophilia—the temptation to use all the fonts on your computer (fig 3). This may impress you, but it will confuse the readers. Select one typeface for the bulk of your text—the "body copy". Reading guidelines from the Royal National Institute for the Blind[1] state that it doesn't really matter if

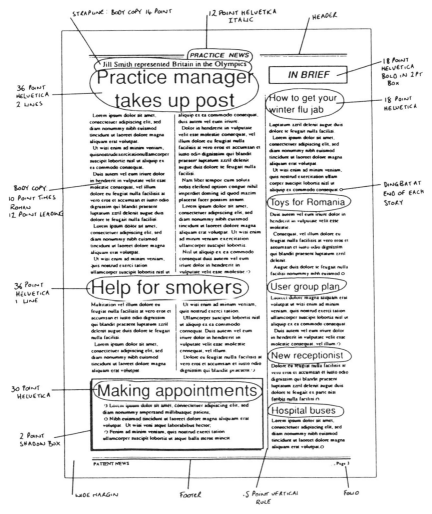

Fig 4 Balanced dummy page

you choose a serif like Times or Palatino or sans serif like Helvetica or Gill. But they stress that many publications use type that is too small. If most of the readers are aged over 40, the minimum typesize for body copy is 10 point. Make sure there is enough white space (leading) between the lines.

Some people use a bold version of the body type for headlines and other devices (display type). Others will use a completely different face. Both work, provided that you are consistent. If you want to vary the effect of headlines, vary the size or lines of the type, not the typeface (fig 4). Don't be timid: a common fault is having headlines too small. Another is using capitals (see fig 3). Using white type on black boxes is an effective device for small boxes but is difficult to read and should be avoided for longer headlines.

Finally, work out a policy on illustrations. The general rule is: if you cannot afford to use them properly, don't use them at all. "Snaps" look amateurish, particularly when they cannot be properly reproduced. The "clip-art" images available in many software packages are technically fine, but they can become visual clichés. It is better to use other devices, such as good strong headlines, "pull out" quotations, and "shadow" boxes, to make a page look interesting. And it will be cheaper.

Write down these style points—and keep to them. This is the only way to build up your publication's personality.

Writing

You should now start thinking about the words for the first issue. Waiting until this stage makes the task less daunting: you now know what space you have to fill.

Do not try to write everything yourself. Using other contributors provides variation and gives you time for leadership tasks such as inspiration and coordination. Be specific when you ask for contributions: give each writer a subject brief, a length, and a deadline, and remind them of the target audience. If you ask someone to write a major article, confirm this in writing. For several articles (for instance, to fill up a news page or a diary section) make sure that you arrange for regular progress reports.

Content

You will soon find that your problem is not which topics to put in but which to leave out. Start listing items that you think will be interesting to your readers. Keep a diary of forthcoming events. Make sure that you receive—and read—as much relevant information as possible, such as minutes and circulars. Decide how each item should be treated—that is, in which section they would be best suited.

Take, for instance, the appointment of a new doctor. You could publish it as a service item, with one or two lines about the new appointment in a "New Faces" column. You could write it as a news story of 200–300 words, giving rather fuller details of the new appointee and the job he or she will be doing. You could run it as a 600–1200 word feature article, in which, for example, a contributor would interview the new person in some detail. Use your flatplan to help you decide the most appropriate treatment.

Do not blur fact with opinion. Saying that the new doctor is the best thing to hit the area since the eradication of smallpox may be valid, but it is not the role of a publication to say so (unless in an editorial). Instead, find a senior colleague and quote him or her. Attribute that comment clearly, and your readers will see you in your proper role of giving out information, not propaganda.

Style

Newsletters must be seen in proportion. They are not documents of record or attempts to advance human knowledge. They are intended to provide a flow of basic information to busy people. This perspective can be difficult in a large organisation, when employees who write are always looking over their shoulders at their bosses or thinking of the possible political repercussions, but it is vital. Good newsletter writing succeeds when it successfully gets across worthwhile bits of information, which is not the same as covering all the angles and the writer's back.

To this end paragraphs should be short, mainly because these are visually less daunting. Sentences should be short—aim for five or six sentences every 100 words—and logical. The words should also be short: use "start" and "pills" rather than "commence" and "medication". Whenever possible use the active rather than the passive. Avoid jargon.

Use quotes whenever you can: these add interest and colour and give you the chance to use opinions. Make sure that your opening paragraph is interesting. Unlike scientific papers, which keep the conclusions until the end, newsletter articles should attract attention immediately. They are competing with many other items for a

---

Common questions on house style

- Do we use British or American spellings (*honour, honor*)?
- When do we use capitals?
- When do we use abbreviations?
- When do we use full points (*Mr., Mr; e.g., eg,*)?
- How do we write scientific terms (*ml/kg/min; ml.kg.min.*)?
- How do we write acronyms (*Unesco, AIDS, or Aids*)?
- How do we use titles?
- When do we spell out numbers (*one-nine, 10, 11, but 2 per cent*)?
- How do we deal with sex (*he, she, s(he), they, chairs, spokesperson*)?
- Do we use single or double quotation marks, and within or outside punctuation: ('. or .')?
- Do we use *-ise* or *-ize*?
- How do we use hyphens (*first-rate card, first rate card*)?

---

reader's attention. Several books deal with the writing techniques needed.[2–4]

Subediting

Deciding in principle whether to accept a submitted article is at the heart of the editing process. Once that decision is made, you will almost certainly need to make some changes to the submitted copy; that is the subediting function. It is important to make this distinction, even though the editor of a small newsletter may be doing both tasks.

Readability

The main purpose of subediting is to ensure that each accepted article has the greatest chance of being read. Apply the guidelines from the previous section. Check grammar[5] and basic facts, particularly names and titles: readers will lose confidence if you write about Jeff Smith when they know it is Geoff Smyth; Mr Smyth may never talk to you again.

Eliminate potentially irritating inconsistencies of style. Readers can be put off by seeing "Dr" in one line and "Dr." in another; in such cases where there are real alternatives write down a house style, and keep to it (see box). Apart from anything else this will cut down on the time spent arguing with pedants: you will be able to say that this is the house style, and that should be the end of the matter.

This will be particularly useful when it comes to the vexed question of initial capital letters. Most readership research shows that capital letters slow the reader down; they also look old fashioned. This does not deter supporters of the Pompous Initial Capital, who will insist that writing the medical management subcommittee without capitals somehow diminishes its status. Think of the reader, and ignore them.

Legality

The two main pitfalls are copyright and libel. In both cases your aim should be to avoid expensive rounds of solicitors' letters, and the best thing is to apply some common sense.

On copyright, avoid taking other people's work without permission. If you want to use words or illustrations that have been published elsewhere, write to the editor, who may well allow you to reproduce them without payment. As for libel, this occurs when you write something about someone that "lowers them in the eyes of right-thinking members of society generally". This also applies to cartoons. Libel is a minefield, which keeps some lawyers extremely rich. The commonsense rule is don't be rude about someone. If you feel you must, then seek legal advice *before* you publish.

Layout

Subeditors are responsible for the look of individual pages, subject to the overall style. They will decide what goes where on each page, and mark up—or format—the copy accordingly. It is unlikely to fit perfectly, so don't be afraid to cut. Do not alter the style to make an article fit, for example by reducing the typesize; this will destroy your newsletter's hardearned personality. Do not be afraid to add extra lines to stories so that they can fit exactly; often, adding extra paragraph breaks will do.

Now is the time to write headlines and other devices intended to attract the reader. Set the style *before* writing the headlines, which will dictate the size of the type and the number of lines. Put the most important (and logically the longest) story at the top of each page. Graduate the size and lines of headlines accordingly.

Headlines are not labels, but marketing tools. They should contain short, interesting words and, whenever possible, a verb. The top line should be longer than the second to draw the reader's eye

125

down into the story. They should never contain information that is not in the story. Avoid whimsical or punning headlines on every story.

Feedback

Newsletter editors find it hard to know how they are doing, but they should try. An obvious method is to send out a questionnaire with the publication, but response rates will be low. Editors must therefore monitor "Letters to the Editor", ask their readers for their opinions, or watch to see how quickly (or slowly) piles of their newsletter disappear. These are not scientific methods but are better than the alternative, which is listening to the opinions of a few people with axes to grind or who have little in common with your target readership. You will have complaints, but see them in perspective: newsletters must be judged on the overall flow of information they provide, not on individual items.

Conclusion

Throwing ill-considered newsletters at a communications problem will probably do more harm than good, and will certainly be a waste of resources. On the other hand, a newsletter that is well planned, adequately resourced, and skilfully executed will be a formidable communications tool. Enjoy it; if you do not, then how can you expect others to do so?

1 Royal National Institute for the Blind. *Making print legible: basic guidelines*. London: RNIB Publications Unit, 1990.
2 Strunk W, White E B. *Elements of style*. 3rd ed. New York: Macmillan, 1979.
3 Goodman N W, Edwards M B. *Medical writing: a prescription for clarity*. Cambridge: Cambridge University Press, 1991.
4 Albert T. *Medical journalism: the writer's guide*. Oxford: Radcliffe Medical Press, 1992.
5 Hicks W. *English for journalists*. London: Routledge, 1993.

20 Prepare a patient education leaflet

J A Muir Gray

Few patients remember all that the doctor has said to them during a consultation. Patients usually remember those parts of the consultation that were most important to them but this does not necessarily include the points in the consultation that the doctor believed to be most important. Many patients are therefore unable to recollect all the advice they were given about treatment and self care.

The verbal aspect of the consultation has its limitations as a medium for transmitting information; the effectiveness of communication can be improved by complementing the spoken word with the written—by giving the patient a summary of what the doctor regards as the most important facts. Ideally, each patient would be given a written summary of the key points that had been covered in the consultation but this is rarely possible and a leaflet that summarises the main points that are of relevance to all patients with a particular problem offers a reasonable compromise to the doctor who would like to give patients some written material but who is unable to write a different set of notes for each and every patient.

Why do it?

Before wondering how to do it, ask yourself "Why do it?" Why prepare a leaflet yourself when there are numerous leaflets available?[1] Your local health education unit should be able to provide information on the leaflets that are available and perhaps provide samples or batches of them, but leaflets and booklets for patients and the public are now produced from so many sources that it is difficult for a health education unit to keep up to date. Other useful sources of information on patient education are the relevant mutual aid groups, for example the Alzheimer's Disease Society or the Parkinson's Disease Society or the community health council. The medical library in the postgraduate centre may be another very good source of information, because many medical librarians are developing an interest in patient information and education.

Published leaflets are, in general, well produced and cheap; many are free. Some of them have been evaluated and most of those produced by drug companies are not used by them to push their own products offensively. There are, however, disadvantages about the use of published material, the principal one being that they have not been produced by the patient's own doctor, for, in spite of the adverse criticism of the medical profession that has become more vehement in recent years, the majority of patients still trust their own doctor's advice on health more than they trust advice from any other source. A stencilled sheet of advice produced by a patient's own doctor will usually be more effective than the glossiest leaflet produced by a third party, because a leaflet, properly used, is not simply a vehicle for information; it can also symbolise the contract between doctor and patient, and thus be an extension and continuation of the consultation.

Writing a leaflet

Having decided to write a leaflet, you have to decide on content, length, language, style, and design.

Content

This may seem self evident, but it is important to think of the objectives that are desired and to include relevant material for all the objectives. If, for example, the objectives are not only to inform but also to encourage a change in behaviour, specific information must be given on the appropriate behavioural change. Therefore ask yourself:

(1) What are the objectives of the leaflet?

(2) What needs to be put in to attain each of these objectives?

The content should include detailed specific advice and not simply vague exhortations. For example, instead of simply exhorting someone to "take more exercise", advice should be given on the frequency, duration, and intensity of exercise that will be beneficial.

Length

Brevity may be the soul of wit but it can also be the source of confusion. Do not make the leaflet so brief that it is superficial or so general that it is ineffective. So much emphasis is put on the need to keep verbal messages short and simple that it is sometimes assumed that all forms of communication should be equally brief. But patients will have time to read the leaflet at their leisure, and to return to it once, or many times, if they wish, so it is possible to give more detail on particularly important points in a leaflet than when speaking to someone. This does not mean that a short book is justified, but 1000–2000 words may be appropriate.

Language

The length chosen is inevitably a compromise, for most doctors have patients whose customary reading material ranges from the brevity of a racing card—the epitome of brief prose—to the prolixity of official documents. Similarly, the reading level of patients ranges from the ability to master only the shortest of words and the simplest of grammar—for example, the English found in tabloids—to the ability to cope with long words and sophisticated sentence structures—for example, the grammar of legal documents or government circulars. In the ideal world a range of different leaflets would be produced; in practice one leaflet must usually suffice. The compromise has to be written for the person who can cope with simple language but that compromise will be welcomed by most sophisticated patients, although a few will feel patronised.

Commonly used words are usually short and should be chosen in preference to longer words wherever possible. This is usually better English in any case; better to "use" a word than "employ" one. Sentences should also be short, with as few subordinate clauses as possible. Take the *Daily Express* or the *Sun* for a few weeks if you are not a regular reader of a tabloid to read well written English of this sort.

Fowler's *Dictionary of Modern English Usage*[2] gives amusing and clear advice on the dangers of, and means of avoiding, "abstractitis" and the "love of the long word".

Style

Case histories, suitably disguised of course, increase the reader's interest and the question and answer format is also an effective style, particularly if the questions are those that patients commonly ask. The humorous approach is best avoided, as humour often falls flat when translated to the written word.

Design

The design of a leaflet is important and the following possibilities should be considered:

- diagrams
- columns to reduce the length of lines
- different type faces.

Patients who are printers, publishers, commercial artists, or designers will be able to offer good advice.

Remember to leave sufficient blank space on the leaflet for writing additional, personal advice when giving the leaflet to the patient.

Theory into practice

The theory is comparatively simple; the practice of leaflet writing more difficult. But the doctor who is considering writing a leaflet should bear in mind two points: firstly, that patients will greatly appreciate, and benefit from, such an initiative and, secondly, when starting to write to remember Robert Graves' famous dictum that a writer's best friend is the wastepaper basket. Do not try to achieve the perfect formula at the first attempt. Draft and redraft the text, viewing each draft as a step towards a useful working document.

Evaluation

Evaluation always improves effectiveness. Even a very simple evaluation of a draft of the leaflet, for example by asking a small number of patients and other members of the primary care team for their comments, will improve the final version. Health visitors' training makes them particularly useful critics or colleagues if the topic is one that is of interest to them, and the health education unit is another very useful source of criticism and advice.

More formal evaluation is, of course, more effective, and the district health authority's research fund or a relevant drug company are sources of finance for evaluation. The health education unit would be a good source of advice for drafting such a research application and one of the health education officers may be interested in participating in such a project.

The use of the leaflet

Leaflets that are left for patients to take have some effect, but a leaflet is more valuable if used by a member of the primary care team in the course of his or her consultation with a patient. The leaflet should not simply be handed to the patient as he or she rises to leave, but should be used during the consultation. At this stage it helps to personalise the leaflet, for example to write the patient's name on it, or underline parts of particular relevance to that patient or to write additional points in the spaces left for this purpose at the design stage. If the opportunity is also provided for the patient to record information on the leaflet, the effectiveness will be further improved.

Conclusion

It is not easy to write an effective leaflet, but the effort is well worth making because a leaflet, properly prepared and used, can be a useful extension of the consultation.

1 Sloan, P J M. Survey of patient information booklets. *BMJ* 1984;**288**:915–19.
2 Fowler, H W. *A dictionary of modern English usage*. 2nd ed. Oxford: Clarendon Press, 1965.

21 Get publicity

Pamela Taylor

When it comes to getting publicity, thinking through the consequences before you take any public action can make all the
difference between sensationalised press headlines, which alienate
your colleagues and alarm your patients, and sensible reports that
accurately set out your position.

Perhaps the most difficult aspect of generating publicity is
recognising yourself what is newsworthy and what is not. Achieving
publicity means simplifying a complex issue and making it readily
understandable by the public. This is not trivialising the subject; it is
the art of communicating with the public on their own terms, just as
an individual doctor should be able to communicate with a patient
on that patient's terms.

Medicine is known as a "must subject" for the press; they must
cover it. Health issues have all the ingredients the public loves: life
and death, human interest, politics, and, crucially, personal health,
which is recognised as being relevant to each one of us.

The first essential step in achieving publicity is to find a "peg". A
peg is journalese for something to hang the story on; that means an
action or event taking place now. You and your colleagues may have
complained about funding for months but the peg for the newspaper
stories would be your letter of protest today to the local member of
parliament.

While the politics of the NHS hit the headlines, remember that
scientific information, too, can be made accessible to the public.
Doctors should be more prepared to explain their work and to help
society to understand developments.

Writing to the press

One of the least traumatic forays into the media can be achieved by writing a letter for publication in a newspaper. Your letter can be in response to an article already printed, but there is nothing to stop you from writing on any aspect of health that you believe will be of interest to the newspaper's readers. You may want to use your local press to encourage women to come forward for cervical screening or you may want to use the national press to alert the public to the problems caused by split site facilities and anaesthetic cover. Either way, the rules are the same.

(1) Keep your letter short, particularly if you are writing to one of the tabloids.
(2) Avoid jargon.
(3) Make your letter relevant to the readers of the particular newspaper.
(4) Before you send the letter, inform your colleagues and double-check your facts.

Ring the letters page and tell them your letter is on its way. Keep a copy. Sometimes the letters editor will ring you and negotiate some cuts to fit your contribution on to the page; sometimes a butchered version is printed without any consultation. Chase the paper up if nothing appears in print, and don't be afraid to send your letter to a second newspaper, provided it is relevant to its readers, if the first one decides against publication.

Local radio

There are countless air-time hours to be filled as the BBC's 39 local radio stations dramatically increase their hours of speech over music, and the public loves to hear about health issues. If you feel brave enough, the opportunities are there for you to put your message out on the airwaves. All you have to do is to ring the local radio station, explain what you would like to say, and ask them if they are interested. You must have something newsworthy to say, but you can rely on the judgment of the local radio staff to tell you whether you are worth interviewing or taking part in a phone-in. Initially, it is as simple as that.

What might they be interested in? National news stories often have a local news aspect that can be highlighted. Smoking is regularly in the national news and many doctors are successful in persuading their local radio stations to run a local interview on young people and smoking, or a phone-in for people wanting to give up.

Now comes the more difficult part—the interview itself. Draw up a checklist of questions to ask the interviewer in advance.

(1) When is the interview?
(2) What programme will it be broadcast on?
(3) Will it be live or recorded?
(4) What will be the venue: surgery, hospital, or studio?
(5) Will others also be interviewed and, if so, will their views be opposed to yours?

Then take time to prepare yourself. Write down a maximum of five key points you want to put over to the audience. Make them positive and informative points, and stick to them. During the interview, listen to the question then select one of your key points in response. If the first question is very far removed from any of your key points, simply say "I think it's more important to say right at the start that . . ." then introduce one of the points you planned to make. So long as your point is positive and relevant, the interviewer will allow this.

If you are a success, they may offer you a regular radio doctor slot. But that is another skill and another story.

Producing a press statement

The easiest way to inform several journalists about your views is to write a press statement and send it to them all. A good press statement is simply written, avoiding hyperbole, and structured to answer the questions who? what? when? where? and why?

What could possibly be of interest to the press that is of help to you? Work involving the community is a sure winner. A joint plea by hospital doctors and general practitioners for adequate meal services and improved home care for elderly patients discharged from hospitals would be of interest to the press, radio, and probably regional television. A booklet available to the public on healthy eating, or new measures to reach ethnic minorities, or a letter to your MP on local NHS funding would all make suitable material for a press statement.

The opening paragraph of your press statement should sum up the whole story:

Blanktown's GPs and hospital doctors have today written to their MP protesting that local cuts in health service financing are threatening the standards of services to patients.

The second paragraph should contain details to expand on the opening paragraph. In this example details of services to be cut could be given.

The final paragraph can be in the form of a quotation where opinions can be expressed:

Dr Joan Smith commented, "We are concerned for our patients . . ."

Make sure there is a contact name and a telephone number, or numbers, so journalists with queries can ring for further information at any time.

Consult your colleagues when necessary; it is no use jumping up and down about a funding crisis if the press hear from one of your colleagues that he or she has no idea what you are on about. Send the press statement, either in the post or, ideally, by fax or by hand, addressed to the newsdesk, unless you have the name of a particular journalist. It helps if it arrives early in the day so the journalists have time to work on it. Ring them and offer to help whoever has been allocated to write a story based on the statement. This often helps to establish the vital fact that your statement has not even progressed beyond the front reception desk.

Press conferences

The information you want to put across to the media may be too complex to be contained in a press statement. What sort of subject would persuade the journalist to come and listen to you? The opening of a new hospital or wing is an obvious, though rare, opportunity. The press would be quite happy, though, to cover the provision of new facilities, particularly if there is some impressive equipment they can photograph. Closures and cuts in services are big news, too. Press conferences announcing fund-raising stunts, deputations, and organised protests are the stuff of local paper front page headlines.

For advice on organising such an event, see "Give a press conference".

Press visits

Why not open the doors and allow the press in? Such an invitation can be disarming, particularly if you have been on the receiving end of some bad publicity. The press would respond to an invitation to see a new service for patients, or to view the poor accommodation for junior hospital doctors. Having the press tramping around disrupting the working routine and accosting patients is what you want to avoid. So a successful open day needs to be planned.

(1) Map out a timetable.
(2) Concentrate on positive points to put across.
(3) Consult internally.
(4) Involve all relevant staff.
(5) Obtain permission from any patients who may be involved.
(6) Hold a dress rehearsal.
(7) Organise the catering (coffee on arrival, with sandwiches and soft drinks for lunch are quite sufficient).

Ensure that everyone who may come into contact with the press during the visit is well briefed on what to say and, just as important, what not to say. An apparently helpful expansion by one doctor on another's views can appear in the press as "local doctors split on the best way to treat . . ."

Television

Television is all about interesting pictures. A row of doctors sitting in the postgraduate centre speaking at a press conference does not afford television the most exciting scenes. If your message is interesting enough, though, TV journalists will want to interview you, but they really want more than what they term "talking heads": they want action.

A well-organised picture opportunity often makes all the difference between no TV interest and hitting the headlines. Even tired old messages can be brought to life.

You will not receive television coverage for warnings about road traffic accidents, but lit candles depicting the number of avoidable deaths should ensure that your message receives attention. Similarly, financial wrangling over the threatened closure of a special baby-care unit is unlikely material for peak time viewing, but a gathering of mothers with their babies who have been successfully treated by the unit should make it on to the screens.

Television pictures take time to organise. Filming is expensive and camera crews' time planned carefully. Make sure you:

- ring the television news intake desk two or three days beforehand;
- discuss in advance the sort of pictures they will want to take;
- discuss timing (you do not want to miss the lunchtime news bulletins);
- find out if they will want to interview someone in addition to taking general pictures; if so, who, where, and when?

Surviving a television interview means acting larger than life. Look interested in what you are saying and be positive. And watch your language. Avoid saying "patient care" when you can say "the care of patients" and "working beyond their contractual obligations" when you can say "doctors and nurses are working very hard". Many doctors on television alienate the viewers when they hide behind such medical clichés.

You will be on air for a few moments, so talk in headlines rather than meticulously building up to a point. Dump most of the information you have in your mind and just concentrate on the major points you want the public to know about. News editors are looking for "sound bites". They want one illustrative sentence that they can pull out of the recording and use up front in the news story, with perhaps a subsidiary sentence slotted into the same news item towards the end.

Using publicity

Publicity is a powerful tool and should be used thoughtfully. At worst it can cause damage and real distress, but used wisely it can help bring about real change for the better.

22 Get a letter in the newspapers

Charles Pither

Giles felt *so* incensed about it that he wrote to the paper . . .

Giles, rather than chaining himself to the railings, lobbying his member of parliament, or hijacking a jumbo jet, has found the ultimate vent for his spleen. Whether it is just another nuance of Englishness like crumpets or cricket, or maybe the hope of restoring the misplaced balance of justice, or perhaps the egotistical motivation of seeing your name in print is uncertain. What is clearer is that ever since there have been newspapers "Incensed of Ipswich" and "Angry of Angmering" have been bashing off letters whenever the mood takes them. For the average man and woman in the street there exists, beyond high dudgeon and extreme annoyance, somewhere between shaking with rage and blinding fury, a state of indignation and agitation adequately extinguished only by picking up a pen and writing to the press.

For most of us this compulsion to share our angst with the readership of a national newspaper is only an occasional phenomenon, motivated by a particular event that we feel we cannot let pass without comment. There are, however, a group of gallant scribes in perpetual competition with themselves, who dispatch letters with the same regularity as they consume their All Bran. For them the game is simply to get into print at any cost, and, although volume of letters is one approach, it is by no means guaranteed to succeed.

Whether a letter published in a national newspaper ever makes any difference to the subject is questionable. At best, it certainly may bring a point to the notice of a wide readership; at worst, authors can feel that at least they did something about the injustice nagging at their conscience. The more pertinent consideration, however, is how to get the editor to publish it in the first place. Having made the decision that sleep will be impossible until the ancient typewriter has been dusted off and loaded with crisp foolscap, what are the mysterious ingredients that secure publication?

There is a tendency to believe that most of the successful authors are dons, lords, members of the Athenaeum, chairpersons of royal commissions, or country curates, but the evidence disputes this. Although there are, not surprisingly, a large number of letters from eminent persons of all walks of life, the majority of letters published come from untitled, ordinary people who never have, nor ever will, be regius professor of Egyptian archaeology at Oxford. A large number of letters do appear from doctors, but it is pertinent to remember PhD, DPhil, DD, and so on, as they frequently enable you to dissociate yourself from a viewpoint totally inexplicable had it come from within the medical profession.

The choice of subject is, of course, dependent upon the motivation of the instant, and I can give little advice about this. The small earthquake in Ongar may, you feel, have deserved greater treatment, or Goethe's original meaning have been misconstrued in a new translation. Your comment may be topical or pertinent enough to merit publication on this alone, but there are several factors that can be helpful.

Headed notepaper is certainly worth while especially if the letter is on the serious side. The editor won't know much about forensic psychiatry and so if your comment appears on paper headed "Academic Department of Forensic Psychiatry" it may carry more weight. The same applies to qualifications; put them all in and hope to blind them with science. Likewise it is worth considering joint signatories, which is a good idea if they add weight to your case. Although the length of the letter in itself is not critical, you are unlikely to repeat Jefferies' 1862 success with his missive to *The Times* of 3000 words on the plight of agricultural labourers. It is more important to be succinct and to the point, conveying, as in a scientific paper, your exact meaning with the minimum of superfluous words.

Lines of approach

When it comes to style, it is worth remembering that there are several styles of letter that appear time and time again, the use of which may modify, for better or worse, the letter's chance of actually appearing in print.

The Tunbridge Wells

This is the letter that from the first line conjures up the image of a bristling moustache upon the quivering upper lip of a retired general. The *Daily Telegraph* letters page consists almost entirely of letters such as this. The subjects range widely from the union jack being upside down on Remembrance Sunday (. . . what's the country coming to . . .) to the union jack being upside down on Boxing Day (. . . what has the country come to . . .). In general not a recommended approach, especially to the more liberal organs.

The Bernard Shaw

In spite of the observations above, if you do happen to be a revered household name of advancing years, it is going to be a very stalwart editor who would deny you column inches in his paper. If you have not been heard from for the past 10 years so much the better. The content of your letter is unimportant but it may as well be on something totally trivial. This will give the nation the pleasure of confirmation that you really are senile and, as they suspected, quietly dementing.

The trireme

This is perhaps the best approach for the enthusiastic amateur. Success depends upon two things. Firstly, knowing a great amount about an aspect of a subject so minimal that most of the population did not know there even was a subject, and, secondly, a lead or introduction. This is the problem; while it is not too difficult to become an expert in a specialised topic, it is all too easy to die waiting for an opportunity to tell the world all about it. The best solution to this problem is obliquity:

> Sir,
>
> Your article on the closure of the Tuileries gallery made no mention of the famous carp to be found in the ornamental ponds of the *jardin*. These fish and others of the family are particularly prone to a fungus *Hyspericillus inpratroides* that over a period of time damages the ventral

fin and thus causes the fish to swim around in circles. While this is not detrimental in the round ponds of Paris the situation in the natural habitat in Xi'ang province . . .

If you are very lucky, somewhere in the depths of a crumbling university a don of great learning, total obscurity, and an age best ascertained by carbon dating will disagree and will write to the editor saying so. If all goes well the whole nation can then delight in the joys of a correspondence of no practical relevance to which most of its premier minds contribute, in thought if not in publication.

The anti

The majority of the letters in all the serious papers. The best way editors have of appeasing their conscience if they have published libel, controversy, or fiction. The letter simply states with convincing evidence that the article or implication was misguided/wrong/libellous/damned lies. The problem is that in these circumstances the mail bag will be full of similar letters and yours must be outstanding to get in with a chance. This can be achieved by taking a totally contrary view, or by being a member of the Athenaeum, chairperson of a royal commission, and so on.

The bottom right hand corner

The traditional position in *The Times* where letters of some wit, originality, or total irrelevance end up. The best chance of publication is to find something of such amusing eccentricity or idiocy that the editor has no option but to publish. If this something happens to be yourself, publication is almost guaranteed.

Luck and judgment

This is, of course an attempt at categorising a subject not very amenable to such treatment. Probably the best way of getting your letter into print is to avoid all these approaches and come up with something completely original and imaginatively different.

Having written the letter, crammed with pertinent comment, brilliant innovation, cutting wit, and a deal of eccentricity, you read it through 10 times, tear it up, and start again. Eventually you end up with a compromise with which you are least unhappy, and rush to the fax machine or to the post office to catch the last post. Then you have the awful waiting. The next few days you spring to the newsagent and scan the letters page even before the cost of the paper has changed hands. Usually it is a progressive disappointment. After a week all thoughts of the editor "saving it for the weekend because it's so good" can be dismissed and the only consolation will be the nice letter from the editor's assistant saying that the editor read your comments with interest. If, of course, yours was one of the 300 letters received that day to be published, the problem is then whether by going out to lunch to celebrate you might miss the call from *Panorama* requesting your appearance on a studio panel. Either way you will dine out on it for weeks, perhaps months, or—for some old bores—the rest of your life.

Many papers nowadays don't reply with the traditional "The Editor has noted your comments with interest" but *The Times* usually still does. But if you are unlucky, nothing matters less. In seismological terms the earthquake in Ongar was a non-starter, and maybe the new translation of Goethe is actually better. The therapeutic effect of writing to a newspaper is in the writing not in the publication. In fact, on odd occasions the letter may not even get as far as the letter box. One of the best letters ever received by *The Times* was from a Major Wintle:

> Sir,
> I have just written you a long letter.
> > On reading it through I have thrown it into the waste-paper basket.
> > Hoping this meets with your approval,
> > I am, Sir,
> Your obedient servant,

Giles, like Major Wintle, will still feel greatly relieved that he did actually write, and he will inform his friends regardless of whether his letter was published or not. Writing to newspapers is an integral part of being a concerned citizen, and, as doctors, we frequently have reason to be concerned. This is a particularly British way of doing things. No other race could have masterminded an effective form of protest that does not even entail getting out of a chair.

In the words of René Gimpel, an Englishman is "a man with a passion for horses, playing with a ball, probably one broken bone in his body and in his pocket a letter to *The Times*."

Long may it continue.

23 Talk to a reporter

Tony Smith

Doctors are mostly ambivalent about the press, radio, and television. Sometimes a series of articles or TV programmes appears that explains a new technical advance clearly, accurately, and with sensible, informed speculation about its future implications. On these occasions doctors join the mass audience in admiring the skill and imagination of the team responsible. But doctors also remember programmes and articles that distorted the truth in the pursuit of sensationalism; several programmes on AIDS have fallen into that category. Sometimes, too, when a new technique has caught the public imagination there may be a siege of a hospital by reporters competing for exclusive rights to interview patients or their relatives—and some using lies and confidence trickery in an attempt to extract confidential information from hospital staff.

Of course the public has a legitimate interest in hearing about medical advances, and often the best way for the story to be presented is with a "human interest" angle; but most doctors have heard horror stories about smooth-talking reporters who try to discover the identity of a patient, who has a right to privacy, and many fear that if they talk to the press they may find an incautious comment given headline treatment.

Ask for time

How, then, should doctors respond when their telephone rings and they find a reporter (from the press, radio, or TV) wanting to talk about a news story—either an incident concerning a particular patient or a technical advance of some kind? My first piece of advice is to ask for time. Few of us are practised enough at public speaking to think on our feet, and I find it invaluable to ask for a few minutes to put my thoughts together. In fact, I usually make a few notes of what I want to say. A 10–20 minute pause will give you time to check a few facts (what exactly is the defect in haemophilia B?), possibly have a quick chat with a colleague, and, if you are in any doubt, to take advice. (What sort of advice? You may want to ask your hospital secretary whether he or she is issuing a press statement and, if so, would prefer doctors to refer all callers to him or her; or you may wish to discuss confidentiality with your defence society. If there is any possibility of litigation you should almost certainly say nothing without having first checked with the legal experts.)

So after 10 minutes the reporter rings back. At this point you may have decided to make no comment either on legal advice or because the subject (such as, say, artificial insemination by donor in homosexual women) is one that you'd prefer to avoid for fear of getting egg on your face. Don't explain why; simply apologise for wasting the reporter's time and say that having had time to think you have decided not to comment. Mostly, however, you'll want to do what you can to answer the questions. So next find out on what basis you are talking. Is the reporter simply seeking background information, talking off the record? Is the reporter wanting attributable statements that will appear (or be heard) with your name attached? Or is he or she sounding you out for a possible interview on TV or radio? The distinction is important, and it is up to you to ask, not the reporter to explain. If reporters ask you for attributable comments on a news story, then you should ask them to read out exactly what is going to be printed. If they tell you that they are still putting the story together, then ask him to phone you later with the final version, including your comment, to make sure that it still sounds right in context.

Studio punch-ups

A reporter may be wanting you to come to talk in a sound or TV studio. Karl Sabbagh, in the following chapter, explains how TV features are made. In general, my advice on the studio punch-ups with a doctor, a lawyer, a sociologist, a trade union official, two coalminers, and a dog is leave them to the experts. Talking one-to-one with a reporter is fair enough; multipanel discussions usually leave the participants angry and frustrated.

On the whole, however, talking to reporters can be fun, intellectually stimulating and worth while. But please don't talk about something outside your range of current knowledge: what you learnt about virology in medical school is not good enough 12 years later. Don't criticise another doctor's treatment—he or she has seen the patient and you haven't. Don't say that anyone concerned is a fool unless you've met him or her and you're certain. Don't seem to assume that patients are invariably ignorant, lazy, and wrong and that doctors are always conscientious, polite, considerate, and right. And don't answer any questions you don't want to answer.

Then, with any luck, you'll get to know your reporters, and they'll come to you again and learn to rely on you—and you on them. Once that occurs you'll be able to forget all the horror stories.

24 Appear on television

Karl Sabbagh

Why should a doctor need to know how to appear on television? Is an invitation to take part in a television programme so frequent that it is worth including in a book like this one? And, even if it is, is there anything the invitee can do that will contribute to the success or failure of the experience?

The answer is "yes" to both these questions. In the United Kingdom alone there are currently four television channels producing factual programmes, and cable and satellite television may bring more. The appetite for programmes in general and medical programmes in particular appears to be voracious, and the chances of some programme seeking your cooperation in a year are quite high. The invitation is even more likely to come if you are (*a*) involved in research, (*b*) active in medical politics, (*c*) a self publicist, or (*d*) negligent, incompetent, or criminal.

Since quite a high proportion of doctors come into one of those categories, so might you. In which case, it is only a matter of time before you pick up the phone to hear an imperious voice on the phone inviting you to be filmed or recorded for a television programme. What, then, should be your reply, and how can you best make use of the opportunity? If you pride yourself on being good with people, and many doctors do, then you should see the invitation as a useful test of your skills in this area. Television is run by people, after all, and if you can quickly establish a personal relationship with the people responsible for the television programme, you are more likely to be treated fairly and to be kept informed about what is going on. Terrorists and hostages provide a useful object lesson in this situation, since it seems that once any sort of good relationship is set up between terrorist and captive, the hostage is probably safe. A superficial knowledge of or contempt for television can lead some doctors to keep their distance, try to exert their authority, and generally remain aloof even if they have agreed to cooperate in a programme. If they do that, I suggest, they are losing the opportunity to use the occasion effectively.

Television personnel

While it is easy to say "establish a good relationship with the television people", it is sometimes quite difficult to find out who they are. You may have a name or two as a result of that first phone conversation but it may be very difficult to find out exactly what role those names play in the production. There is an understandable tendency for each member of a television team to claim personal responsibility for both the idea and the work behind a programme. This is not always true. There are actually four main job descriptions you will come across: researcher, director, producer, and, occasionally, executive producer. Each of these is involved in some way with production and each will persuade you that he or she holds the reins of power. If you know the functions of each of these you can actually use one against another to find out what you need to know about the programme to help you decide whether to appear at all.

The first person to call you is likely to be the researcher, trawling the professional world connected with the topic of the programme. Treat him or her politely, give an impression of great depth and originality, but don't waste too much breadth, particularly if you are in the middle of a busy surgery or outpatients. Do, however, offer to send some printed material that describes your views or your work, and, unless you are dead set against any appearance on television for any reason at all, keep the channels of communication open.

The reason you are not spending too much time talking to the researcher is that he or she won't really be able to give you the answers to the important questions that you need to have answered before you can make your decision to help. These are: Who else will be appearing? Why was the topic chosen in the first place? Is it film or studio? Will it be edited afterwards? Will you be told how much of your contribution is finally to be used? Will any independent medical adviser see the programme before it goes out? And so on.

These questions can only really be answered by the producer, one

147

or two rungs up the ladder. The researcher may give you answers, but you cannot hold this person to them because he or she doesn't make the decisions. The research is passed on to the producer, or producer/director who is in charge of the programme, and who will have some control over the answers to the above questions.

One of the most puzzling distinctions to outsiders is the difference between the functions of a producer and a director in television. Confusion arises because, while production and direction are separate functions in a television programme, they are often performed by the same person.

A television programme usually starts with an idea by a producer, who then writes a treatment, prepares a budget, gets together a team, and starts work. Decisions relating to staff, finance, and content are usually all his or hers. One member of the team could be the director of the programme. His or her job is to ensure that the pictures and sound that will be needed to tell the story arrive in a suitable form for transmission. If it is a film programme, this will involve planning to shoot the film, directing the film crew on location, and supervising the film editing in the cutting room. If it is a studio programme the director's role is concerned with the placing of cameras, the design of the set, and any subsequent editing of the videotape. In either of these media the director will be responsible to the producer. Any decision about your role in the programme, how the material is to be edited and the overall arguments to be presented are made or approved by the producer.

Different jobs, different objectives

What sort of people are television producers, and what do you need to know about them and their job to make the most of your television opportunity? In the main they are people who believe that television has a different role in society from the one many doctors think it should have. You must remember, if approached to appear on television, that broadcasting is not an arm of the public health services. One of its roles, and the one you are most likely to be consulted about, is to act as an honest reporter of the society we live in. So television producers are continually on the lookout for things that people do not know about and that, in their judgment as journalists, they think people would like to know about. In the health area this can range from new treatments to hospital closures, from drug disasters to prevention of heart disease. But a topic is rarely chosen because the producer feels that the viewers should know about it for the good of their health. Unfortunately, since the good of the nation's health features largely in the priorities of many doctors, there is a source of conflict in the different approaches to the publicising of health matters, which will exist until we have government—or BMA—controlled television.

But why is an appreciation of this conflict useful to a doctor who is invited to appear on television? Well, I believe that the best approach is a realistic one, and doctors who have low expectations of what they will achieve on television will come away far more satisfied than those who see it as a long-sought chance to (*a*) publicise their life's research, (*b*) increase their grant, (*c*) improve the figures for their hypertension clinic, (*d*) get a dig in at their rivals.

Optimising the opportunity

If you are invited to appear on television your participation is likely to be in the form of an interview, unless you can juggle or do card tricks. Few programmes are transmitted live these days, so your contribution will probably be either filmed or recorded on videotape some time before it is transmitted as part of a programme. Although doctors are suspicious of recorded programmes because of the opportunities provided to the television production team for editing, I believe that prerecording allows a greater flexibility for participants as well as producers. I have known of producers who have spent hundreds of feet of valuable film filming several attempts by inexperienced interviewees to put over their points as well as possible.

Here are a few suggestions to help you make the most of an invitation to appear on television.

• Be limited in the amount you expect to get over. You are likely to be seen or heard for seconds rather than minutes, and if you cannot say something brief and useful about the topic of the programme, then don't accept the invitation. Bear in mind, however, that if you were asked to summarise your life's work by an acquaintance in some social setting, you would probably come up with quite a useful account, clear and comprehensible to a layman, in a couple of minutes.

• Accept the need for some editing of your contribution. After all, if you spoke to a newspaper reporter for ten minutes, you wouldn't

149

expect the paper to print every word you said, 600 or so. You do have a right to be edited fairly, and you should certainly make it clear to the producer that you would like to be informed about what portion, if any, of your contribution remains in the final version of the programme. This is a courtesy you are entitled to, but is unlikely to be offered spontaneously to you. As well as giving you an opportunity to make a final plea for reconsideration if you don't like what the television people have done to you, it helps to avoid the embarrassing situation of your whole family sitting around to watch a programme from which you have unaccountably disappeared.

• Never address the camera—see it as an observer of the events of the programme, rather than as the focus for your remarks. Even if an interviewer is not seen in vision with you, there will usually be someone, the director or the researcher, to address your remarks to.

• If you are taking part in an interview or discussion don't be afraid to correct the interviewer or chairperson, or to lead the discussion into areas that you would rather deal with. Many interviewees are too polite, and feel they must play according to the rules set by the television programme. This can lead to a situation where a participant saves up until after an interview something he or she should have pointed out.

I may have given the impression that if you want to appear on television, you have to wait for someone to invite you. But increasingly, doctors themselves are suggesting opportunities for themselves or their colleagues, by building on contacts that they have made professionally or socially. No television producers mind receiving a well thought out programme suggestion from a viewer. What they do mind is receiving a suggestion for a programme that is identical to one transmitted in the last few weeks. If you feel there are things that television should be doing in your subject area, make sure first of all that these things aren't being done already, by watching television occasionally.

In fact, if there's one piece of advice I would offer above all others to someone invited to appear on television it is to watch as much factual television as possible before you take part. Note what you find irritating or insincere or confusing or difficult to understand, and make a mental note to avoid those pitfalls yourself. You might even find the experience of watching television enjoyable in itself, and if you treat the medium seriously, so will your viewers when you appear on it.

150

25 Give a press conference

Pamela Taylor

Never call a press conference if you can cover all the information in a written press statement or by telephoning the newspapers. Journalists will not thank you for calling them away from their desks unnecessarily.

A press conference must be planned, whether you have weeks of time or the journalists are milling around outside the door. Your checklist should be:

- The invitation
- Timing
- Invitation list
- Venue
- Badges and signing in
- Personnel
- The conference
- Picking up the pieces.

The invitation

Depending on the event, you may send embossed cards for a formal conference, issue a written invitation, ring round frantically giving an hour or so's notice, or call out, as the press jostle you, that you will be commenting in the hospital board room in 20 minutes.

For the embossed card, formal event such as an after dinner speech by a minister, give the journalists plenty of warning. Send the press a covering letter giving fuller details and remember to inform them about dress.

A written press invitation should contain enough information to encourage the journalists to attend. Once written, your invitation may be hot news, so put an embargo (figure) on it for the time of the conference.

151

> PLEASE DO NOT BROADCAST OR PUBLISH IN ANY FORM
> BEFORE 11.30 AM THURSDAY 13TH OCTOBER 1984

Embargo notice for the invitation.

Time may be too short for written invitations. Jot down the essential details, grab some volunteers, and ring round the journalists or their newsdesks.

Timing

A good time for a press conference is 11.30 am, giving the journalists time to write up their stories afterwards, before their late afternoon deadlines. Make special arrangements to meet deadlines for evening and local newspapers and magazines; you can brief them in advance under embargo, so they can write the bulk of their stories and attend the conference for quotes and the finishing touches. Remember, too, the needs of broadcasters and offer embargoed interviews for their lunch-time news bulletins.

Any day of the week will do. Weekend conferences are not unknown, but the daily press work on Sundays, not Saturdays, and the Sunday newspapers will want some convincing to give you space at short notice.

Invitation list

Press

Draw up a list of those journalists you and your colleagues know and invite them by name. Then compile a list of the remaining publications and send invitations to their newsdesks.

Invite press representatives from as many relevant publications as you can. There are paramedical and scientific journals, local newspapers and national press. Resist considering a publication or a programme from one of these categories as unsuitable to invite. The journalist is the best judge of what the public wants.

Invitation lists for press conferences called on the spot are out of the question. Round up the press who are milling around and ask someone to telephone quickly any special press contacts you have.

TV and radio

Invite representatives of independent and BBC radio and television. Television interviewers and their crews need advance warning, and special consideration must be given to the requirements of both television and radio journalists who will have to sit anxiously through the press conference watching their looming deadlines. Try to record embargoed interviews before the press conference, but remember that the press will not want to be kept waiting while you give the BBC special treatment.

After the press conference, make sure there is a quiet place you can escape to for follow-up interviews.

Record the interviews according to deadlines. The work can be shared if more than one person took part in the press conference.

You may be asked to go to the studios to record an interview, or appear live. Ask them to send a car to pick you up, and to take you on afterwards.

Photographers

Photographers invite themselves without warning. They stand in the front and pop electronic flashguns in your face. You may wish to limit numbers by providing a photographer of your own who will make arrangements to supply all the interested publications, meeting their various deadlines.

Photographers door-stepping are a fact of press relations life. If you take part in delegations of national interest or announce major medical advances, you must expect to be photographed.

Venue

The success of a major public relations event will depend heavily on the venue. Many conference centres and hotels provide good facilities and staff trained to try to cope with your every need. Bear in mind transport facilities, car parking, and hotel accommodation for out of town sites, and catering and visual aids.

The best place to hold a news press conference is on your own premises. You need a room, a table and chairs for the speakers, and enough chairs facing them for the journalists. Journalists now come complete with cell phones and laptop computers, but some will want access to the nearest telephone and typewriter. Prop up some name plates in front of the speakers, even if they are written in felt-tip on plain cardboard. Tea or coffee is appreciated on arrival and you may run to refreshments (not alcohol) afterwards.

Badges and signing in

It is useful to give journalists badges so everyone knows who they are talking to. Journalists can be checked off against a list of acceptances and given badges with their names and publications. On less formal occasions journalists can write their own names on stick-on badges. Don't waste time on badges for a hurried press conference. Just ask them all to sign in; a sheet of paper with two columns headed "name" and "representing" will do. A record of attendance is useful if a resulting story needs following up; it also helps you build up a press list, and check numbers for the catering bill.

Personnel

The set-piece conference needs a programme for the chairperson's welcome, minister's or other guest's contribution, and questions. Too often a press conference is a time when the person at the top puts in a rare appearance, giving an overlong speech. When you know you are dealing with such an event, give timings in your invitation so the journalists know what they are in for. Invite enough staff to keep the show running smoothly and brief them on the special responsibilities of talking to the press (no off-the-record asides).

The final choice of speakers is often dictated by internal politics, rows behind the scenes and, occasionally, common sense. Ideally, the most senior person with a detailed knowledge of the subject should be present. Add a chairperson, essential for keeping control, and perhaps one other person with specialist knowledge.

However short of time you are, a rehearsal is essential. You must know who is to cover which aspects of the information to be given and how questions are to be dealt with.

The conference

Introductions from the chairperson should be followed by short speeches from the participants. Speeches should be kept to the minimum necessary to explain the position. Overhead projections, with journalists plunged into darkness, are not a good idea; use hard copy, and make sure television lights are not going to render any film unviewable. Avoid in-phrases, abbreviations, and jargon. If you are reading from a prepared statement, let the press have copies just before you speak; this helps them report you accurately.

The style of press conference will dictate the type of written material given out. Speeches typed up or photocopied from hand-written notes will be enough for a news conference, but photographs, biographical details of the speakers, diagrams, and background material may also be made available at the time, or in advance under embargo. If you are launching a publication, detailed report, or the results of research work, an easily understood synopsis should be made available.

Take all questions at the end. During questions never openly disagree with your fellow participants; correct something said tactfully. Tell the truth and don't try to dodge any questions. If you don't know an answer, say so.

Picking up the pieces

Planned follow up to a press conference is essential. Immediately following the conference, during any refreshments, in the corridor, or over the telephone go over points with individual journalists, particularly if you did not handle a question well during the conference.

Check the resulting press coverage and clear up any errors or differences of opinion, either by submitting a letter for publication, or having a word with the journalist, asking for your particular point to be included next time the subject is written on.

Remember, you will be competing for column inches and air time with many others, and, despite all the advice, there is no guarantee of success.

III SOMETHING DIFFERENT

26 Associate with community groups

Lilias Gillies

Doctors, like policemen, have traditionally tended to mix only with their own profession. Recently, many doctors have come to the view that they must go outside the profession to seek support for their patients' needs. This may be with housing associations to help provide housing for disabled patients, with self-help groups who can give support to sufferers of a particular disease, or with groups who might raise funds or otherwise campaign for the development of a service that the doctor and the group agree is needed.

How do you go about it? As chief officer of a community health council I suggest that a good starting point is the community health council.

Sounding out

Community health councils recruit at least one third and often more of their membership from voluntary bodies. They also usually make it their business to know and be known by as many voluntary bodies in their area as possible. They have lists of these and their current secretaries, which are updated every two years for the election of members of the community health council. So your first port of call could be the community health council office to discuss your project with the staff there, who might be able to give you some useful contacts.

The community health council would also be interested in your project because of its interest in improving health services. The easiest first contact is the chief officer, and that could lead to some publicity either through a notice given out at the council meeting or inserted in the mailing to council members, which usually also goes to a number of local people interested in the health service. The mailing from my community health council goes to 150 people who also receive a monthly newsletter, and this is also distributed to health clinics and libraries. A short paragraph in that could identify supporters for your cause.

A council for voluntary service would be able to help with lists of organisations and people to contact, and might also have a newsletter. A volunteer bureau would be able to help with finding volunteers. These organisations are usually aided by grants from the local authority, which would be able to supply their addresses. Some hospitals and some social services offices have volunteer organisers who might be helpful. If you work in general practice a patient participation group will be a useful source of people to start self-help groups or provide volunteers for helping others.

You might also write a letter to the local newspaper or issue a press release. The free newspapers have the advantage of being delivered to every house.

You may, for example, be a rheumatologist who needs supported housing for people who have become very disabled. There might be a local group such as SHAD (Support and Housing Assistance for People with Disabilities)[1] interested in such housing to which you could be introduced. It will be glad to have medical advice and a source of clients and you will have a group of people with contacts in housing associations, the expertise for adapting the housing, and the means of providing support.

If you join a committee, do attend, if not all the meetings, at least fairly regularly. If you miss a meeting or two, keep in touch with the people concerned and the ideas that are being discussed. Contribute to the discussion that you have seen in the minutes with a letter or phone call.

Meeting the public

If there is not an already existing group you will have to set one up. Calling a meeting is the best way to do that. If you have gathered a few interested supporters they will help you. The community health council might help organise the meeting or there might be some other group with related interests, such as a disability association or league of friends. Community organisations, residents' associations, women's institutes, and townswomen's guilds have regular programmes of meetings and might be willing to have you as a speaker or your project as the topic for one of these.

Having decided to hold a public meeting or been invited to an organisation, you must organise what is to happen. If you are not confident that you can hold interest on your own for the whole time, is there a suitable film you could use or another more accomplished public speaker? Perhaps it is a new idea or one that has fairly local interest. Then you can add to the interest of your presentation by asking several people to join you on the platform. If, say, you want to start a self-help group for patients with cancer and their relatives, you could have a treated patient who is doing well but has to live with the fear of recurrence, and a relative of someone who has died. It would be best for the three of you to get together beforehand to talk about what you will say so that it is coordinated. You might find that there is a national group, such as, in this case, CancerLink,[2] which will be happy to send a speaker along. A national organisation might do all the speaking but it is better if the presentation is made by local people and yourself to bring the subject more directly to the notice of local people.

In preparing for a local public meeting, going to a conference of a national organisation or a local meeting elsewhere could help you organise your arguments and get ideas for improving the impact of your project. If you have found some supporters, perhaps you could take them with you. You may find that that organisation fits what you want and you could then aim at setting up a local branch. You will in that case benefit from national publicity and national advice. Suppose you want to support the relatives of elderly, confused people. The Alzheimer's Disease Society might fit the bill and you would benefit from the advice of their development workers and could use their publications.[3] Suppose you want to give more practical help with relief carers. Crossroads Care Attendants might be an organisation to which a local group could affiliate.[4] You may find that none of the existing organisations meets your ideas or the ideas of your group but you can still benefit from them even if you only learn what you do not want.

What do you want?

Having organised your public meeting you should have clear in your mind what you want out of it. If you want to set up a campaign

161

for a new voluntary body, you will need a committee. It is best to strike while the iron is hot and collect names of interested people at the meeting. You should invite to the meeting individuals and groups who might have an interest in, or stand to benefit from, your project. If you hope to set up a housing association for people with learning disabilities, ask the parents of teenagers with disabilities in the local schools and the parents of people in local hospitals for learning disabilities, who will naturally be concerned about the issue and will have an interest in working towards your aims.

If you want to set up an advisory service on alcohol, you should also contact social workers, general practitioners, nurses, and probation workers, all of whom are bound to be aware of alcohol misuse among their clients.

Community health councils frequently carry out surveys on a variety of health related topics and might be persuaded to do work relevant to your project. This could be carried out by council members or students from a local college, or by a paid researcher if money can be raised. This would then provide the focus for a campaign to launch the project. Of course there is always the possibility that the research will show that your favoured project cannot be justified, but that is not likely if you have already done your homework. Nevertheless, research could modify your first thoughts and refine your ideas to meet the community's needs. Though time-consuming and not immediately productive, research may be well worth while and should not be neglected. It could go on alongside other developments.

You will need to raise funds for the project. You may in fact be interested in fund raising only for a piece of equipment for your department or an adaptation to a building. Fund raising requires quite a lot of time and preferably a few people to generate ideas and do the letter writing or organising.

One of your earliest objectives should be to get a committee organised so that the amount of time and effort you put in is reduced. Your efforts may produce a group of enthusiasts with time, ideas, and experience to get the project going, raise funds, and cope with the responsibilities of managing the money and staff. What is much more likely is that you will have a few enthusiasts and some of the necessary expertise will be missing. You or the members of the new committee must seek out individuals with the expertise that you require and persuade them to join your committee. The ranks of the newly retired are one of the best groups to recruit from and there are organisations that might help you find the people you need, such as REACH (Retired Executives Action Clearing House)[5]—which exists to put retired executives in touch with charities that need their particular expertise—or local churches, local Rotary clubs, Lions, or Soroptimists.

Keeping it going

When the committee has done its work and got the project going, you must be prepared to take a lesser role. Nevertheless, you must not leave it all to them and thereby have the project move away from your concept and what you perceived as the need. Nor must you direct everything yourself and risk alienating the committee, because they have not got enough to do, and also overworking yourself. Remember that people work best with rewards, so regularly point out the benefits that are coming from the project and endeavour to make sure that everyone feels that they are part of it and are contributing something useful. Social gatherings and celebrations are very important in welding a group together and keeping it going. Training is also important if you are providing a service, particularly one using volunteers.

Associating with voluntary groups may require a lot of unaccustomed effort from you at first but it can be rewarding to you as well as your work, and associating with your patients or their relatives in different ways can be enriching to your practice of medicine as well as to the service to your patients.

1 CancerLink Ltd, 17 Britannia Street, London WC1X 9JN; telephone: 0171 833 2451.
2 SHAD (Wandsworth), Nightingale Centre, 8 Balham Hill, London SW12 6EA.
3 Alzheimer's Disease Society, Gordon House, 10 Greencoat Place, London SW1P 1PH; telephone: 0171 306 0833.
4 The Association of Crossroads Care Attendants Schemes Ltd, 10 Regent Place, Rugby, Warwickshire CV21 2PN.
5 REACH, 89 Southwark Street, London SE1 0HD; telephone: 0171 928 0452.

27 Run a pressure group and change the law

Madeleine Simms

My own experience of law reform is confined to a quarter of a century's work with a single political pressure group, the Abortion Law Reform Association (ALRA). What I have to say will inevitably be influenced by my experience with this particular cause, which I will draw on for examples to illustrate more general points.

First essentials

Three things are initially required: a clearly defined cause; a group of lively, intelligent, and committed people; and money—preferably lots of it.

A clearly defined cause

The broad aim of ALRA in the early 1960s when I joined it was clear and straightforward and could be understood without difficulty by everyone: to change the law to enable women to obtain legal and safe abortions more easily. Nevertheless, when a group of lively people get together they are bound to have some differences of opinion, interest, and emphasis. Thus, some of our members simply wanted to extend the medical indications for abortion; others were concerned to introduce social grounds for abortion; others were chiefly anxious to help women avoid giving birth to handicapped babies; while the more radical favoured abortion at the request of the patient. So a degree of consensus needs to be established. People must be prepared to compromise on acceptable minimum aims and to work as a team. Those who demanded too much or were satisfied

164

with two little eventually dropped out or formed their own splinter groups. There is room for all opinions to be expressed, though not necessarily within the same organisation.

A lively, committed, and intelligent group of people

This is the core and lifeblood of any political pressure group. The people need to be intelligent in order to recognise the need for reform, to be able to translate it into political terms, and to argue and debate their case in public. They have to be committed because once they are attached to the cause their private lives may cease to exist for a number of years, as flexibility and the ability to seize the moment are of the essence in this kind of political activism. Political crises do not always occur at convenient moments. This means that spouses or partners must also be sufficiently committed to put up with a high degree of domestic disruption. Behind nearly every effective lobbyist there is a long-suffering, unflappable, tolerant, and committed partner.

Money and power

In this respect ALRA was largely a failure, as by comparison with the huge sums raised more recently by some religious and antifeminist pressure groups with national networks based on parishes, ALRA had no natural source of either organisation or money other than individual, relatively low-paid women and the occasional philanthropist—a rare bird indeed. We never solved the problem of money, as successful fundraisers are like gold dust and we were not the sort of fashionable cause likely to attract them. Money is power in politics. It enables you to print elegant, illustrated, easy on the eye literature with a distinctive house style, expounding your cause to many different types of reader. It enables you to take influential political figures out to lunch to put your case in civilised surroundings. It enables you to invite distinguished speakers from far and wide to add their experience to your own on public platforms. It enables you, the committed lobbyist, to travel round the country in reasonable comfort spreading the word, meeting influential supporters, cheering on the troops. It enables you to commission films aimed at a variety of audiences—medical students, women's clubs, schoolchildren, and so on. Lacking the necessary kind of resources and organisation, ALRA members could do only little of any of this, and what they did do was generally undertaken at their own expense—hence the importance of commitment.

The second stage

Having defined the cause, gathered the core of the committee that will run the organisation, and collected such money as is available from well wishers, the next stage is to distribute the jobs.

Who does what

An effective chairperson must be elected who commands the total respect of the small group initially assembled, who is clearsighted about the aims, shrewd in assessing the character and available talents of the team, and able to pour oil on troubled waters when this is required—as it often will be in a group of dynamic activists; able also to judge situations coolly and impartially, and to enforce a degree of internal discipline and uniformity when necessary—no small task among a group of unpaid, opinionated volunteers. Such a paragon is hard to find, but because ALRA with singular good fortune did find one in the person of Lady Houghton it was ultimately successful.

The secretary needs to be down to earth, practical, efficient, methodical, and able to use common sense and initiative. The treasurer has the hard and thankless task of trying to raise money from whatever sources might be thought to have some natural sympathy with the cause, and of using whatever is raised to maximum effect. This often puts paid to bright ideas produced by other members of the committee, so the treasurer is not always deeply loved and must not mind this too much. The membership secretary works in close association with both the secretary and the treasurer, making sure that membership files are kept up to date and that the particular talents and qualifications of the members are carefully noted in case they are needed, answering queries about membership, ensuring that speakers at meetings remember that recruiting new members is part of their task, and constantly trying to think up new ways of increasing the membership.

There needs to be someone interested in undertaking the research, information, and editorial function, to find out the facts, both historical and current, which have a bearing on the present political campaign and to communicate these to the membership at large so that it can deploy them in local contexts. Thus, some kind of newsletter or house journal is essential for providing information and exchanging news and even gossip.

Two other key officers are required for this committee. One is a press and public relations officer, who will mastermind and organise the public aspects of the political campaign, helping to educate the public and being on tap for the media. Publicity stunts and demonstrations may also come into this person's sphere of operations, though ALRA in the '60s always rather priggishly scorned such activities as being in bad taste and inappropriate to the subject, until members saw with astonishment how effective in crude publicity terms the mass demonstrations of the antiabortion lobby in the '70s were.

Finally, the committee needs a political secretary or parliamentary officer, who will regularly communicate the views of the association to a group of key parliamentary supporters, feed them with the latest information and statistics that they have not the time to search out for themselves, and write first drafts of speeches for them on request and often at short notice. During parliamentary debates the political secretary has to ensure that enough sympathetic MPs are present in the House to make speeches in support of the cause and are prepared to stay late, even all night if necessary, in order to be present to vote.

Eminent persons and experts

Above and alongside the executive committee are the eminent persons who will serve as presidents and vice presidents and occasionally perform ceremonial, media, or even down-to-earth advisory functions for the pressure group, and the outside experts who will command respect and influence in the relevant professions. In the '60s, ALRA was fortunate in having the loyal and energetic support of one of the most eminent doctors and one of the most distinguished lawyers of their generation in Sir Dugald Baird and Professor Glanville Williams QC, and their active presence encouraged many able young doctors and lawyers to lend their support also. This was long before publicly supporting abortion law reform was considered safe or respectable, when the BMA and the RCOG were still opposed to reform and when *The Times* refused to publish letters in support of abortion law reform even if they merely corrected the inaccurate figures produced by the other side. Only the signatures of VIPs could, on rare occasions, break through this embargo if they were eminent enough or had smart enough addresses, such as the House of Lords or the posher gentlemen's clubs. The aspiring social reformer will have to learn the hard way that from the point of view of much of the press it is not what you say that matters, however true or important, but who says it. So having eminent names on tap to append to letters will, more than anything else, determine whether or not they are printed.

Planning and patience

When all these officers are installed, they need to draw up a realistic plan of action involving parliament and the media, prepare pamphlets, train speakers, encourage people to write letters to the press, and respond to correspondence from the public. And they need to exercise constant vigilance with regard to the stunts, scandals, and disinformation that opponents will try to perpetrate. In the week before an important parliamentary debate on abortion the gutter press could always be relied upon to produce alarming abortion headlines about "scandals" that generally shrivelled out of sight on closer examination. Meanwhile the damage, in public relations terms, had been done. An educated and informed membership can help to counteract propaganda of this type.

Patience and determination and long-term commitment are the essential qualities that social reformers need. In a democratic society changes do not come quickly. Years of public education and public debate precede any major reform—and that event is rarely the end of the story. The Abortion Law Reform Association was founded in 1936 by a group of farsighted and courageous women. Only one of them, Alice Jenkins, lived long enough to witness the passing of the 1967 Abortion Act. Since 1967 nearly twenty parliamentary attempts have been made to restrict or, if possible, destroy the right to legal abortion. The fight to maintain the Abortion Act has been tougher and more exacting than the battle to bring it into being, because it lacks the glamour and excitement of the original campaign. The necessity for this *post hoc* struggle is often forgotten by reformers in their excitement at the passing of reforming legislation. It requires dogged persistence, sticking to one's last, and rather boringly keeping one's hand to the plough. None of this is very exhilarating. The press and media find it tedious and now regard the antifeminist lobby as better value in publicity terms if they are making the running in trying to destroy a piece of existing legislation. Even the *Guardian* women's page no longer bothers about this old-hat cause. So changing the law is only one half of the battle; maintaining it in the longer term, and improving on it, is the other, and often the more exacting, half.

Fighting for social reform is like planting a great tree. You are unlikely to see the full results in your own lifetime. It is the next generation that will benefit. So a long view is necessary, as is the conviction that in the very long run rationality and benevolence will prevail.

Hindell K, Simms M. *Abortion law reformed*. London: Peter Owen, 1971.
Marsh D, Chambers J. *Abortion politics*. London: Junction Books, 1981.
Simms M. Parliament and birth control in the nineteen twenties. *J R Coll Gen Pract* 1978; **28**:83–8.
Simms M. The politics of fertility control. *New Humanist* 1981;**96**:73–5.
Wilson D. *Pressure*. London: Heinemann, 1984.

28 Raise funds

A K Thould

"Can anyone remember when the times were not hard, and money not scarce?" Ralph Waldo Emerson

Desperate times beget desperate remedies. When no money is available from conventional sources, there are only two courses open to you: either find funds by other means or give up in despair and take it out on your garden. However, if the project of your heart's desire still eats at your soul, then lesson one of fundraising is that if *you* are convinced that the enterprise is worthy and the plan is viable, don't let anyone put you off, and don't be disheartened because the country is bankrupt. It is never the right time to raise money, so go ahead and do it anyway.

Lesson two is that if you think fundraising is merely a matter of saying to yourself "There are 300 000 people in this county, so if everyone gives 50p we will be home and dry", forget it, go home, and tend your roses instead. Nobody is interested in handing over their hard-earned cash unless you can convince them that the whole scheme is sound, necessary, and appealing to *them*. After all, why should they? Fundraising is grinding hard work. You must be prepared to kiss your spouse and the baby goodbye for many evenings, because you will need to address any number of lay meetings. You will spend many hours at the kitchen table with your spouse signing letters and putting them in envelopes. You will go through agonies of self doubt and many crises of morale in your organisation. You will learn to endure the hunted look of your friends as they see you approach, hot with the news of your latest disaster or triumph. Fascinating for you; boring for them. If all this appears too much for you, with the seemingly endless hours of repetitive, slogging work, then don't go fundraising, not at any price—it is not for the faint-hearted.

Basic organisation

If you have lasted this far, and are still convinced of the rightness of your cause and the glamour of your appeal, then the next step is to set up your basic organisation. First of all, you will need a small but select band of trusted (voluntary) and dedicated hard-working helpers. You *must* have a very good secretary/typist, because you are going to need to send out a great many letters: thousands will be needed for a major appeal. Next, you need to gather together a small committee you can trust. The members will need to be long-suffering, industrious but enthusiastic, and, if possible, experienced in this sort of thing. They should, if possible, be well known and respected in the community, with many contacts in the business and professional worlds. Do not have a big committee. I suggest about ten as the maximum. You will need a good solicitor to set up your trust and do the legal work—for nothing, if you're lucky. You must have a good, painstaking treasurer, used to handling large amounts of money without getting nightmares, and able to keep proper accounts. Above all, you must have a good, decent chairperson, well known in the area at large, and carrying with him or her the aura of trust.

You ought to be the secretary yourself, and be prepared to do the dog work of arranging the committee business. You will need a bank account, and all cheques must be signed by the treasurer and yourself. Next you must get your solicitor to set your organisation up as a charitable trust. The procedure is tedious, but not particularly difficult, and be prepared for the Charity Commissioners to ask some searching and highly pertinent questions. When drawing up the articles of the trust, be sure you look ahead, so that you can continue to raise funds by way of the organisation in the future and can, within the articles, pursue whatever long-term projects you wish. Your solicitor will advise you. If you are successful, you will be given a number, and you must quote this in all your correspondence. If you don't, some charitable trusts may not be prepared to give you money.

171

Where to start

It is a good idea to start with a meeting to which you invite all the heads of the known fundraising organisations in your area, that is, the Women's Institute, Rotary Clubs, Lions, and so on. You will be surprised how many there are; you must find out who they are from your committee and local contacts, then draw up a list. Have your meeting in the early evening and provide sherry and whatnots to eat, but don't be too lavish. They will be looking for evidence that the money you raise goes to the appeal, not towards wasteful window dressing. Try not to be mean, however—the balance is important. Make up a brochure setting out your aims and objectives, not glossy and expensively produced, but workmanlike and readable. A small book on the subject is unnecessary and will not be read. It needs to be short, informative, and to the point. Most of all, when someone asks you to go and give a talk on your project, then go, however inconvenient, and go at their time and convenience. Be prepared to answer questions and, above all, be honest and frank. If you feel your project needs a million pounds, then say so. The dissembler is soon mercilessly exposed and rightly so. Never underestimate your audience or talk down to them. They are probably more experienced at the game than you are. They are usually hard-headed but great-hearted people, and they need to be convinced of the essential worthiness and practicality of what you are doing.

Some fundraisers prefer to set up a local organisation of ardent supporters of the cause. If your project is a large one, then this may be a sensible course. An effective way is to divide up your parish into districts and appoint a local committee for each district under a suitable leader. However, these district leaders need to be chosen with care. Enthusiasm is a necessary attribute, but good organisational ability, staying power, and the ability to lead and encourage but not bludgeon people are equally vital properties. A good district committee can safely be left to get on with local fundraising efforts. You will need to show regular and highly visible interest in its efforts, however, and regular coordination meetings are essential.

A further step is to get from the public library the published list of registered charities (there may be a waiting list to get it), then go through the 3000 or 4000 listed there and see which ones may be interested in your cause. Write them a short letter setting out the facts and enclosing your brochure. About 95% of them will throw your application in the wastepaper basket. The other 5% may give you some money. If you can, and they will let you, offer to go and see their trustees in person.

Some recommend trying to raise money from the top 1000 companies, but I have found this a waste of time. Only local industry seems to be interested in contributing to local causes, and this is all that one can expect. If there are large industrial combines near you, write to the managing directors and go to see them. They will usually be courteous and give you a fair hearing. Just possibly, they may even advise their company to give you some money. Look up local businesses in the yellow pages of the telephone directory; then write them a letter. The letters themselves are important. They can be printed, using your appeal's logo at the head, but you must personally enter the name of the person you are writing to, and sign it personally.

This will mean signing many hundreds of letters, possibly thousands. If you are not prepared to give the personal touch, then don't expect to get much money. Nothing is worse than the cold, printed impersonal letter. It looks as if you are not prepared to take the trouble, and, if you don't sign it yourself, this is probably true.

You must be prepared to go to endless donkey derbys, band festivals, sponsored walks, fêtes, and whatever. After all, if they are prepared to go to that much trouble to raise money for you, the least you can do is turn up, and make a short speech of thanks. Anyway, it is all enormous fun for most of the time.

Publicity and costs

The local press will probably be interested and, in my experience, helpful, but they like to be kept informed of how things are going. In return, they will give you a few column inches of publicity at intervals. Be careful, however, about self advertisement. It is a good idea to check with the Medical Defence Union about how far you can go. Almost any publicity is valuable, unless your treasurer makes off with the funds. It is worth asking to have a stand at the local county show—they will probably give you a site at cheap rates.

Costs should be kept to less than 1% of the money you raise, so spend as little as you can on your organisation. Your worst expense will be on postage—the costs of printing should be relatively trivial (use the office photocopier). Car stickers are worth while and cheap—if you can persuade people to display them. The Charity Commissioners will expect you to have your accounts properly audited and these must be readily available. So keep good records; don't be like Samuel Johnson, who observed that he had two very cogent reasons for not printing any list of subscribers—one that he had lost all the names; the other that he had spent all the money.

When it is all over, invite your subscribers to see what their money has bought, and be generous in your thanks. Do not forget to announce that your fundraising appeal is now over, at least for the time being; otherwise people may go on raising unnecessary funds for you to the detriment of other equally worthy appeals whose turn it now is. The reward for you will be the immense satisfaction of seeing your project completed. It will have been very hard going and at times discouraging, but the glow of satisfaction is very warm. Good luck.

29 Admit that you are wrong

David Morris

To err is human . . .

At one point in the preparation of this chapter I thought of writing to the editor "Dear Sir, I admit I was wrong in accepting your tempting invitation to write 2000 words on 'How to admit you are wrong' because . . ." It had sounded stimulating and challenging, but it did not prove as easy as I had thought. According to the *Oxford English Dictionary*, wrong is "out of order, in bad condition, contrary to law or morality, wicked, other than the right or suitable or the more or most desirable, awkwardly placed, in a difficulty, at a disadvantage, *mistaken, in error (wrong opinion, guess, decision, hypothesis)*." These words in italics became my brief. I found it intriguing that 21 lines were devoted to "wrong" and 80 to "right", "To admit" is, by definition in the *Oxford English Dictionary*, "to accept as valued or true".

We have all at some time or another been wrong. The list that each of us could make would be interesting reading. The *Observer* once republished part of an editorial written 30 years earlier over the Suez affair and condemning the government's action, which had "incurred the fury of readers and advertisers". Some years later the late Iain Macleod commented, "You can be wrong by being right too soon"—illustrating the complexity of the topic.

Realising it

We each have our own set of ideas and values, and we function according to them. We build up beliefs and convictions that direct

175

our actions and practices. We all cherish our point of view, our allegiances, and the things we believe in. Our everyday life requires us to make choices and decisions, and though often easily and readily made, they can prove onerous. Choice entails deciding between different possibilities or preferences. Decision making entails making up your mind, arriving at a conclusion after formal judgment. There are those who find this so difficult that they drift into careers where they can easily pass the buck, thus avoiding both responsibility and authority.

When our concepts are challenged, we instinctively try to defend them. When they are proved to be wrong, the integrity of the system we have taken so much time and trouble to construct is threatened. How we cope with such a situation will depend on the circumstances and the implications of the mistake that we have made. There are circumstances when there is no room for doubt—a wrong dosage, an error of commission or omission. But it is not always precise and clear cut and without room for a different point of view. Extenuating circumstances can mitigate the wrong done. A house officer who has made a mistake may be pardoned if he or she had been up three nights running or had stayed on duty in spite of being unwell, not wanting to let his or her colleagues down.

What effect the realisation that we have made a mistake and are in the wrong has on us will be determined by what the error means to us and to those who may be concerned. Our reaction is part of our personality and character, our self esteem and confidence, but, above all, the degree of strength and tolerance that we have that enables us to be wrong and not be too seriously affected by it. How we feel in relation to others and what they think of us will colour the emotional effect of our error.

What kind of person are you?

The admission is another matter, but intimately connected with these subjective feelings. There are those who both realise that they have made a mistake and can admit it without undue difficulty. By contrast, there are those who find it impossible to believe that they are wrong and cannot admit it. They will produce argument and counterargument and fight ruthlessly to win the day, revealing much of themselves and their emotional fabric. There are those who realise that they are wrong but share this realisation with no one. What an emotional burden of continuing guilt this must be. There are those who too readily and easily accept that they are wrong and almost proffer admission before it is due, which may indicate a form of masochism.

Reactions vary from immediate or delayed acceptance to denial, and there are varied accompanying emotions. For the experience is intimately part of our self esteem and our susceptibility to the opinions of others. This is an essential part of the process of reaction to approval and disapproval that starts at birth and never leaves us. Constantly and consistently, we are influenced to learn about right and wrong, about truth and honesty, telling lies and cheating, and, above all, to cope with the mistakes that we make. These concepts are not easily acquired, for they are often accompanied by strong emotional overtones that confuse us and interfere with our ability to see the events in their right perspective. Why should disapproval and scorn, criticism and fault finding have so much greater effect on us than approval and praise, flattery and success? The pangs of loss, I contend, outstrip the joys of discovery.

In the practice of medicine when errors are made we have to ascertain if the doctors took the necessary steps to acquaint themselves with the patient's story and carried out the necessary examination. In the light of these, they arrive at an opinion, which determines their action. No court would find fault with such individuals simply for failing in the first two steps. What makes the mistake more serious and difficult to deal with is the risk to reputation and social and professional standing.

In recalling past incidents of being wrong, the one that comes immediately to my mind was to do with the first baby that I was asked to see on being appointed as a consultant. "A baby of 6 weeks old in extremis," said Mr Geoffrey Parker's registrar. I had never met Mr Parker nor had I been to the hospital before. As I examined the baby I could not for the life of me feel the tumour that I suspected of causing pyloric stenosis. I rang Mr Parker and told him what I thought and suggested that he operate on the baby. His reaction was explosive, which as I learnt later was typical of this extraordinary surgeon-parachutist to the Maquis.

"Right," he said. "But if you are wrong I shall never speak to you again, and if I am wrong I shall never speak to myself again." Strong words for a debutante to carry until the tumour was found. At the end of the operation he cut me down to size with, "Well, you can't always be wrong."

Experience the best teacher

It is said that fools learn by their own mistakes and wise men from the mistakes of others. How true is this aphorism? While there is an element of truth in it, our own personal experience teaches us more by direct involvement than wise counsels of perfection. There are instances when we may be wrong but are unaware of the error of our ways. It is only when it is brought to our notice that we are shocked to learn. A lot will depend on how we are told, who does the telling, and the importance of the error.

So where between the extremes of never being wrong and being too quick and ready to admit it do the well-balanced, healthy individuals come, those who can see when they are wrong, accept it, and admit it without letting it take too much of a toll of them? The necessary elements are, I contend, a level of self esteem that can accept the human error to which we are all subject and the confidence in yourself to see the situation in perspective as being only part of the whole and not an entity on its own. Pride and vanity are always at play and vary according to the company we keep. It is a personal, very subjective, issue and has to do with how we feel about ourselves and how dependent we are on how others feel about us.

30 Be a patient

B T Marsh

I shall be forever grateful to Stephen Potter for his four classic books on how to cope with the vagaries of life, namely, *Lifemanship*, *Gamesmanship*, *One-Upmanship*, and *Supermanship*.[1-4] *Lifemanship* was written in 1947, and in my schooldays reading the first three books was *de rigueur* in the sixth form. In fact, you could almost do an A level in the subject, and I still find his advice both apposite and welcome some 40 years later. Many other larger and more erudite treatises on how people react to life have been published over the succeeding years, yet I doubt if any have bettered Potter's acute, albeit exaggerated, observations on how to make the most of one's opportunities and better the opposition, whoever or whatever that may be. I have no intention of making this article a poor man's Potter or an exposition of his various gambits, but I am aware that throughout my experiences of being a patient I have both consciously and subconsciously tried to beat the system with a form of "patientship".

As an opening gambit, "Don't" or "Be lucky" is the best advice I can give to anyone contemplating being a patient, but this fails to take into consideration that most of us have very little choice in the matter. If you are worried about your health it is sensible to consult an expert. Once this consultation begins, inevitably you become a patient and are drawn, either willingly or unwillingly, into a whole new world of instability and anxiety, indeed a role reversal with a vengeance. Although I have suggested that you should not be a patient if you can sensibly avoid it, by the same token you should avoid acting as your own physician. This is not because of any

179

doubts about diagnostic competence, as you may get it right, but you may do so for the wrong reasons, in the wrong order, with the wrong conclusion, or with the wrong sense of urgency.

Nobody knows how you feel

I think it important to state that being a patient is an intensely personal experience that we all approach for differing reasons and with differing expectations. Because of this, one thing I have learnt is that no one can truly say, "I know how you feel". Indeed, as a patient I became quite angry when well-meaning sympathisers made this statement. It is one that should always be associated with some indication that the speaker does not know, but is at least making some attempt to appreciate the situation. This usually prevents the upsurge of anger and frustration that may otherwise be provoked and allow the patient to explain in great detail what he or she does feel, which certainly helps him or her, if nobody else.

In June 1984, after a pleasant dinner, I developed severe retrosternal chest pain that was relieved by metoclopramide and antacids. This pain, although less severe, recurred over the next two weeks and was related in my mind to food and to bending. Angina was clearly a differential diagnosis but I was quite unable to provoke the pain by exercise, and it came well below plain indigestion, reflux oesophagitis, and hiatus hernia in my estimation of likelihood. As indigestion was an unusual symptom with me, I was eventually persuaded by my wife to make an appointment to see a physician, and I was on the path to becoming a patient. The day before my appointment I had a massive myocardial infarction.

My indigestion had turned out to be oesophageal angina, which has a reputation of being both a mimic and unpredictable. After the infarct I successively underwent cardiac arrest and resuscitation, admission to an intensive care unit, intracardiac pacing, septicaemia, infective endocarditis, insertion of an aortic balloon pump, and, finally, 15 days after the initial event, cardiac transplantation. Discharge home came 12 days later with a convalescence of six months before I returned to work. Regular outpatient visits are still necessary (and will be, presumably, for ever) with, at yearly intervals, an exercise electrocardiogram, a 24-hour electrocardiographic tape, thallium scan, echocardiography, heart muscle biopsy, and a coronary angiogram. A smaller number of investigations are performed every six months, but may be expanded if an abnormality is detected. I have described my experiences in greater detail elsewhere,[5] and much of this advice will be specific to these experiences, but I hope that there will be a generic basis that will help those yet to be patients confirm some of the impressions of those who have been patients, and, for the rest, allow some insight into the feelings of a reluctant but lucky patient.

What is going on

The first thing to realise is that although being in the profession does have many benefits, you are still a pawn to be moved around the chessboard under the aegis of—you hope—a benevolent dictator. Life as a patient is totally different from what you expected, what it was like in your day as a medical student, and what you would like it to be. Day merges into night and nights seem to go on for ever. Time has no relevance and it is quite astonishing how you can lose track of the date and overall time scale. If you are really ill, meals lose their importance at the same time as their taste. This is no reflection on the catering staff, who labour valiantly to excite your appetite. Patients' appetites are still, I think, one of the best indicators of their state of health. Night-time sedatives or hypnotics become highly important. Long periods in bed mean frequent naps and consequent difficulty in getting off to sleep at night, with a very light and disturbed sleep pattern, especially in a busy ward or intensive care unit. Judicious use of sedatives helps, but a vicious circle is often set up if the sedative is not a short acting one. The patient is then sedated during the morning, often confused, and then becomes even more awake in the evenings.

Even if you have your own room, there never seems to be enough easily accessible space to put things on. Grapes, other fruit, and flowers are really only good for visitors, and "get well" cards are nice to receive but difficult to keep on show. Do not consider your stay in hospital as a chance to catch up on that heavy reading you have been putting off. Solzhenitsyn is definitely out and it will take you all your time to stagger through the most basic newspapers and magazines. A radio cassette player such as a Walkman and, especially, a television with a remote control are absolute musts. The television programmes both entertain—using the word in its broadest sense—and take your mind off your current discomfort. The remote control allows you to jump from station to station, as concentration rarely lasts longer than a few minutes, particularly with some of the more erudite programmes.

Information on what is happening to you is often at a premium even though you are in the trade. Do not be frightened to ask what is the real diagnosis and what is the plan of treatment. Invariably you will get a full explanation and be brought into the discussion. It is more difficult, however, to get from your advisers the results of your electrocardiogram, chest radiograph, and other investigations. If you feel aware of what is going on within your body, do not hesitate to suggest a diagnosis, particularly if you think that something is going wrong or if you are conscious of a change. You may not be believed and you may be wrong, but at least you should stimulate further examination and thought. Do object if two-way conversations occur across the bed between relatives and the attending doctor and you are not included. This is usually inadvertent and arises because it is thought that you are too tired, or sedated, or unwell. Always have your say, as you may want to say "I told you so" at a later date.

Tricks of the trade

There are certain things you should not believe, such as: "It will be just a small prick and it won't hurt"; "We are only going to put in one stitch and there is no need for a local anaesthetic because the injection would be just as painful"; "Everything is fine and don't worry"; "The doctor will be along in a minute"; "You aren't written up for it, so you can't have it"; "We have no idea when you are going to be discharged"; "No, you are not going to be moved from this bed or room"; "You must take this drug, it is essential" (for something that you well know is not essential, such as a vitamin C tablet).

There are other things that you should always ask for if you want them, such as sedatives or hypnotics at night, and analgesics if you are in pain or discomfort. Long periods in bed inevitably lead to a tender sacrum and buttocks and an aching back and neck. Despite what some nurses declare, regular massage of the buttocks and sacrum is a tremendous relief, nay, pleasure, even if there is no sign of skin deterioration. A rubber ring and a lambskin undersheet also help to relieve the problem. If you are a male, always have at least one spare urine bottle available, and if you have a bedpan, ensure that the emergency call button is within easy reach, as sitting on one of these for half an hour is not to be recommended.

A sense of isolation may occur if you are in a room on your own, and the frequent popping in and out of nurses and domestic staff is a great comfort. Needless to say the visit of your spouse plus or minus other sundry relatives and friends is often the highlight of the day. This event becomes so important that at times unreasonable pettiness on the part of the patient can erupt. Comments such as "Why are you late?" when your spouse has moved heaven and earth to get the family fed and clothed, friends and relatives informed, and other essential jobs performed, are not conducive to harmony. In the same vein, the simple "Thank you" is all that most of the nursing, paramedical, medical, and domestic staff require for the countless small favours that they perform for you during a stay in hospital—it is so easy to say, but so often forgotten.

There are certain essential items that you should take into hospital with you, and tricks that you should know. Always have an adaptor plug set with you. You can bet that the one on the ward doesn't fit, won't work, is lost, or is being used by someone else. Have a mirror with you, preferably a polished metal one. The mirror in the room is rarely in the best spot for shaving, hair drying, or whatever else you are trying to watch yourself do. Have soap, toothpaste, flannel, talcum powder, and other toiletries of your own choice with you, as the make you prefer is never on the trolley. Heels often feel sore after a long period in bed, and it becomes impossible to get your legs in a comfortable position. Ask for a frame to keep the bedclothes off your legs and suggest that someone fills up two rubber gloves with water and ties a knot in the wrist ends. These "donkeys" provide wonderfully gentle supports for the heels, but be prepared for rubber fatigue and a wet bed from time to time. If you have difficulty in pulling yourself up, a knotted rope to the foot end of the bed makes it much easier. Depending upon your particular problem, there are many other tricks of the trade that are available—if you ask the right nurse.

Getting out

As you come to discharge time never underestimate the weakness from weight loss and loss of muscle mass that will have occurred if you have been seriously ill and bedbound for some time. You will need help from the physiotherapy department, and this is always readily and efficiently given provided it is asked for or is routine for your type of case. It is remarkable how quickly you can lose strength, particularly for such everyday tasks as getting out of a chair unaided or walking upstairs. This is particularly important, as most bedrooms and bathrooms are on the first floor of a house. This is the time also to ensure that you know exactly what medicine to take, what exercises to perform, and what to avoid when you are discharged. Don't forget to ask what the drill is if an emergency occurs—do you go back to your own general practitioner, ring the consultant, or get yourself admitted to the hospital? When you are being driven home, usually at a sedate 20 to 30 mph, be prepared for this to seem as if you are taking part in a Formula 1 Grand Prix race. I suggest sitting in the rear seat with your eyes closed.

Finally, a word about outpatients. Find out the critical timings and days associated with your outpatient clinics. Which ones are overbooked or underbooked, always have plenty of nurses present or appear to be as unpopular with the nurses as they are with the doctors? Is it better to go for radiograph, electrocardiogram, or laboratory tests before or after your consultation? Find out the people who determine the pace of the clinic—what is known in the Royal Navy as "making your number" and in hospital as "getting on the right side of Sister". Ensure that you know the treatment and investigation protocols and then keep a check on these and the results. Familiarity breeds contempt, and minor slips can quickly build up into major problems. When in doubt, ask. Follow the instructions unless they appear to be clearly wrong. If they do appear wrong, you will often be proved correct. Make a note of your symptoms, reactions, and problems, especially if they are related to something like drugs or food. Pass them on to the physician or nursing staff on your next visit. Much of the lore about a particular condition or its progress is often anecdotal from patients (although many findings get confirmed in the waiting room), and you never know if your experience will be helpful to someone else. If you need regular admissions it is worth suggesting the most convenient dates for you—surprisingly, it often works.

If you become a long-term outpatient, keep watch on the main markers determining the progress of your condition. Be prepared to be classified as an "anxious" patient when you insist on seeing the results of your regular laboratory and other investigations after each visit. This epithet is even more likely to be applied if you then insist on someone taking notice and doing something, particularly when you provide a printout of the test results that show a clear deterioration over time. It is easy for both you and your advisers to become complacent and miss changes that may have been occurring over several months or even years. Attempts to reverse a deterioration may seem like trying to stop a runaway train. It takes a long time and a lot of effort to get back to anywhere near the original state. The NHS as an organisation is still suspicious of patients who want to know exactly what is going on and want to be actively involved in the management of their disease. Mention of the Patients' Charter should and does provide at least some back-up to your demands if you meet problems.

Being a patient is a major step that should not be taken lightly. It is an enormous psychological experience that will in most cases entirely change your outlook on life and certainly make you more understanding and sympathetic to other patients. Most patients undergo at least one period of self-pity, sometimes many. There is no answer to the querulously put "Why me?" Each must work out his or her own rationale for what has happened and what will happen in the future. It is also important to realise that your illness might have been equally upsetting to your spouse or relatives and that they may be asking the same questions. Luckily, most people are optimists and although such a question is not unreasonable, it is not too difficult to persuade oneself that all is going to be well. This attitude is essential if there is to be any return to normality. On the other hand, there is no doubt that being a patient can become addictive and may damage your health.

1 Potter S. *Gamesmanship*. London: Hart-Davis, 1947.
2 Potter S. *Lifemanship*. London: Hart-Davis, 1950.
3 Potter S. *One-Upmanship*. London: Hart-Davis, 1952.
4 Potter S. *Supermanship*. London: Hart-Davis, 1958.
5 Marsh B T. A second chance. *BMJ* 1986;**292**:675–6.

31 Attend an inquest

R A B Drury

A true presentment make of all such matters and things . . .

Occasional attenders at a coroner's court may feel that they have
found in the inquest an unchanging aspect of our otherwise rapidly
altering scene. But though the Victorian building may be the same as
when you were a house surgeon—or even when your grandfather
was—a light breeze of change has been blowing through the
courtroom and its far older proceedings.

In 60 years the number of deaths reported to the coroner has more
than doubled, but the number of inquests has fallen by a third. The
coroner's jury virtually disappeared in 1978, following the implementation of one of the recommendations of the Brodrick Report.[1]
The calling of a coroner's jury (part of whose oath is quoted above) is
now an exceptional occasion for rare inquiries, such as those into
deaths in prison or fatal industrial or railway accidents. With no
jury, the occasional committal for manslaughter also becomes a thing
of the past.

The absence of a jury has led to speedier completion of an inquest,
with less formality and no banging on doors, often in less august
circumstances, since inquests may be held in many places, such as
offices or hospital committee rooms (but not on licensed premises).
The cast and procedure remain largely unchanged, and those present
will be the legally or medically (and sometimes both) qualified
coroner, who will certainly have considerable knowledge and insight
into the seamier side of medicine; the coroner's officer, usually a
police officer with criminal investigation department experience, but

sometimes a rural police officer at his or her first inquest; relatives of the deceased; one or more medical witnesses of the events leading to death; and others who will be called (occasionally subpoenaed) by the coroner's officer to attend.

Before the inquest

You will be told of the time, date, and place of the inquest. In cases of unnatural or violent death necropsies are now universally carried out, and the clinician will know where, when, and by whom the necropsy will be performed. Attendance at this is desirable, as both the clinician and the pathologist can learn much from each other, though their evidence will be independent and be based on their own observations at the bedside and in the postmortem room. With a knowledge of the circumstances leading to death and the findings at necropsy, clinicians should ask themselves whether any complaint about lack of medical care could arise. In the event of this rare possibility medical witnesses are "proper interested parties" and are entitled[2] to be legally represented at an inquest; they should inform their medical defence organisation at once by telephone and be guided by them. If doctors learn that relatives are to have legal representation, this does not automatically dictate that the doctors should be legally represented unless they know that criticisms are to be levelled at them. The vast majority of inquests have no such problems and the purpose is to inquire into the cause of death rather than matters of civil liability.

The clinician and pathologist should both be fully informed about the case before they attend the inquest because they will be asked questions of fact as well as of opinion. Retain the medical records of the patient and be familiar with the medical and nursing records as well as details of treatment. An incomplete grasp of the facts casts doubt on the validity of a witness's opinions.

At the inquest

It is not only courteous to the coroner and to the deceased's relatives to arrive in time and suitably dressed (not funereally attired), but also prudent, as many coroners take the medical evidence early and allow doctors to leave if their evidence is not controversial. Make your arrival known to the coroner's officer and tell him or her if you wish to affirm rather than take the oath: the act of the renunciation of the Testament still causes a slight stir in the proceedings while a prearranged affirmation is accepted as a matter of course. In addition to the relatives, whom you will have met, and the pathologist, with whom you have already spoken, there may be solicitors acting for the deceased's family or other interested parties, and there will be one or more press reporters.

When your case starts you may be surprised at the informality of the proceedings. Coroners' courts are not bound by strict rules of evidence and the inquiry may include leading questions and hearsay evidence. Ensure that the court hears your evidence clearly and understands it, especially if names or diseases are unusual or difficult to spell. Speak in terms that can be understood by intelligent lay people, avoiding jargon. If details of rare clinical and pathological findings are necessary, it is usually possible to lead up to these with a few explanatory words. There is always much consideration for the relatives, and in many inquests general medical findings are sufficient, with gruesome or harrowing medical evidence being avoided; likewise, coroners avoid publicising personal tragic details, and suicide notes are seldom read out in full.

After your factual statements, you will be questioned by the coroner, and possibly by solicitors or "properly interested parties". Usually it is possible to give straight answers, but medical witnesses are sometimes asked questions that they can answer only on hearsay evidence, if at all. If your reply is based on the observations of someone else, who is not in court, make this clear. Speak from memory with assurance, but refer to case records for details; avoid inaccuracies, however minor, as these may need correction later. An unexpected question impugning a lack of medical care is unlikely to be permitted by the coroner, or need not be answered. An allegation of negligence without warning can make a doctor a "properly interested person" and the coroner can allow that doctor to put relevant questions to witnesses,[2] but doctors will normally prefer to seek an adjournment of the hearing to arrange legal representation.

In traumatic deaths medical witnesses may be able to give a valuable opinion on the type and degree of violence that caused the fatal injuries. In addition, evidence of previous disease or disability that would have made the deceased more prone to an accident or susceptible to its consequences may be highly relevant to the coroner's inquiries and will be of interest to insurance companies. Pathologists will be asked to comment on the circumstances leading to death and it is in these cases that a full understanding of the final illness is essential. Be prepared to sign a statement of the salient points of your evidence before you leave the court.

At the end of the inquest, have a word with the relatives, whose inarticulate gratitude for your unsuccessful efforts will be more rewarding than the coroner's officer's payment for your attendance. As you drive back to the land of the living you will appreciate that the roots of some of our recent social legislation, the recognition of hazards in industry and adverse reactions to drugs or the contraceptive pill spring from medical evidence given at coroners' inquests.

1 *The Brodrick Report of the Committee on Death Certification and Coroners*. London: HMSO, 1971.
2 *Coroner's Rules*, 1984; Rule 20(1).

32 Give evidence

Bernard Knight

The witness box is commonly held to be the place that most doctors shun with distaste and even trepidation. Even so, an appearance in court as a medical witness need not be an ordeal if doctors observe a few simple rules. This applies equally well to both criminal and civil cases in the crown courts and to a lesser extent in magistrates' courts and coroners' inquests, the latter the subject of another chapter. Certain doctors, such as police surgeons and forensic pathologists, make such frequent visits to the witness box that it might be thought that they become immune to the tensions and pitfalls of the courts; nevertheless, they can just as easily come to grief if they ignore the basic precautions.

There has long been a facetious saying that doctors in court should "dress up, stand up, speak up, and shut up", and there is considerable merit in this advice. Doctors in the witness box should dress like professional people and not like disc-jockeys or lumberjacks. Not only is a fairly sober appearance more appropriate to the many cases in which there was a fatal outcome, but an opinion uttered by someone who at least looks like a medical expert will carry that much more conviction.

Similarly, as long as it falls well short of condescension or arrogance, a confident demeanour will add weight to the substance of the evidence. As to speaking up, if the doctor's evidence is worth hearing, it is pointless to have it mumbled and muttered. This tends to give the impression that the witness is so unsure of the substance of the testimony that he or she is reluctant to have it heard. Inaudibility will not only lengthen the proceedings but irritate judge and counsel.

As to "shutting up", there is a further well known saying that "if one opens one's mouth, one puts one's foot in it". Any amplification should be limited to the matter under discussion; loquacious witnesses are a delight to opposing counsel, who will encourage doctors to tie themselves in knots with their own tongue.

Importance of original statement

These general matters apart, the most important part of giving evidence takes place not in the court itself but in the original circumstances that generate the evidence. More than any other single factor, it is the original statement given to the police or to a solicitor—sometimes months or even years earlier—that determines whether or not the doctor is to get a rough ride in the witness box. It is vital that this first statement—which is a formal declaration of the facts known to the witness and, where appropriate, the witness's opinion on those facts—should be exactly what the doctor is prepared to say when he or she stands before the court.

Therefore, doctors must decide at the outset what are the limits to which they are willing to testify. They must consider all aspects of the case and decide on the factual demarcation beyond which they are not prepared to step. They must be prepared to "put their mouth where their pen was" when the time of trial arrives. So often, in the security of the consulting room, doctors will dash off a sweeping statement, drawing unwise and perhaps unwarranted conclusions and opinions. Then, when they are on their feet before a crowded court, the previous literary bravado tends to drain away and they fail to "come up to proof", as their legal colleagues would term it. In these circumstances not only will they do the court and justice a disservice, but they will almost certainly have a very uncomfortable time from opposing counsel and possibly the judge or magistrate. So often one has seen a barrister waving a sheaf of papers at the discomforted medical witness, saying, "But doctor, let me read what you said last February".

It cannot be overemphasised that medical witnesses should never commit themselves to opinions that they are not willing to maintain. This is not to say that they should never admit to being wrong in the face of new facts or interpretations from elsewhere, but they should not back off at the time of trial from their own earlier opinions.

Preparing the facts

The second necessity is the preparation of the facts. Whether they are attending as a witness to fact or as an expert witness with opinions, medical witnesses should have done their homework sufficiently to be seen in the witness box to have at least an adequate grasp of the matters under discussion. Too often, the sorry sight is seen of doctors standing sheepishly in the witness box, giving the impression that they have never heard of the person about whom they are being questioned and have no idea of any medical facts relating to the case. Under such circumstances, counsel becomes sarcastic and the judge incensed to the point of apoplexy. Doctors should bring all records relating to the patient; they should have read them beforehand; and they should refer to them when questioned, rather than mutter and stammer in a vain attempt to remember the relevant details. Such records must be originals, such as actual case notes or the contemporary reports made by the witness.

The use of such records in the witness box may have to be approved by the judge, who may wish to see them, to check that they are originals. Judges will always allow doctors to refer to the records for the purpose of "refreshing their memory", so that it is as well if medical witnesses avoid shuffling them and searching as if this were the first time they had ever set eyes upon them.

Thirdly, doctors should never trespass beyond the bounds of their own skill or competence. Junior house officers are not expected to give opinions that might tax the capabilities of a senior consultant —if they do so, they are likely to be destroyed by opposing counsel. Senior specialists are equally vulnerable when they transgress the boundaries of their own specialty. The classical example was the comment of Mr Alec Bourne, the well known gynaecologist, when Sir Bernard Spilsbury unwisely gave an opinion about clinical obstetrics. Mr Bourne said that, however eminent Sir Bernard was as a forensic pathologist, when he spoke of childbirth his evidence should be treated with contempt. Doctors who are pressed to answer questions that they consider to be beyond their sphere of skill should draw a firm line and indicate to the court—by appeal to the judge if necessary—that they feel unable to give a useful opinion.

Courtesy and consideration

The days of blood and thunder advocacy are thankfully past and counsel today are almost invariably courteous and considerate, especially to witnesses in a sister profession. Nevertheless, this does not detract from the penetrating intellect and piercing questions with which they can nail medical witnesses to the courtroom wall. When doctors have allowed themselves to stray on to the thin ice of doubtful fact or the swampy ground of unwise opinion, the best course is to cut their losses and regain terra firma as gracefully as possible, by admitting that they do not know some fact or that they allow that a contrary opinion may be correct.

Whatever happens, embarrassment and loss of face should not tempt doctors into anger, sarcasm, or even impertinence. Not only will this earn a rebuke from the judge, but it delights opposing counsel, who can run rings round an angry witness like a matador around a bewildered bull. Nevertheless, this state of affairs is rarely likely to happen if doctors are well prepared, have kept within the perimeter of their original considered opinion, and give their evidence and responses to questions calmly and responsibly.

There are two last points. Firstly, evidence needs to be given slowly and in short instalments, especially in the crown courts, as the judge will be writing it down longhand. Some doctors have suggested that barristers who are on their feet suffer from intermittent catalepsy, but in reality they are watching the end of the judge's pen before putting the next question and experienced medical witnesses will do the same. Secondly, doctors should use comprehensible language in court, free from medical jargon. Even though the barristers and the judge may know almost as much about the medical aspects of the case as the doctor, the rest of the court—including the jury, if there is one—may not have the slightest idea of what the witness is talking about. From motives of sheer thoughtlessness, from professional pomposity, or even because a retreat into the familiar terminology is comforting during the uneasy vigil in the witness box, many doctors relapse into the jargon of our mysterious medical language. Good witnesses will translate their evidence into everyday English. Often the more junior doctors are the worst offenders; two of their classical gems are "periorbital haematoma" for "black eyes" and "biventricular myocardial hypertrophy" for "a big heart".

33 Beautify your old hospital

J H Baron

Why should hospitals be beautiful?

Sir Henry Wootton is usually remembered for defining an ambassador as "an honest man sent to lie abroad for the good of his country". But he equally pithily paraphrased Vitruvius's qualities of a building (strength/utility/beauty), "Well building hath three conditions, commoditie, firmenes and delight".[1] A hospital is designed to work as a health care factory, and does so more or less effectively. Not all contemporary hospitals fall down from lapses of design and execution soon after they are completed, but how few people expect a hospital to be designed and built for delight. I find it curious that those who like their homes to be elegant, who museum crawl and sightsee on holiday at home and abroad, are amazed when I suggest that a hospital should be beautiful, and provide a life enhancing experience for staff, patients, and visitors.

It is only during the last half of this century that my ambitions are considered eccentric. No one thought it odd that Hogarth should have painted murals at Bart's. The Victorians expected their town halls and railway stations to be objects of wonder and beauty; the walls of some of their children's wards were covered with fairy tales and nursery rhymes in Doulton tiles; even a workhouse might have pictures on the walls (fig 1). Those who trained at Middlesex will remember its elegant panelled front hall, with Cayley Robinson's *Acts of Mercy* murals, the central circular table with the daily change of flowers, the brass-buttoned, frock-coated uniformed porters, and the singular lettering of the ward names on the direction boards. Think of most hospital entrances today.

If you accept my premise, then this chapter will help you to

194

Fig 1 Sir H van Herkomer (1849–1914). Eventide: A scene in the Westminster Union, 1878 Walker Art Gallery, Liverpool.

beautify your old hospital. If you want your new hospital to have works of art, you may find ideas in a separate article.[2]

Apathy and antipathy

Do not be put off by lack of interest. Achievement is still possible in the face of amused tolerance so long as you press on regardless.

Although apathy can be brushed aside, actual antagonism will stop you. You will fail if you meet explicit opposition from any power figure. I made hints at two hospitals world famous for their clinical science. In one, "The sad facts are, even in periods of financial boom, no one would consider art as a necessary portion of hospital expenditure." In the other the dean did consult his advisory committee and heads of department: "There wasn't a very enthusiastic response. Perhaps we are all a bit overwhelmed with the general gloom, particularly on the NHS side. . . ." Faced with these reactions, give up and wait for a new dean, who is "interested in changing what is unquestionably one of the most squalid hospitals in all Britain."

The committee

In any facet of British public life, and especially in a hospital within a bureaucratic health service, you need a committee for any

195

new venture to succeed. Some hospitals use conventional names: an art or arts committee, a fine arts board, a history and works of art committee; I was forthright and called ours the beautification committee. You need terms of reference, which should be as wide as your interests. You must report to someone, such as the unit management team of a hospital, or the special trustees if they are the prime paymaster.

The other reason for a committee is to spread the aesthetic reponsibility. The directors of the National Gallery and the Tate may buy nothing on their own decisions: the trustees have to approve every purchase, so that the responsibility for acts of expenditure of public money can be spread among, and any obloquy borne by, many broad shoulders. Similarly, in a hospital there will be strong criticism of anything you do: let it be clear that decisions have been shared and conclusions reached by thoughtful people.

The committee must be small and meet regularly on a specific day and time. If you are chairperson you need an interested administrator, interested nursing officer, and the key figure, the committee secretary, who must have a devotion to the topic, and can come from any discipline—for example, the voluntary services organiser if you have one, or an outside art lover in an honorary capacity.

What to beautify

Buildings

Every hospital was designed by an architect with skill, devotion, and artistry. Often the original drawings or engravings survive or can be found in illustrations in old books, local newspapers, the topography collection of your library, architectural journals, or national periodicals such as the *Illustrated London News*. These designs will grace an entrance hall or corridor, framed as pictures or as black-and-white photographic enlargements blown up to whole wall size.

All too many British hospitals were built a century ago as Victorian workhouse infirmaries for the sick poor. The nineteenth-century buildings have usually been altered, or extensions of every style added, leaving a mishmash of an architectural jungle. But sometimes the original buildings have not been so disturbed. If you can persuade the works department to remove decades of grime you may be pleasantly surprised at the splendours of Victorian brickwork, detailings, and architecture. You may find your principal work of art is your own building. If so, cherish it. See that there is an overall colour scheme for the exterior woodwork and drainpipes, that the roofing is repaired in colour and texture similar to the original: if you cannot afford new real slates, at least have simulated ones. If there are original iron railings, fences, balconies, or walkways, try to keep them and prevent their replacement by barbed wire or chicken fencing. Similarly, the original lamps may have been gas lit and can be adapted to electricity rather than replaced by concrete posts.

In lieu of a brand new hospital you will probably be given new additions for outpatient or x-ray departments; if you are not careful some prefabricated concrete box will rise up and mar the old ensemble. Try to persuade your district to set up a design panel that must see and approve aesthetically, and not just functionally, all new additions to any hospital in the district, so that representations can be made before it is too late and the juggernaut of the NHS planning process rolls over you.

Gardens

Gardens are best left to garden experts, one or two of whom are bound to be found in your committee or can be co-opted. Your garden subgroup should take a look at the whole hospital campus and make recommendations via your committee to the unit management team about the outside lawns, trees, paved areas, benches, tubs, climbers and plants, ponds and fountains, not to forget litter bins. There may be scope for some indoor plant schemes, but every scheme must be manageable either by named and interested volunteers from staff or friends, or by contract with a garden firm.

Hospital entrances

Hospital entrances come in all sizes and shapes, but are rarely welcoming. The casualty department is often approached through a tiled tunnel or corridor lined with wheelchairs. The outpatient department may be hidden down a side street and the waiting hall filled with broken chairs, tattered magazines, blaring television, ashtrays, and countless notices, hortatory or admonitory, ranging from injunctions to tell the desk if you have changed your name or your family doctor to warnings about smoking, drinking, and the problems and consequences of life after sex.

Most visitors come into a main courtyard and are immediately made unwelcome by a kaleidoscope of notices forbidding them to park (reserved for consultants), or warning that they park at their own risk, or telling them how to get to the special clinic or the mortuary.

Inside, the main hall is cluttered with more notices, telephone booths, fire extinguishers, post boxes, flower stalls, newspaper kiosks, and sometimes a reception desk with pigeon holes for letters, fuseboxes, and a keyboard. A sympathetic architect should be commissioned to design a comprehensive plan for refurbishing, lighting, and decorating your front hall. It may be possible to bring the porter's desk forward and flank it with a general shop and a flower stall with telephone alcoves at each end. The clutter of objects and notices can be removed and tidied up visually. It is often helpful to lower the ceiling, install concealed lighting, and bank the direction signs into blocks of colours to complement the whole colour scheme.

Notices

Notices spring up everywhere and can mostly be removed. A map is ideal with a plan of the hospital or even a model. Obviously directions are needed to the different wards and departments. Most hospitals have been persuaded by the Department of Health to use their standardised lower case sanserif typeface for every sign. Some people like it. It is a matter of taste. Such lettering is ideal for motorway signs for clarity and ease of reading as you rush past in your car. I am depressed by seeing the same institutional lettering in every hospital. It may suit hospitals that look like motorways. For your hospital, look at other typefaces in the catalogues of notice makers—perhaps Times New Roman will suit your own buildings best.[4] Look at the British Museum and the National Gallery.

Ideally your hospital, and indeed your district, should have a corporate image, with a logo and an elegant typeface for everything it presents to the public, from the flags flying overhead and the names on the vans going through the streets to the signs over the entrance, the writing paper, and the mail franking.

Corridors

Until recently most district and many university hospitals were designed on the Nightingale pattern, a long corridor off which branched several two or three storey ward blocks. This design allowed natural light and ventilation to enter the wards from two

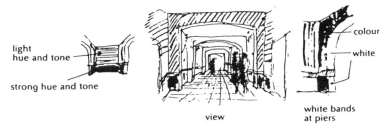

light
hue and tone

strong hue and tone

view

colour

white

white bands
at piers

Fig 2 Corridor colour scheme by Robert Radford, 1984. The objective is to provide a linking line of colour to the chair rail and a sequence of hues to each bay emphasised by the strong hues below the chair rail punctuated by white elements.

sides, and separated each ward from another by a distance sufficient to lessen cross-infection and noise. Another happy consequence of this design is that staff meet each other walking up and down the corridors, and do not spend their time in isolation waiting for, or crowded into, the lifts of the vertically designed hospitals of today.

However, long main corridors are often the most aesthetically depressing part of a British hospital. Visitors' hearts sink as they see a gloomy prospect with the end scarcely in view, frequently in a grubby decorative state, or, even when freshly painted, in a drab single colour.[5] Ask your architect to consider breaking the corridor into different coloured areas. He or she may want to coordinate and to classify the colour on some such scheme as the Munsell system, and then give you a linking line of colour with a sequence of hues to each bay (fig 2).

How to beautify

Murals

You may have an entrance stairway or foyer, or a busy corridor leading to outpatients. These can be key areas visually and cry out for murals. They are places of continual movement, where it is perhaps undesirable for people to stop, stand, and scrutinise recognisable representational objects in a mural. Perhaps an abstract pattern could be used to better advantage. The mural must work as a simple immediate effect unfolding as the visitor walks past, and by its optimism relieve the tension of those who are worrying about themselves or others. In other departments, such as a visitors' waiting area, or for those sitting in chairs or lying on stretchers (for example, outside radiotherapy) pastoral scenes or flowers may be

199

more restful. Day areas might be cheered by local topography, past or present. The needs of children's units are obvious.

Pictures

Pictures can adorn most walls, but need to be chosen for size and colour for a specific site. They are particularly needed in long corridors, in waiting areas, in day rooms, and in foyers outside wards. Persuade your colleagues to donate, or at least pay for, framed photographs of the notables who give their names to the wards (Addison, Fleming, Churchill, etc). You may be asked for pictures for individual offices, in which case you should have an operational policy that pictures are provided from hospital funds only for public spaces—that is, where the public walks and in offices where patients or visitors come: other office holders should certainly be encouraged to have pictures—their own.

Hospital wards have surprisingly little space for pictures, usually only a few walls are sufficiently bare for hanging because most walls in a ward are taken up with windows, cupboards, or have wires trailing and tubes attached. Even in side-wards you should be careful not to trap a patient face to face with an incompatible picture for days or weeks on end.

Conservation

Pictures cannot be left to look after themselves any more than laws can be left to enforce themselves. An institution should not buy, and certainly not borrow, works of art unless it is prepared to catalogue, conserve, and generally keep an eye on them to prevent loss and damage. This task should be assigned to one interested and obsessional individual, who could be an expert volunteer or from the administrative, nursing or paramedical staff.

If you do borrow from public bodies, you will have to insure the work at their valuation: few hospitals have either the time or expertise to deal with such administrative problems. For example, in 1965 the Walker Art Gallery lent pictures that were hung in the entrance hall of the Liverpool Royal Infirmary: the security arrangements were later considered inadequate and the gallery withdrew its pictures.[6] Pictures continually disappear from hospitals. Theft is probably rare: more often the pictures are taken down and not properly stored when a ward or corridor is to be cleaned. When the decorations are completed, the pictures are not rehung: they are mislaid, discarded, or lost. The donor who in 1912 gave tens of thousands of pounds to each of at least eight hospitals to bear the name of his widow, Annie Zunz, also gave a portrait to hang in the ward. Who can find Annie Zunz today?[7]

Anything hanging on a hook can all too easily be carried off. The pictures need to be fixed firmly to a wall by screws—with mirror plates, for example. If the hospital engineers cannot spare appropriate staff for this task, then professional picture hangers will be needed. The pictures must not be exposed to intense light or heat, wind, rain, or humidity.

All pictures need framing, and all watercolours and engravings and some paintings need glazing too. Works on paper need mounting on acid-free boards. Even a large occupational therapy department is unlikely to be able to cope with such requirements, and professional framers should be used, with thoughtful and individual consideration of the type of mount and frame suitable for each work.

Pictures need labels to tell the viewer at least the title and the artist. These are best pinned to the lower horizontal of the frame, and the size, colour, and lettering will depend on the colour and texture of the picture mount and frame, and again is usually best done professionally. Large works such as murals deserve a large wall-mounted label giving not only title, artist, and date, but also the occasion of its commissioning and the donors; a few lines explaining the composition may be helpful too.

Quite apart from the simple labels you need a card or computer index, detailing for each object the artist, with dates of birth and, where appropriate, death, the date and title of the composition, the medium (oil, watercolour, engraving, etching) and the material (canvas, board, paper, etc), the date of purchase, the cost and source of funds (or from whom borrowed and when and for how long), and its location. Some of these data can be turned into a catalogue, which can be duplicated or printed, according to your resources.

Finance

The old board of governors voluntary hospitals all had endowment funds, which have been preserved in the care of special trustees. You may be able to persuade them that they should spend some of their income, or even their capital, on works of art. Some have allotted tens of thousands of pounds for initial purchases, and then provided up to £10 000 a year for staff, further purchases, and conservation. Others spend nothing on art.

If your special trustees refuse you money for works of art, or you are in an old municipal county council hospital without special trustees, you may find your district has some free money, their share of the old area health authority's trust funds. Your unit too may have some free money from donations or legacies from grateful patients and well wishers. Funds may be raised by friends or volunteers, specially for specific purposes like pictures for a refurbished day room.

Study some of the available publications[8-21] for ideas and funding. There are national organisations—Healthcare Arts[22] and Healthcare Arts in Scotland[23]—that will advise. Discuss your requirements with the visual arts officer of your regional arts association and the director of your local art gallery. In London the King Edward's Hospital Fund[24] and Public Art Development Trust[25] may help. The Manpower Services Commission may help you with a project for training the unemployed, as craftsmen in the arts, or you can approach the industry, and national foundations. Pictures can be borrowed from Paintings in Hospitals.[26]

You can steel yourself against criticisms of your aesthetic judgment and taste in any beautification you promote. You will probably be wise to avoid, even if you are able to obtain, exchequer funds from the hospital budget. However, if there were any payment for a work of art, you may find "the correspondence columns of the local newspaper immediately filled up with letters from Mr Disgusted Taxpayer (who else?)—a man who didn't know anything about art, but knew what he disliked. If this money had not been wasted on so-called modern art my grannie could have had her teeth taken out and a new gas stove put in."[27]

The visit

The NHS, like all great institutions, has an inertia of its own, which will stop all your initiatives from starting, and prevent the completion of any which began. You may speed up your project by the usual wheedling and negotiations, but faced with an impasse, play your ace, the visit. Arrange for some dignitary (be it royalty, the regional chairperson, or the mayor) to come on a specific date to open one of your schemes and unveil an appropriately worded plaque in the presence of an invited audience. You will be pleasantly surprised how the impossible begins to happen at once, that timetables of work are kept, and that the hospital, or at least the professional route of the tour by the visitor, has been cleaned.

Conclusion

Now that you have read this article, do you still want to beautify your hospital? You can do so, just as you can achieve anything else in the health service given vision, energy, time and patience, a lack of enemies, a working committee, and sufficient guile to know both the regulations that run the NHS and how to outwit them.

Acknowledgements

Many have helped and are thanked elsewhere.[8]

1 Wootton H. *Elements of architecture.* London: John Bill, 1624: 1.
2 Baron J H, Greene L. Funding works of art in new hospitals. *BMJ* 1984; **289**: 1731–7.
3 Warner S B, Baron J H. Restorative gardens: green thoughts in a green shade. *BMJ* 1993; **306**: 1080–1.
4 Baron J H. How to signpost your hospital. *BMJ* 1987; **295**: 482–4.
5 Agate J. Colour in hospitals. *World Medicine* 1969; 20 May:13–17.
6 Brewer C. *Liverpool Royal Infirmary, 1887–1978.*Liverpool; Area Health Authority (Teaching), 1980; 131.
7 Rosse E M. The lady missing from St Mary's. *Nor West* 1984; **2**(3): 2.
8 Baron J H, Hadden M, Palley M. *St Charles Hospital works of art.* 2nd ed. London: St Charles Hospital, 1993.
9 Baron J H. Art in hospitals and for the disadvantaged in New York and London. *Lancet* 1986; ii: 1438–41.
10 Baron J H, Miles M F R. Art in hospitals. *Contemporary Review* 1991; **259**: 137–41.
11 Coles P. *The Manchester Hospital arts project.* London: Calouste Gulbenkian Foundation, 1981.
12 Coles P. *Art in the National Health Service: a report by the Department of Health and Social Security.* London: DHSS, 1983.
13 Hyslop R. *Art in hospitals: conference report.* London: DHSS, 1983.
14 Miles M F R. The pool of Bethesda: art in British hospitals. *Scot Med J* 1991; **36**: 55–8.
15 Moss L M. The arts as healing agents in recovery from operation: a critical review. *Theoret Surg* 1986; **1**: 96–102.
16 Moss L M. *Art for health's sake.* Manchester: St Mary's Hospital, 1987.
17 NHS Management Executive. *Demonstrably different.* London: Department of Health, 1991.
18 NHS Management Executive. *First impressions, lasting quality.* London: Department of Health, 1992.
19 NHS Estates. *Environment for quality care.* London: HMSO, 1993.
20 Reed F. Art in hospitals. *Arts Review* 1983; 13 May: 259.
21 Townsend P, ed. *Art within reach: artists and craftworkers, architects and patrons in the making of public art.* London: Art Monthly/Thames and Hudson, 1984.
22 Healthcare Arts, Pegasus House, 37/43 Sackville Street, London W1X 2DL; telephone 0171 333 0660; fax 0171 434 3332.
23 Health Care Arts, 23 Springfield, Dundee DD1 4JE; telephone 01382–203099; fax: 01382–27304
24 King Edward's Hospital Fund for London, 14 Palace Court, London W2 4HT; telephone: 0171–727 0581; fax: 0171–727 7603.
25 Public Art Development Trust, 3rd Floor, 12/14 Whitfield Street, London W1P 5RD; telephone 0171–580 9977; fax: 0171–580 8540.
26 Paintings in Hospital, Samaritan Hospital, Marylebone Road, London NW1 5YE; telephone and fax: 0171–723 7422.
27 Keep P. Having an art attack. *World Medicine* 1983; 25 June: 22.

34 Commission a portrait

Imogen Lock

For many of us the prospect of having our portrait painted is quite daunting. There may be no choice in the matter if the portrait has been commissioned by an outside body to commemorate your life's achievements. Even if you are a willing participant commissioning a portrait for yourself, the process must be carefully considered. The past decade has seen a tremendous upsurge in interest in all types of figurative art, and portraiture especially has been given a new impetus. The resultant wide choice of artists and styles makes the task of commissioning both more simple and more complex. No longer limited to a formulaic photographic likeness or "society" portrait, you may choose a style of painting and format to suit your mood and budget. You might want to commission an established portraitist whose clients may range from academics and aesthetes to pop stars and politicians. Or you might be more adventurous and seek out young talent from an art school's diploma show or tailor made exhibition such as the annual BP Portrait Award for portrait painters under 40.

There are two overriding considerations in commissioning a portrait. What is it for and how much can it cost? Purpose and budget will affect all other criteria. Is it a formal portrait to be placed alongside those of fellow worthies? Or a private commission to display at home, intended to record your personality, not status? Have you a free reign in the choice of medium, size, format, and style? Or are these dictated by the nature of the commission? Is the portrait part of an existing series to which it must conform? Will your budget cover the considerable costs of an established society

> ## Points to consider when commissioning a portrait
>
> • Type of artist: young inexperienced, experimental, established, fashionable
> • Medium: oil, acrylic, pastel, watercolour, drawing, limited edition print, mixed media, sculpture, photograph
> • Size and format: full length, three-quarter length, half length, head and shoulders, miniature, lifesize, full face, three-quarter face, profile
> • Style: photographic likeness *v* artistic licence
> • Setting and dress: home, office, studio; academic gown, informal, iconography, association

portrait painter or would you prefer to test younger talent or a more experimental artist?

Homework

Having a portrait made is quite an undertaking in terms of both time and money, so you must do adequate homework to ensure the smooth running of the venture. This begins well away from the artist's studio in your acquiring a grounding in portraiture. Visit a number of exhibitions in which portraits are included and take a historical overview at the National Portrait Gallery. Looking closely at historic and contemporary portraits helps an educated approach to your chosen artist and will also help you decide on the right format. Specialist exhibitions include the annual BP Portrait Award at the National Portrait Gallery and the Royal Society of Portrait Painters' annual exhibition, both of which show a wide spectrum of contemporary work. Photographic dossiers on many portrait artists are kept at the National Portrait Gallery, the Royal Society of Portrait Painters, the Royal Society of British Sculptors and at other specialist galleries, such as the New Grafton Gallery, London. These can be examined by appointment.

After viewing exhibitions and photographic records, you should have some idea of whose work you would like to see in detail. It is important not only to visit the artists themselves but also to view collections of their work and to talk to previous sitters about their experiences and misgivings. During informal studio visits you should discuss your expectations for your commission. What do you want from the portrait—mere likeness (in which case why not have a

---

Points to consider when budgeting for a portrait

- Trips to exhibitions, artists, previous patrons
- First sitting, subsequent sittings
- Studies, maquettes
- Finished portrait
- Varnishing, glazing, framing, casting, mounting, unveiling or exhibiting, lighting, hanging, entertainment

---

photograph instead) or a record of past achievements? Do you wish to include professional or personal iconography? What kind of setting had you envisaged? Whether there is empathy between you or a personality clash will soon become apparent, an important consideration as the portrait making process can be quite intense and exposing.

Sorting out the details

Once you have found a sympathetic artist whose work you admire, you must have another, more formal meeting to discuss the contract, budget, and timescale. How many sittings will there be? What happens if one of you has to withdraw because of other commitments? What happens if the first sitting or subsequently finished portrait is not acceptable. Which stages of the commission require payment? Some artists make no charge for the preliminary sitting and sketches. Others will not charge if you reject the finished portrait. You are most unlikely to do so, as they will usually agree to alter or repaint the work. Your contract is a "gentleman's agreement" not a legal document—all the artist has to do is supply a finished portrait, but she or he will most likely accommodate your suggestions so as not to damage her or his reputation. If an artist accepts defeat entirely and chooses to add the portrait to her or his store of works for exhibition, you must start the commissioning process from scratch and pay the artist's expenses. Bearing in mind the "gentlemanly" nature of the agreement, you should also offer part of the fee. Artists belonging to the Royal Society of Portrait Painters ask for a third of their fee in advance and the rest on completion. Finally, does the final bill include framing and varnishing, or casting in the case of a portrait bust?

The first sitting

The next stage is the first sitting—at home, at work, or in the artist's studio—the setting depends on the purpose of the portrait and your choice of iconography. Artists' working methods vary enormously. Some will produce a finished portrait "on the spot" with few sittings. Others will take many photographs, make numerous drawings, and produce the finished work in your absence. Most will produce a study or series of studies at the first sitting. In some cases an artist produces rapid, loosely worked pencil or charcoal drawings as you talk. Others may require total silence and a fixed pose and go for a much more finished piece—even a small watercolour or oil study or a sculptured maquette. Work produced at this stage gives the subject an opportunity for a useful exchange of views; the artist can tell you how she or he envisages the finished work and you can discuss reservations.

If the first sitting is a success, you will be invited to have subsequent sittings and then to view the finished work. Ask your closest friend to give you an honest opinion of the portrait—not just in terms of physical likeness and recognisable iconography but to assess whether the artist has captured your essential character. It should not be too late for amendments to be made or indeed to reject the commission, but you should remember that the purpose of a portrait is not to flatter the vanity of the sitter but to stand as a summation of career or personality or in its own right as a strong and solid work of art.

Think of posterity

If the portrait is not acceptable (for example, to you or the commissioning body) you should say so. It will be almost impossible for you to reject it on artistic grounds—you chose the style, you saw previous work, it is a risk you have to take. What criteria separate a bad painting from a good one, can you argue your case through? There should be fewer problems justifying rejection on the grounds that the portrait is not a true likeness, though sitters are not always the best judges, as they never see themselves as others do. If, for example, the commissioning body is really unhappy, you should have a "full and frank" discussion with the artist about points you think that she or he has got wrong. Most artists will probably arrange further sittings, make new sketches, and alter or completely

207

Portrait of Dorothy Hodgkin by Maggi Hembling, 1985

repaint the portrait, charging only for additional expenses incurred. On the other hand, if you are presented with a portrait that is a poor likeness but a wonderful work of art, think of posterity. Will it really matter what you looked like? Won't future generations be all the more respectful that you had the foresight to choose such a talented artist?

The task of commissioning a portrait does not end here. The painting will need to be framed and eventually varnished (six months

208

later) or the plaster be cast, stages that add quite considerably to the cost unless budgeted from the start. Many artists, particularly young unknowns, prefer to frame their work themselves. You should ask to see examples of their framing; it can often be unprofessional and detract from an otherwise good painting. Professional framing is expensive but worth doing. An artist may have a preferred framer, and she or he may wish to visit the framer with you to advise on what is needed—for example, rococo gilded plasterwork or plain stained wood with canvas slips. Some artists may wish to paint the frame themselves, sometimes extending or "bleeding" elements of the painting on to the frame. Or they may wish it to be carved with motifs reflecting passages in the painting. Whatever the case, you should be sure that you will be happy with the end result. A portrait bust will require a plinth or stand. The artist can advise on your choice: an antique, or a cast of an old style, or something more up to date.

If the portrait is intended for home consumption, the story is almost over. Once the finished article has been approved, a nice touch is to invite the artist to a small party at which friends and family can view the portrait and ask about its evolution. If the commission is a formal one it must be presented to the commissioning body, most usually at a private viewing or unveiling. Guests should include the artist, you the sitter, your peer group, the commissioning committee, family and selected friends as well as former and future patrons of the artist. An enthusiastic press officer will ensure that a private viewing becomes a media event and may cajole you and the artist into making a formal statement about the commission. Discuss any misgivings about this kind of circus before it is too late. Check that this stage of the proceedings is covered by a separate entertainment budget, as the costs can be quite high. The portrait will need to be displayed and lit for the event. Possibly unveiling will take place away from the portrait's eventual location or for ease of viewing it may be displayed on an easel. It will still need professional lighting and to be hung and relit after the event.

If you have the time, money, and inclination having your portrait painted can be a challenging and rewarding experience. The more effort you put into it—in terms of adequate preparation and research, facilitating the number and length of sittings required, and being open with the artist—the better the end result. Anything less than total commitment will result in an unsatisfactory commission, and you should think of sitting for a studio photograph instead.

Factors to consider when planning timescale

- Basic research
- Number and duration of sittings
- Length of time required to complete portrait
- Framing or casting and mounting
- Is the unveiling to take place before or after varnishing?
- Does the artist intend to exhibit it elsewhere afterwards?

Useful information

BP Portrait Award June–September, National Portrait Gallery, 2 St Martin's Place, London WC2H 0HE; telephone: 0171 306 0055. Open Mon–Sat 10–6, Sun 12–6. Admission free. Catalogue available. The annual exhibition for artists under 40 provides a forum for painters from all over Britain. Information from the National Portrait Gallery's competitions office.

John Kobal Photographic Portrait Award May–June, National Portrait Gallery (as before). The award, open to photographers over the age of 18, aims to further the artistic and technical understanding and appreciation of portrait photography.

The Royal Society of Portrait Painters Annual Exhibition May, The Mall Galleries, The Mall, London SW1 (near Admiralty Arch, telephone: 0171 930 6844. Open daily 10–5. Admission free. Open exhibition dominated by work of members of the society. Catalogue includes names and addresses of all members. Further information from the Secretary, Royal Society of Portrait Painters, 17 Carlton House Terrace, London SW1Y 5BG; telephone: 0171 930 6844.

The Royal Society of British Sculptors 108 Old Brompton Road, South Kensington, London SW7 3RA; telephone: 0171 373 5554. Holds portfolios of work by members of the RBS and will advise on all aspects of public and private commission. Periodic temporary displays on premises.

Portrait Centre, New Grafton Gallery 48 Church Street, Barnes, London SW3 9HH; telephone: 0181 748 8850. Open Tues–Sat 10–5.30. Admission free. Portrait booklet available including artists' biographies and lists of previous portraits. Examples of work and portfolios held at gallery.

210

35 Organise a reunion of your undergraduate classmates

Colin Kenny

How and where do you begin to trace up to 150 medical graduates, firm friends and daily companions for six years, but now scattered worldwide? How to inform, inspire, and then encourage them to travel miles—all for an evening, a day, or a weekend's immersion in nostalgia for the time before mortgages, children, and on call began? The initial answer is simple—start early and form a committee, ideally 18 months before the desired date of the reunion.

Most reunions are based around decades. The 10-year reunion is the most enthusiastically supported, and interest diminishes during subsequent years.

Should you put yourself in charge of procedures, then the first step is to appoint 6–10 people to the committee. Inevitably, no one will have experience in this area, so go for people who are enthusiastic and who live within driving distance for the frequent meetings that will be required. Much of the organising and attendant paperwork for the reunion will require secretarial, photocopying, and word-processing resources, so if these are not directly available to you, choose your committee members to include someone who has these facilities. General practitioner members are most likely to help by raising funds for the event from pharmaceutical companies, whereas a hospital consultant is more likely to have access to the secretarial skills.

The long run up

Once the committee has convened, the first meeting will have to tackle the inevitable questions of who, what, when, and where, preferably in that order.

The "who" calls for some detective work. We found the best way to get an initial list of the graduates in our year was to approach our university's examinations board for the names of all those who sat finals with us. Doing this identified those who were definitely in our year and avoided the embarrassment of missing those who failed to graduate. This then gave us an initial database. Fortunately, our profession requires us to keep ourselves on various lists, such as the principals list in general practice and particularly the *Medical Register* and *Medical Directory*. Consulting these will immediately throw up 90% of the year's full names and addresses, the "lost lambs" being those working abroad, those not practising, or those who have reregistered under a married name. Put these names on a separate list and send it out along with the letter to everyone. In most cases someone will know where they are, even if it is the opposite side of the world.

The questions of when, what, and where are best taken as a single question, as ultimately they will be interrelated. There are a number of factors to consider, but a good place to start may be the duration of the event. Would there be enough interest for a full weekend, or is it better to concentrate on a single evening's get together? Initially keep your options open—if you are sure of the reunion dinner taking place, then build other events around this, depending on the response to the mailings.

When choosing the venue, gather information from those who have organised previous reunions in the area. They will provide useful advice about which hotels were courteous and helpful, and which proved to be expensive mistakes. You may also get guidance on suitable dates, such as whether to choose or avoid bank holidays and school holidays. Ultimately, let the committee make this important decision on the hotel and date.

When the data and venue are decided, make a booking for flexible numbers and construct your first letter. As well as details of the arrangements we found it useful to include in the first mailing a request for a career résumé, a passport-style photograph, and a deposit of 10% of the anticipated cost. We also requested further information on our "lost" list. We discovered that our year was fairly representative of the medical profession's response to correspondence: some replied immediately; some replied eventually, even if it was with the Christmas cards; and some probably never even read our letter but discarded it along with their junk mail.

Several important things need doing during this early stage. Meticulous record-keeping is important. A separate bank account should be opened and all deposits entered and recorded. All personal profiles should be stored, ideally in a computer, to facilitate eventual publication in a "yearbook". It is worth investing some time and effort in this publication, as it will be brought away from the reunion and mulled over later. The résumés will be as diverse as their authors. The act of consigning 10 years of one's career to a single page proved impossible for many, and much editing was required before producing a book that was both informative and entertaining.

In the long run up to the reunion the drug firms should be assiduously courted. If a full weekend event is envisaged, then these companies will certainly provide the icing on the cake. Those who express an interest through their local representative should be followed up in writing and invited to take part in trade exhibits around a postgraduate medical meeting. Adopting this framework also permits those graduates from abroad to claim travel and accommodation expenses.

The meeting

So with a good deal of cajoling, much telephoning, and some surprise at those who are coming and those who are not (with some coming from the west coast of America and others not coming from the west side of the city), the reunion will be upon you sooner than you imagine.

The staff in the hotel we chose were very professional in their approach, so we allowed them to handle many of the administrative details, including allocation of rooms and distribution of the yearbook. This left the committee free to concentrate on collecting the money and ensuring accurate bookkeeping.

If there is enough interest in the reunion to fill a complete weekend, it is a good idea to break the ice with an opening event, such as an afternoon of golf, followed by a reception, and then some light team games—for example, a table quiz. The hidden agenda here is to get everyone relaxed and talking, as inevitably you will remember faces but not names. This is especially important for the spouses, who may never have met this bunch of extroverts who keep drifting off, arms round shoulders, murmuring "Do you remember that ward round with old what's his name?"

The first full day should include the postgraduate meeting. This

213

should read well on the programme but be short and stimulating. Ideally, the presentations should be by year members on their own specialties or interests. A number of group activities might follow on from this, such as a treasure hunt, clay-pigeon shooting, and, of course, a year photograph. These all precede the reunion dinner, which is after all the *raison d'être*.

The reunion dinner will include the inevitable toasts, and once these are out of the way, the organising committee should be able to relax and enjoy a good meal, good company, and a good band. If the band can be persuaded to play contemporary music from your student days to get everyone on to their feet and in the mood, then the event should go with a swing.

Just when you have got yourself, and everyone else, into the right frame of mind, when old friendships have been renewed and gossip exchanged, the reunion dinner will be drawing to a close. On the morning after, for those still lingering on, ensure there is some lively music to offset the inevitable sad farewells.

Successfully organising a reunion of classmates takes time and energy. It should be approached with care and attention to detail, with important tasks delegated to members of an enthusiastic committee. Leafing through a copy of the yearbook will provide another 10 years of nostalgia and make all the effort seem worth while.

36 Start and run a medical dining club

J H Baron

British medicine has many curious customs. One of the least known and most idiosyncratic is the Dining Club. A club can be scientific, semi-scientific, or simply sybaritic. I explain here the origin of these clubs and give detailed advice on how to start one and run it successfully. I do not cover alumni or surgical travelling clubs: they present no problems. Nor do I discuss groups such as the Breathing Club, whose members respire and cerebrate, but neither eat nor drink.

History

Most of our famous professional societies began as a small group of friends with a common interest, who discussed, drank, and dined together regularly: Aubrey's "sodality in a tavern", or Dr Johnson's "an assembly of good fellows meeting under certain conditions". With a small membership renewed only on resignation or death such clubs may survive for centuries. Once the membership of the club expands into hundreds or thousands with the advance of the particular specialty, then the members cannot all dine together intimately. There is then a need for a club within a club and a new small fraction of the larger society comes together to meet, drink, and dine with one another. Thus the British Society of Gastroenterology began with 39 members in 1937 but now has 1500, so that on the evening before its annual dinner smaller groups meet, each with its own theme.

Clubs go back three centuries. Robert Boyle's Invisible College of

> **Menu of the Royal Society Club**
> **24 March 1747**
>
> Fresh Salmon   Lobster Sauce
> Cods Head
> Pidgeon Pye
> Calves Head
> Bacon & Greens
> Fillett of Veal
> Chine of Pork
> Plumb Pudding
> Apple Custard
> Butter & Cheese

Fig 1 Menu of the Royal Society Club, 24 March 1747.[2,3]

experimental philosophers met weekly from 1645, often in the Bull's Head Tavern in Cheapside. By 1648 it had a satellite, the Philosophical Society of Oxford, a 30-member Greate Clubbe. In 1660 these two amalgamated to become the Royal Society, with 55 members, now grown to 1105.

After the Wednesday meetings groups of Fellows supped at different taverns, such as the Crowne Taverne Club, the Club at the Sun, Halley's Club and the Virtuosoe's Club at Jonathan's Tavern in Cornhill. The records of the present Royal Society Club date from 1743, with eight members dining on fish and pudding with porter for half a crown (12.5p).[1,2] Membership increased to 40 in 1748, 66 in 1900, and later 75. The club now meets for dinner twice a year, with no formal business except the toast to the "arts and sciences". At its 7573rd dinner in 1974 it was agreed that women should be granted membership.

A group of scientists and technologists in Birmingham met together in 1757 and became a formal circle in 1766. Dinner at Matthew Boulton's house was always followed by scientific discussion. This Lunar Society met every full moon for ease of travelling at night. Engineers started to dine on Friday evenings in 1771 at the King's Head Tavern before forming the Smeatonian Society of Civil Engineers. The Society of Antiquaries started their dining club in 1774. The Royal Society of Edinburgh, founded in 1783, had its own club from 1820, and others briefly (New Club 1832–40, Supper Club 1834–5).[3]

Of the social clubs that have their own buildings, the oldest is White's (1693), and there are several others of the mid-eighteenth century, such as Brook's (1746) and Boodle's (1762). Dining clubs, however, usually began in taverns, such as the Dilettanti (1732), now meeting at Brook's, or the artist-governors of the Foundling Hospital (1746), the forerunners of the Royal Academy of 1768. Dr Johnson and Sir Joshua Reynolds founded the Literary Club in 1764 with nine members dining each Monday at 7 pm at the Turk's Head.[4]

The Royal College of Physicians of London had at least two dining clubs, the younger of which was founded before 1764. They merged in 1834 and were still going strong in 1909.[5] Many of the early minute books of these clubs have not survived. The early records of the Medical Club, afterwards known as the Sydenham Club, are said to have been stolen by a footpad from one of the first secretaries walking home across the park, but its account books date from 1796. Wagers were common—for example, in 1854, "that Miss Nightingale is not married by the next meeting", and "that Miss Nightingale has a child by this day twelve month".[6] The club still numbers 18, 6 each of physicians, surgeons, and "apothecaries". The St Alban's Medical Club, named after the tavern where it first met, has records dating back to 1789.[7] It now has seven each of physicians, surgeons, and apothecaries, dines three times a year, and has occasionally dined together with its old rival the Sydenham Club.

Several other clubs have mixed family doctor or specialist membership. The Chelsea Clinical Society was founded in 1896 with nine members for informal discussion about medical problems: "whisky should be provided, but no women".[8] By 1910 there were over 100 members, and formal, clinical, and pathological presentations and volumes of published proceedings. It now has 300 members dining formally (with spouses) five times a year. The Hunterian goes back to 1819 and now has 500 members with 10 dinners a year, as well as the Hunterian Oration at the Royal College of Surgeons.

Some clubs are confined to a particular city or hospital, or specialty. Thus Oxford has the Circle of Willis (1920s) and the breakaway Republic of His (1966): each dines every term. Cambridge has the Carphologists Club, and Edinburgh has the Aesculapian Club (1773) with 11 FRCP and 11 FRCS members dining twice a year. Other clubs in Edinburgh are the Royal Medico-Chirurgical, the Coulston, and the Harveian. Guy's Hospital Physical Society began in 1771. General practitioners just south of

Carte de Vins	
Old Chablis	Huêtres au Citron
Milk Punch	Tortue claire Tortue liée
Madeira (1857)	Saumon de Christchurch
Johannisberg (1862)	Blanchailles
Perrier Jouet	Ris de Veau à la Montpensier
(1874)	Chaud-froid de Cailles à la St James
Amontillado	Selle de Mouton de Galles
Chateau Lafitte	Selle d'Agneau de Sussex
(1875)	Petits Canetons rôtis
Martinez Port	Petits Pois
(1865)	Asperges en Branches, Sauce Mousseline
Boulestin's Cognac	Pouding à la Burlington
(1810)	Tarte aux Pommes
Kümmel	Pailles au Parmesan
Café	Dessert

Fig 2 Menu of the College Club, Burlington Hotel, 22 February 1897, when the Prince of Wales dined.[6]

Hyde Park formed a Sloane Medical Society in 1973. Among the orthopaedic clubs are the Girdlestone, Lippman-Kessel, Arbuthnot Lane, Percival Pott, Sesamoid, Innominate, and Nibblers, some of which were started by peer groups of trainees who continue to meet once or twice a year to discuss clinicopathological problems, followed by dinner with spouses.

The Dublin Biological Club was founded in Trinity College Dublin in 1872 "to consider the morbid and healthy conditions of animal and vegetable life".[9,10] Members originally numbered 14, then 18, and later 30. The club met weekly from October to June, and each member had to present a paper at least once a year. Refreshment was at first limited to light ale, but later there were annual dinners, followed by kite-flying, quoits, and firing with .22 bore rifles at empty champagne bottles.

One medical club was started by the government. After the first world war the Ministry of Pensions was faced with major economic pressures from those said to be disabled from heart disease. In 1920 the ministry appointed regional cardiological advisers, who also met in committee in London from time to time. In 1922 John Cowan turned this group into a 15-member Cardiac Club, which became the British Cardiac Society in 1937.[11,12]

The "42 Club" was founded in 1942 by 12 clinical professors (medicine, surgery, and obstetrics) but now covers the whole clinical academic field.[13] The first meeting was at the Euston Hotel and discussed the effect of the war on clinical teaching. Further meetings in 1942 and 1943 provided evidence for Sir William Goodenough's Interdepartmental Committee on Medical Schools. The club also lobbied successfully in 1946 in the House of Lords for an amendment to the National Health Service Bill to make explicit the duties of teaching hospitals to provide facilities for teaching and research.

The Ratio Club was founded in 1949 as a dining club of young physiologists, engineers, and mathematicians interested in cybernetics and advances in computing.[14]

Most clubs last only for the active lives of their founders and then are forgotten in the absence of any surviving papers. Fortunately, some are documented. The Hexagon Club[15] was founded for six neurologists by Sir Charles Symonds at a dinner at his Wimpole Street home on 30 April 1930 with Russell Brain, Hugh Cairns, Macdonald Critchley, Derek Denny-Brown, and George Riddoch. All were connected with the National Hospital for Nervous Diseases, Queens Square. They chose to meet regularly at a neutral site, the Great Central Hotel. Conversation was general before and during the dinner, but after dinner at each meeting one member (in turn alphabetically) gave a 20 to 30 minute paper followed by a fierce discussion. Many of these papers, much improved by this rehearsal, appeared in *Brain*; others disappeared without trace. The club occasionally had foreign guests: Foerster (1931, 1932), Lhermitte (1934), and Broewer (1936). The club ended when the second world war broke out.

The Keppel Club[6] was started in 1952 by a group of radical young lecturers at the London School of Hygiene and Tropical Medicine at Keppel Street. The founder was (Sir) John Brotherston (later chief medical officer Scotland) and it met monthly in term on Fridays from 5.30 to 7.30 pm for formal presentations. At any one time there were never more than 25 members: economists, physicians, general practitioners, psychiatrists, and medical officers from the Department of Health such as (Sir) George Godber. John Fry[16] attributed the death of the club in 1974 "because there was no young generation of leaders ready to take up the baton". I wonder whether the club might have prospered and survived if it had followed the precedent of centuries and eaten and drunk heartily after each meeting instead of mere "informal discussion at a local pub".

There may well be similar clubs in other countries. The most intriguingly named is the St Anthony Club.[7] St Anthony (or Antony) the Great (251–356) was a hermit tempted by fornication, food, and drink, and it was these last two habits that the Brotherhood of St Anthony of Philadelphia adopted. A Guthrie game dinner was a stag affair, with ladies dining elsewhere. The mainstay of the principal courses were quail, pheasant, grouse, and venison shot by Dr Donald Guthrie (founder of the Guthrie Clinic) and served rare to raw. However, before even the game course was served some of the brethren had already slipped under the table.

Conclusion

If you work in an exciting new field and want to talk freely in a congenial ambience with a few colleagues, then consider starting a medical dining club. Find an equally gregarious and obsessional friend to help: the more literate of the two can become secretary, the more numerate, treasurer. Then write round to suitable prospective members to come to a dinner to discuss your proposal and the future is yours. The following appendices may help.

Appendix: Model rules for a semi-scientific club

1 *Name* This association shall be called the Navel Club in honour of Sir Nathaniel Navel, 1750–1851.

2 *Object* This club is constituted to provide opportunities for those interested in the secretions of the umbilicus to meet for discussion and fellowship.

3 *Meetings* The club will hold at least one, and as many meetings each year as the committee decide. Meetings will usually be held on the evening before the annual meeting of the British Society of Omphalology. Each meeting will consist of a dinner, of which members will be given due notice by the secretary so that they can pay the treasurer in advance if they are attending. Members may bring to the dinner, by prior notification, guests interested in the secretions of the umbilicus. Speakers and topics for discussion will be decided by the committee.

4 *Ordinary membership* Persons domiciled in Britain with a major interest in the secretions of the umbilicus are eligible for ordinary membership of the club. Founder members will be selected at a foundation meeting. Additional members may be elected at any meeting of the club after prior notice to the secretary with the candidate's name and umbilical interest and with the signatures of a proposer and seconder. Ordinary membership is limited to 50.

5 *Senior members* Ordinary members automatically become senior members on their 65th birthday.

6 *Honorary membership* The club may elect to honorary membership because of domicile abroad. Honorary members have all the privileges of membership but shall not pay a subscription.

7 *Corresponding members* Ordinary members who take up domicile abroad automatically become corresponding members with all the privileges of membership.

8 *Subscription* On election each member shall pay to the treasurer a life subscription of £5.00.

9 *Finance* The club shall be financed by contributions from its members. Grants from other organisations and donations from persons desiring to support the club shall be accepted at the discretion of the committee.

10 *Management* The business of the club shall be conducted by the committee, which will have sole control in all matters relating to the club. The committee shall consist of the president, the secretary, the treasurer, and two additional members. Two members of the committee shall constitute a quorum.

11 *Election of officers* The president shall be elected annually and is not eligible for reappointment. The secretary and treasurer should be elected annually and be eligible for reappointment. The two other members of the committee shall serve for three years and shall not be eligible for immediate reappointment.

12 *General meetings* The club will hold an inaugural meeting to draw up the rules of the society, and thereafter shall hold an annual general meeting at which 10 members shall constitute a quorum. At the annual general meeting reports of the treasurer and secretary shall be presented and the officers elected.

13 *Amendments to rules* The rules of the club can be amended at any annual general meeting when notice of proposed changes has been given to each member at least two weeks previously. No changes shall be made unless two thirds of the voting membership are in favour.

Notes to rules

Rule 1 A constitution is essential for any club, if only to satisfy a bank manager on opening an account.

Rule 3 Ensure that members pay in advance. A scientific or even a semi-scientific club should have a theme to each dinner, either a discussion paper by a member or guest or a debate carefully argued by a proposer and an opposer on a topic made known to the membership in the annual notice. A toast to "the Queen" can be followed by one in honour of the founder: "the memory of Nathaniel Navel". This provides an opportunity for some historical references to the development of omphalology in the city in which the club is dining, or the country of origin or domicile of the guest of honour, with some appropriate remarks on the life and times of the founder.

Rule 4 Do not have ordinary members from abroad. Scientific or semi-scientific societies should not blackball new members, and in practice it is advisable for the committee to recommend to the post-prandial annual general meeting candidates to fill vacancies arising from death, resignation, emigration, or seniority. Members need not come every year: it is more enjoyable and intimate if they do not, so that the members, including guests, are less than 40. Members who stop coming usually resign voluntarily, or can be so persuaded.

Rule 6 Limit honorary membership to those from overseas, usually one each year, and avoid the invidious task of selecting Britons for honours.

Rule 8 The club finances itself from the monies gained from dinners, but needs a small working capital obtained from an entry fee, which avoids the effort and expense of collecting annual subscriptions.

Rule 9 Clubs are often offered hospitality by industry. The committee should consider carefully whether doctors should dine at the expense of others.

Rule 10 The business of the club can usually be managed by the secretary in, say, 10 hours a year. The committee need never meet, but its members can be asked by post to nominate the next president, guest of honour, new members, topics, and debaters. The secretary and the treasurer should stay for years if they are efficient but must be subject to formal reappointment each year.

Appendix 2: Model rules for a sybaritic club

1 The club shall be called the Sir Lancelot Spratt Dining Club.

2 It shall be limited to 15 members who shall be proposed and elected by the members.

3 It shall hold not less than one dinner each year, at which members will preside in rotation.

4 One member shall be elected as president for one year only; another shall be elected as secretary/treasurer for one year and be eligible for re-election. The secretary shall keep the minutes,

incorporating the menu of the dinner and the signatures of the members present.

5 A member absent over two consecutive years shall be deemed to have offered his or her resignation.

6 Members attaining the age of 70 (or 65) years shall become senior members and will not be counted within the limits of 15 members of the club, nor will they be liable to forced resignation under rule 5.

7 Each member may propose one name for any vacancy. The secretary shall send a list of such proposals to all members, who shall record their vote(s) according to the number of vacancies and return the ballot paper to the secretary. A member may vote against any name on the list by striking it out, and one such adverse vote shall exclude that proposal. A second ballot shall then take place on those proposals that scored most votes on the first ballot, and the list on the second ballot should contain one more name than the number of vacancies. This list should be circulated to all members to vote as before, but no name can be excluded on the second or subsequent ballot. Any problems in election shall be solved at the next club dinner under the direction of the president, who shall have a casting vote.

8 Any changes to the rules shall be forwarded to the secretary, proposed and seconded, so that a postal ballot can be conducted with two thirds of the membership being necessary for the change to be agreed.

Notes to rules

Rule 2 A sybaritic dining club must be small enough to dine around one table, about 6 to 18 in number.

Rule 3 Most clubs dine annually and some three or four times a year.

Rule 4 The president should be changed annually. The secretary should remain in post for years.

Rule 5 A small closely knit club does not want members who come only occasionally. Their membership should be deemed to have lapsed after their absence for two consecutive years.

Rule 6 Older members may find it difficult to come each year and should be encouraged to come whenever they can.

Rule 7 New members must be acceptable to everyone else, and most clubs operate a "one blackball excludes" rule. Some are more tolerant and two blackballs are needed as veto.

1 Geikie R A. *Royal Society Club: the record of a London dining club in the eighteenth and nineteenth centuries.* London: Macmillan, 1917.

223

2 Allibone T E. *The Royal Society and its dining clubs*. Oxford: Pergamon, 1976.
3 Guthrie D. *A short history of the Royal Society Club of Edinburgh 1820–1962*. Edinburgh: (privately printed), 1962.
4 Murdoch T. Talk of the Town. *Country Life* 1988;**182**:180–1.
5 Payne J F. *History of the College Club of the Royal College of Physicians of London*. London: (privately printed), 1909.
6 Wellcome Institute for the History of Medicine. The Medical Club. In: *A vision of history*. London: The Wellcome Trust, 1986;24.
7 Price R. St Albans Medical Club. *J Internat Wine Food Soc* 1979;**6**:7–17.
8 Harvey W. *A history of the Chelsea Clinical Society*. London: (privately printed), 1962.
9 Bewley G. An account of the Biological Club. *Irish J Med Sci* 1960;**409**:1–15.
10 Foot A W. Reminiscences of the Dublin Biological Club. *Dublin J Med Sci* 1892;**93**:425–41.
11 Cowan J. Some notes on the Cardiac Club. *Br Heart J* 1939;**1**:97–104.
12 Campbell M. The British Cardiac Society and Cardiac Club: 1922–61. *Br Heart J* 1962;**24**:673–95.
13 Booth C C. Friends and influence: the history of the '42 club'. *J Roy Coll Phys* 1993;**27**:187–191.
14 Foster C, Bates J A V. *BMJ* 1993;**307**:1278.
15 Critchley M. Posthumous papers of the Hexagon Club. In: *The citadel of the senses and other essays*. New York: Raven Press, 1985;109–20.
16 Fry J. The Keppel Club (1952–74): lessons from the past for the future. *BMJ* 1993;**303**:1596–8.
17 Beck W C. Dr Donald Guthrie: clubman and gourmet: the Brotherhood of St Anthony. *The Guthrie Journal* 1990;**59**:179–181.

37 Survive a dinner

Clifford Hawkins

Public dinners provide an occupational hazard for VIPs such as presidents of royal colleges, vice chancellors, deans, and others. The risks to health are minimal: obesity, bowel upset, and, rarely, hepatitis (a severe outbreak of this followed a dinner held at an ancient medical society in London). Formerly, there were dangers. Max Beerbohm described how, in the fifteenth century, some members of the renowned family of Borgia laid down rare poisons in their cellars with as much thought as they gave to their vintage wine. An invitation to dine at the Palazzio Borgese was regarded as the highest social honour, but whereas the snobbish Roman might say in an offhand way "I am dining with the Borgias tonight", it is unlikely that he would say "I dined last night with the Borgias".[1] I will consider here, however, the irritations and frustrations that afflict habitués of dinners, especially the problems of the after-dinner speaker.

The reception

A hardened and distinguished diner described the reception as the pre-prandial cacophony. People speak louder and louder to compete with the general clamour, and this makes communication more and more difficult. An ear trumpet would be useful, or perhaps a gong should sound periodically to proclaim a moment of silence so that conversation could start again quietly.

Joining the reception when it is in full swing presents no problem on home territory. When it is elsewhere, the usual advice is to obtain a drink and then approach someone you know or think you recognise. This can be risky. The story goes that a guest went up to a woman whose appearance seemed familiar and the following conversation took place:

"How is your father these days?"
"Oh, he has died".
"I'm so sorry; when was this?"
"Thirty-five years ago".
"Tell me about your brother".
"I haven't got a brother".
"Sorry, I meant your sister".
"Oh, she's still on the throne".

Small talk does not come easily to everyone, and the energy drain of light polite conversation with strangers in a confined space can be considerable. Moreover, the impaction of bodies makes it difficult to extricate yourself and to circulate, so that you are sometimes rooted to the spot until every topic has been exhausted—and there is seldom anywhere to sit down. The background chatter makes it difficult to catch the name of those to whom you are introduced, and it is easy to forget this when passing on the introduction to another: the legible lapel label is a blessing. Forgetting the names or appointments of those met only occasionally is easy, especially for public figures, who meet so many. The cliché "I remember your face but have forgotten your name", which is usually true, is preferable to "I remember your name but have forgotten your face". Americans help by introducing themselves with a brief biographical sketch, such as, "I'm Casper Fitzwater, married with four children, live in Boston, and my special interest is pneukalgiography".

Background music creates a relaxed ambience. But it should be gentle chamber music and not (as happened at a reception I once attended) a boisterous wind ensemble that obliterates human voices. The musicians, perhaps from the local music college, must be told that guests may not take any notice of them. A few chairs should be provided for those who wish to listen or just to sit down.

Time spent in reconnaissance is seldom wasted: studying the seating plan and, when necessary, finding out about neighbouring diners. When there is no plan, the temptation to join colleagues whom you see regularly is best avoided: either seek out friends who are otherwise seldom seen or take pot luck and sit anywhere. Wine, if not included in the cost of the dinner, should be ordered early; once the dinner has started the busy staff will be difficult to corner—a point that explains the epitaph suggested for the tombstone of a waiter: "God finally caught his eye".

At the dinner

A seating plan is essential for the top or high table, otherwise diners will shun it, and unless tables are clearly marked some diners may be wandering around when the VIPs come in or as grace is starting. Talking is limited at the top table, where no one sits opposite; sometimes long tables are too wide for conversation. Separate round tables are increasingly a feature of public dinners and avoid the isolation of the top table; but vision should not be obscured by a bowl of flowers. Isolation is also caused by empty places, and doctors who accept invitations but fail to turn up and give no warning or apology are a particular annoyance to pharmaceutical firms that provide hospitality at medical meetings.

Whether or not grace will be said must be made clear, otherwise diners may be caught halfway between sitting and standing. Some think that grace is an outmoded ritual, and a wit considered it odd that the Lord should be thanked before you know what has been provided. Latin graces beginning with "Benedicite" are seldom understood, and several lines of Latin are hardly more than an ego trip for the speaker. A fundamentalist Christian grace seems inappropriate in our multiracial society. A suitable form of words may be "Let us give thanks for the food and drink we are about to receive and spare a thought for those who are less fortunate"—not that a thought alone may be of much help to them.

Dinners are often remembered by the company that has been enjoyed. Prowess in conversation varies; a cynic said that a gossip talks about others, a bore talks about himself, and a brilliant conversationalist talks about you. The evening can be spoiled if the diner never sees other than the back of his or her neighbour, who is concerned with two or three others interested only in shop talk. On the other hand, however interesting an enthusiastic talker may be, it is helpful if he or she, like Macaulay, "has occasional flashes of silence that make his conversation delightful",[2] as one object of a dinner is to enjoy the food. Conducting a dual discussion with someone on each side could be risky: choking might be caused by attempting to answer a question with a mouthful of, perhaps, sherry trifle garnished with brandy snaps, as no one may be capable of performing the Heimlich manoeuvre.

The food

Meals have improved over the past 20 years owing to deep freezers and microwave ovens. But public dinners are not for the gourmet, for, as Rose Macaulay wrote, "another sad comestive truth is that the best foods are the products of infinite and wearying trouble",[3] and preparing them is impossible when catering for large numbers. It is difficult to please everyone, and some diners may be vegetarians or have religious taboos. Tastes vary; some like beef well done and others prefer it rare. Lamb was once a safe choice, but the vogue now is to have it underdone. Many foods spoil if reheated and go off if kept warm; casseroles such as coq au vin and beef stroganoff are an exception. Thin tasteless slices of electrically cut meat steeped in lukewarm gravy fail to tempt the appetite, and portions are often too large for the average eater. Those brought up to leave the plate clean feel guilty, but others reared in the affluent society leave food uneaten without feeling this.

Slap-handed service is a rare hazard. On one occasion the guest speaker and the wife of a distinguished guest were both doused with soup; if this happens the head waiter apologises and the caterers' insurance puts right the damage.

The drink

Gone are the days when some, having wined well, would slump into their cars, somewhat inebriated, and drive home. Such behaviour no longer provides a macho image and is socially unacceptable. Wine that "maketh glad the heart of man" has to be taken in moderation and—what sacrilege—orange juice instead of port if you are driving home. Happy is the diner whose spouse remains teetotal for the evening and can act as chauffeur. Water, which as Mark Twain said, "taken in moderation cannot hurt anybody", should be on the table and not need to be asked for.

The essential interval after the royal toast allows a visit to the "comfort station". Anyone intent on smoking should ask whether any at the table are misocapnists, especially now that many more hate tobacco smoke because of the possible risk of passive smoking.

Listening to after-dinner speaking

After-dinner speeches can make or mar the evening.[4] Sometimes, when the wine and good food have created a climax of conviviality, a dull silence falls and the jovial atmosphere disappears as the speaker delivers a speech that has cost him or her restless nights in its conception and anorexia during the meal. Occasionally, the victim makes a speech that holds the audience in interest and mirth—a fine ending to a meal and a good prelude to the rest of the evening. If speeches are dull and long, the diners get stuck in their places and opposite the same old faces.[5] They are a captive audience and there is no time limit or chairperson to call a halt. About eight minutes is the customary length, but 20 minutes or more may be expected from the solo guest speaker. There is a good case for limiting speeches to two.

Listeners expect to be amused, but humour is not everyone's forte. One result is a forced funniness and, at the worst, a series of worn out and irrelevant jokes, some of which may be risqué and embarrass the audience. Listing the top 10 phrases used by speakers, Miles Kington gave the winning phrase as "In this context, I am reminded of the story . . ."; others were "An anecdote comes to mind . . ." and "Which reminds me of an incident . . ." He suggested that an after-dinner speech should be brief, witty, and clean.[6] Jokes are useful to illustrate serious ideas, and humour should be natural, original and unpredictable, if possible, and appropriate to the audience. Shakespeare understood this: as Viola remarked in *Twelfth Night*, "This fellow's wise enough to play the fool and to do that well craves a kind of wit: he must observe their mood on whom he jests, the quality of persons, and the time." Excellent speeches can be made without a single joke, the best being casually witty although basically serious.

Some speeches put the listeners to sleep. This can happen at the annual dinner when the chairperson decides that he or she has to report on "the state of the union" and dwells endlessly on unnecessary details of the year's activities. Members have no time to circulate; they slink home exhausted to bed. Sir Francis Walshe wrote, "The toast of the guests is always the nadir of after-dinner oratory. It would be a healthy custom if every proposer of this toast who started on the *Who's Who* tack were swiftly and silently removed from the room. Nothing else will save us from these unimaginative bores".[7]

Plight of the after-dinner speaker

Few leap with joy when they receive an invitation to "say a few words after dinner". A colleague who lectures in this country and abroad was concerned at having to speak at a formal dinner after he had received an honorary degree from a university. A distinguished professor of medicine stated that after-dinner speeches should be given by those who are gifted and that others should never speak, but there were some like himself who are required to speak and need advice. A cabinet minister who appears regularly on television said that he likes going to dinners except when he has to speak, although he is pleased to get up at any time and talk about politics.

Enjoyment of the dinner may be spoiled by apprehension. No trial has been done on the effect of β-blockers. Alcohol helps, but too much is disastrous: speak first and drink later. The call to begin is especially alarming when announced by the thunderous decibels of the crimson jacketed toastmaster on a formal occasion. The speaker stands alone, a pinnacle in a sea of expectant faces, and may have to begin while waiters and waitresses flit around serving coffee or noises come from the adjacent kitchen.

Some believe that good speaking, like good writing, comes easily, but for most mortals hard work is needed for both. This certainly applied to Richard Asher, physician, writer, and scintillating talker. I once looked forward to enjoying the company of Dr T F Fox, a distinguished former editor of the *Lancet*, whom I had arranged to entertain before his speech at our annual medical society dinner, but he apologised and spent those 30 minutes or more with his head buried in his notes. Yet when he spoke it seemed as if it were an impromptu talk. Mark Twain stated that it usually takes no more than three weeks to prepare an impromptu speech. No doubt the high standard of many of the speeches given today is due to a similar devotion.

The ideal speech should be friendly, slightly discursive, appropriate for the occasion, and to some extent lighthearted to avoid destroying post-prandial conviviality. Lack of confidence is an asset, and the best speakers get nervous beforehand; the worst speeches are given by those who suffer from overconfidence and enjoy listening to the cadence of their own voices.

Hazards of speaking

Whether invited as a guest speaker because of his or her distinction or because of the office held, the speaker is likely to address an amiable and sympathetic audience whose receptivity has been increased by the food and wine. A modest start endears the speaker to the audience and is usually sincere, but must be put carefully. A risky way of invoking the "weakness of the chosen vessel" theme is to begin with "Goodness only knows why I am making this speech" or "No doubt you must be hoping that the old bore will shut up and sit down." The morale of even the most self-confident person will be disturbed if this is received in sullen silence, perhaps broken by a few mutterings of "Hear, hear" instead of laughter.

Notes are useful for moral support and as reminders in case of speaker's block. They can be written on record cards, kept as simple as possible, made legible (as they will be further away than the customary lectern), and held loosely together (by treasury tags or rings) in case they are dropped. The cards can then be placed unobtrusively behind a bowl of flowers or the wine glasses, or held in the hand if small. Even Sir Derrick Dunlop, a most polished and experienced speaker, believed in having notes; once he was delivering a memorial address in Edinburgh cathedral without notes when he had the appalling experience of his mind suddenly going blank.

Worst of all, as Girdwood aptly described, is to be asked to speak off the cuff without warning.[8] And nearly as bad is to be the last speaker. To be called on at a very late hour after several long speeches have been made is a nightmare. As Norman Birkett, the distinguished judge, wrote, "Many of the diners are hurrying from the hall before the speaker rises so that they can catch the last train home, and there is a general air of having-had enough-speaking-for-one-night abroad". He quoted the solution of another judge, Lord Hewart, to whom this happened. He told his audience that, fearing this situation, he had prepared two speeches in order to meet any eventuality. One speech was a short speech, the other was a little longer, and he was considering what he should do. After keeping the listeners in suspense for some moments he announced that he had decided to give them both; here the audience uttered a long,

231

collective sigh. He then went on, "I will begin with the short one, which was 'Thank you', and I will also give you the longer one, which was 'Thank you very much'". He then sat down to the longest applause of the evening.[9]

Finally there comes the vote of thanks, which should be limited to a minute or two. It is pleasant to hear a few flattering words but disheartening when the speaker goes off on his or her own tack and forgets to mention your effort—or starts on a long recap of the speech just heard. Every speaker should end before the attention of the listeners has started to wane.

Needs of the speaker

A good organiser appreciates the needs of the speaker and briefs him or her clearly about the occasion: whether the audience will be medical, or mixed with lay people and spouses, whether there will be the one speech or several, and whether a toast will be required. Most speakers are looked after well, but lapses are possible.[10]

The speaker should be cosseted: recognised on arrival instead of having to force a way through the crowded reception to find the host and given a good send off. Even professional after-dinner speakers have their trials and tribulations. Basil Boothroyd wrote, "He enters their life for an hour, filling a speaker shaped space like a fairground cut-out. How should they guess that it's not an hour but a week out of his life, mostly with bad nights and delirious mutterings? Why, when he's gone, should they give him another thought, as he lurks at a cabless Euston or sprints for the Cincinnati plane?"[11]

1 Max Beerbohm. The incomparable Max. In: Roberts S C, ed. *Hosts and guests.* London: Heinemann, 1962;**248**:244–57.
2 Holland S. *A memoir of the Reverend Sydney Smith by his daughter, Lady Holland.* Vol 1, 2nd ed. London: Longmans, 1855;366.
3 Macaulay R. Personal pleasures. In: Ray C, ed. *The gourmet's companion.* London: Eyre and Spottiswoode, 1963;323.
4 Hawkins C. After-dinner speaking. *BMJ* 1988;**297**:1693–5.
5 Anonymous. After dinner [Editorial]. *BMJ* 1958;**ii**:904.
6 Kington M. *Independent* 30 June 1987;14 (col 1).
7 Walshe F. After dinner. *BMJ* 1958;**ii**:1039–40.
8 Girdwood R H. Performances that went wrong. *BMJ* 1987;**295**:1668–90.
9 Birkett N. On saying a few words after dinner. *Punch* 2 November 1959:12–4.
10 Lock S. Nice people with no manners. *BMJ* 1978;**ii**:1774–5.
11 Boothroyd B. *Accustomed as I am: the loneliness of the long-distance speaker.* London: Allen & Unwin, 1975:12.

38 Retire

David Waldron Smithers

There are no rules. Thankfully, no two people are the same, so it is impossible to impart any formula for retirement; it is an enterprise that each must plan and carry out personally. Nevertheless, some thoughts on a change that may turn out to be a predicament or a jubilation, a deprivation or an indulgence, a shock or a planned enhancement of living may set the mind to work on the subject, if only in tabulating omissions or in angry disagreement.

Get ready for it

One thing is certain; namely, that the best advice about retirement is "Be prepared." Leon Trotsky in his *Diary in Exile* wrote that "old age is the most unexpected thing that ever happens to a man". It certainly does tend to creep up on the retired. There are plenty of books about such preparation and a magazine called *Choice*, which offers help to those about to come to grips with it. Taking first things first: being financially padded as far as the available resources will allow for the foreseeable future will not cause any problems to vanish but will make nearly all of them seem less pressing. For those who do not command financial wizardry, the British Medical Association runs investment, tax, and retirement planning seminars for members and spouses—who are offered lunch as well for £50 each or £80 a couple—that set about these fundamentals at most reasonable cost.

Perhaps "when" should not intrude on a "how" article, but there are a few doctors—among such branches of medicine, for example, as ophthalmology, dermatology, and general practice—who are able,

233

if they wish, to continue in practice into their 80s and so never really retire at all. This I understand, though it seems a sad waste of a wonderful opportunity. So "why" enters the lists at times. I once sat next to a courtly, balding, white-haired surgeon at his introductory tea ceremony in a Canton hospital, who presented his colleagues to us in Chinese through an interpreter and then turned to me, speaking faultless English, to say that we did not understand retirement in Britain. He said that he no longer operated but, for as long as he wished, he would take some outpatient sessions and do some teaching. He then added, with sparkling glee, "and I am on full salary".

For most of us "when" is 65—still time to start a new career, if a little late. Sir Harold Himsworth became a philosopher, but I suppose he always was one. In my time I have advocated a series of most sensible changes in medical and nursing practice, generally regarded as totally impracticable. My notion on retirement was that the heads of hospital departments should abandon their administrative responsibilities in their 50s to allow younger people to plan the future they will have to cope with. Older consultants, happily freed from a great deal of planning and committee work, would then be better able to deploy their hard-won experience, so valuable both in practice and in teaching. Whenever the time does come for retirement, however, it would be wise to listen to Alexander Pope:

> You've play'd and lov'd and eat and drank your fill.
> Walk sober off before a sprightlier age
> Come titt'ring on, and shove you from the stage.

Natural breaks

In retirement there are some dangers to avoid. One of these is to go on too long speaking at meetings; medicine advances fast today, doctors can soon get out of date on retirement, and most junior colleagues are kindly people who will applaud and keep you in the dark because you were once worth listening to. Another danger is to cut yourself off too suddenly from caring for others; personal or community care is in a doctor's bones and an unhappy feeling of being useless after a lifetime of service can be quite distressing. Another danger is embodied in a proposal to move from home. If this is the plan, you would be wise to spend as much time as possible at the new location well in advance of the move. A sudden separation from friends and familiar surroundings, even to a lovely place in the sun or, as in Plato's retirement, "Where the Attic bird trills her thick-warbled notes the summer long," does not always work out too well and seldom comes up to expectation without careful preparation. It was a doctor who wrote:

O blest retirement, friend of life's decline,
Retreats from care that never must be mine,
How happy he who crowns, in shades like these,
A youth of labour with an age of ease;

but not necessarily blest if too much ease or too strange or distant the shades. You will, of course, pay attention to keeping fit. We should all aim to live until we die. Exercise and a modicum of restraint pay dividends.

Freedom to act

The most important aspect of retirement is activity. The individual's own inclinations and abilities will determine what activities are pursued; the best often prove to be those long thwarted by the pressures of the daily round. Retirement activities should be enjoyable. Bertrand Russell put this with his accustomed clarity in *Portraits from Memory* when he wrote: "There is need, first, of a stable framework built round a central purpose and second, of what may be called 'play', that is to say, of things that are done merely because they are fun and not because they serve some serious end".

Inner resources are the thing; with these there can be no cause for concern—activities abound. It is, however, creative activities that most certainly promote happiness, even when, as usual, they are laced with frustration. If you can paint, write music, sing in a choir, play in an orchestra, or write acceptable prose or poetry, you are fortunate indeed. I have often had to remind sceptical friends that gardening is a creative activity. Some remarkable group activities have been set up. I recently heard of one most successful theatre group and club, run exclusively by retired people, that puts on a new show each month for which it is often difficult to get a seat.

One oddity is open to you. If you harbour a qualm that your full worth may not have been appreciated, or more seriously that you have been recognised only for your less important contributions, the *British Medical Journal* encourages you to compose your own obituary. These are, of course, chiefly written for the nearest and

235

dearest at home and at work, but that need not stop you from trying, without too much earnestness, to avoid being one of Hardy's "Spectres that Grieve":

> We are stript of rights; our shames lie unredressed,
> Our deeds in full anatomy are not shown,
> Our words in morsells merely are expressed
> On the scriptured page, our motives blurred unknown

Of the essence

You must, and you will, do your own thing, but some of the suggestions I would put forward are:

(1) Take care to prepare for retirement well in advance.

(2) Arrange for continuing financial stability at whatever level is open to you. You may live a very long time.

(3) Make no too sudden break in your habit of caring for others or with your familiar surroundings.

(4) Remember that the key to happiness is activity, preferably creative.

(5) Give some thought, but not too much, to maintaining fitness and avoiding over indulgence.

(6) Have fun.

To me the essence of successful retirement was embodied in a charming, courteous gentleman, who was the ear, nose, and throat surgeon to the Brompton Hospital and the Royal Academy of Music among his many appointments. Sir James Dundas-Grant lived to be 90, and in his 80s, when as a young man I knew him, he conducted an orchestra, was straight of back, sharp of eye, and quick of thought. When asked how he managed to seem so young at his age, he replied, "I say something pretty to my wife every day".

39 Fly

Ian Capperauld

There is only one way to fly and that is first class. However, not all of us can afford to fly first class and it should be remembered that first-class treatment starts only when you reach the airport and stops when you reach your destination. The object of this paper is to give a few practical hints on how to fly in the most comfortable fashion prepared for all eventualities no matter whether you are flying Concorde, first class, "tourist", or Super Apex.

Preparation for the journey

It is not my intention to tell you how to pack or what to pack but there are certain points that must be remembered.

(1) Do not put a copy of your lecture or slides in the hold baggage. Carry them with you.

(2) Carry a spare bag in your suitcase to bring back literature and goods you have purchased since they will not cram into your hold baggage.

(3) Carry a spare string carrier bag with you that will accommodate your duty free on the way out and your duty free on the way back. The string bag is not so inclined to give way as are the normal plastic bags given away at duty-free shops.

(4) Carry a briefcase. Ideally, it should contain the following articles:

● A wallet specially fitted with compartments to carry your passport, airline tickets, travellers cheques, boarding card, receipts, vaccination certificates, and any other documents that you may require for the journey. (Keep your luggage reclaim tags separate rather than affixed to the ticket.)

• A screwdriver, or preferably a Swiss Army knife, which will allow you to change plugs in your hotel room. It is impossible to carry all types of adapters, but taking one plug off a lamp in the room and fixing it to your own electrical gadget will enable you to use this equipment.

• Have a pen that enables you to fill in your landing card. People usually leave their pens in their jackets, which are hung up, and there is a scramble at the time of landing to fill in the landing form. Incidentally, always make a point of completing the landing form immediately you receive it. This is in case you are unable to complete it coherently because of liberal supplies of alcohol.

• Carry dollars in single dollar notes, as these are invaluable for porters and to obtain taxis in most countries.

• A shoehorn is invaluable to put your own shoes on following a long flight. You will find that this is also more than useful to your travelling companions.

• A toiletries bag, containing, for example, toothpaste, toothbrush, and cosmetics or a shaving kit, allows you to arrive fresh at your destination.

• A clean shirt or blouse will allow you to change before landing and to arrive fresh.

Incidentally, both the toiletries bag and shirt or blouse become invaluable in the event that you are diverted to another destination without access to baggage in the hold.

(5) Medicines: At an early point in the preparation for the journey a decision has to be made, since you are a doctor, about the medicines you take with you. The decision is that of taking medicines to treat yourself or taking medicines to treat any or many of your travelling companions. Because of the implications of international laws and the areas over which I may be flying, I restrict the medicines I take for myself. Some of the medicines can be carried in your briefcase and others in the hold baggage.

Certainly, it pays to carry aspirin or paracetamol and, if you have difficulty in sleeping on an overnight flight, some form of hypnotic such as Temazepam. Other medicines that are particularly useful are:

avomine	travel sickness
imodium	diarrhoea
maxolon	nausea or sickness in gastroenteritis
antihistamine	allergic conditions
paludrine ⎫	
maloprim ⎬	antimalarial
chloroquine ⎭	
septrin	urinary infections
tetracycline	respiratory infections

Although essentially not forming part of a medical kit as such, I find it useful to carry the following in the hold baggage, which can make life bearable in otherwise adverse conditions:

• a solid rubber ball, which will act as a bath plug or a sink plug,
• soap,
• toilet paper,
• insect repellent and room freshener spray,
• stain and spot remover for spills on clothes,
• presept tablets, which are a form of sodium hypochloride or bleach and which are invaluable for putting down the toilet or bath in hotels where the plumbing and the cleaning leaves a lot to be desired.

At the airport

Determine whether the plane is going to take off on time and, if it is not, the alternatives for rerouting to get to your destination at the time you want to be there. There are warning signs of impending delay, such as the flight number not appearing on the board, and if the announcement detailing the delay is "indefinitely", this can often be interpreted as at least a six-hour delay.

When reserving your seat, try to get one beside an emergency exit, which, apart from giving you an element of safety, also gives you an element of comfort, since by law the space at the emergency door is always 50% greater than in the rest of the plane.

Buying duty free is not always now a bargain or even necessary, since in countries such as America alcohol is usually cheaper, and in countries like Russia and Poland there are duty free shops in which you can buy any form of alcohol by using hard currency and at a rate cheaper than at the airport.

While it may be tempting to have cups of coffee or alcohol before boarding the plane, there is usually a queue after take off for toilet facilities and, therefore, it is better to restrict your intake.

On board the plane

There is a lot of advice written on how to fly in comfort and, indeed, many exercises that can be performed do help to pass the time or to prevent deep vein thrombosis. One of the best ways of relieving boredom and of trying to prevent deep vein thrombosis is to make an active effort to get up out of your seat and wander round the plane. To this end, therefore, you will be less of a nuisance to your travelling companions if you choose an aisle seat rather than a window seat. If you are not fortunate enough to travel first class where slipperettes are provided, carry an extra pair of socks or obtain a pair of slipperettes to put on your feet, since no matter how fit you are or whatever your age group, inevitably some form of gravitation oedema does occur when sitting for long periods. Walking around the plane also helps to dispel the effects of sitting. If you are flying from west to east overnight and, because of the time lag, you will be arriving at your destination early in the morning while it will be late in the evening at your point of departure, it is extremely important that you do not have an excess of food or alcohol on that journey. Going through customs and immigration tired is one thing, but bloated and merry is another. Try to consume at least a litre of water on any journey over five hours.

Arrival

Get a porter. It is money well spent: a porter will get you a trolley, get you through customs, and get you a taxi. When considering what to pay for this service always pay $1 per piece of luggage carried and you will not go far wrong. If you are in any doubt as to whether you are being charged properly or overcharged for the taxi ride, get the driver to carry your luggage into the hotel or get the hotel to pay the taxi for you and put it on to the bill, especially if you have not changed money into the local currency. If possible, change your money at the bank rather than the hotel, as there is usually a charge of $7\frac{1}{2}$–10% levied by the hotel for changing currency. If you wish to avoid bringing back local currency, buy your duty free with this, and make up the difference in price with a credit card.

Conclusions

Flying can be fun, but arriving at your destination safe, fresh, and comfortable, knowing that your slides and your lectures are with you, and that you are prepared for all eventualities, be it friend or foe, can be a comfort and a consolation; as I said at the beginning, first-class treatment often stops when you arrive at your destination.

Index

Related title

HOW TO WRITE A PAPER

Edited by G M Hall

This short book provides all the practical information on how to get a paper accepted. It has chapters on each section of a scientific paper, from Introduction to Discussion. With contributions from editors of international journals including the *BMJ*, *British Journal of Anaesthesia*, and *Cardiovascular Research*, it explains in a refreshingly direct way what journal editors are looking for in a good paper.

Readership: all medical professionals, scientific researchers

ISBN 0 7279 0822 7 128 pp 1994

For details of this book and our full range of titles write to Marketing Department, BMJ Publishing Group, BMA House, Tavistock Square, London WC1H 9JR or telephone Diana Chapple on 0171 383 6541